# ENCYCLOPAEDIA OF INDIAN GOVERNMENT: PROGRAMMES AND POLICIES

# ENCYCLOPAEDIA
# OF
# INDIAN GOVERNMENT:
# PROGRAMMES AND POLICIES

Vol. 15

Petroleum and Natural Gas

*Edited by*

**Satish Tiwari**

**ANMOL PUBLICATIONS PVT. LTD.**

**NEW DELHI - 110 002 (INDIA)**

**ANMOL PUBLICATIONS PVT. LTD.**
4374/4B, Ansari Road, Daryaganj
New Delhi - 110 002

*Encyclopaedia of Indian Government: Programmes and Policies*

First Edition, 2000
ISBN 81-261-0515-1 (Set)



PRINTED IN INDIA

Published by J.L. Kumar for Anmol Publications Pvt. Ltd., New Delhi - 110 002 and Printed at Mehra Offset Press, Delhi.

# Contents

# Preface

Encyclopaedia of Indian Government: Programmes and Policies contains authoritative information on about fifty departmental policies and their future developmental programmes.

Organised to be completed in 40 volumes, this gigantic work covers Agriculture; Atomic Energy; Chemicals and Fertilizers; Coal; Commerce; Communication; Culture; Defence; Education; Environment and Forests; External Affairs; Finance; Food & Consumer Affairs; Food Processing Industries; Health and Family Welfare; Home Affairs and Internal Security; Human Resources; Industry; Information and Broadcasting; Labour; Law, Justice and Company Affairs; Non-conventional Energy Sources; Ocean Development; Parliamentary Affairs; Personnel, Public Grievances and Pensions; Petroleum and Natural Gas; Planning and Programme Implementation; Planning and Statistics; Posts and Telegraphs; Power; Rural Development; Science and Technology; Social Justice and Empowerment; Space; States Affairs; Steel; Steel and Mines; Sugar and Edible Oils; Surface Transport; Textiles; Tourism; Urban Development; Water Resources; Women and Child development etc.

Based on the information derived from authoritative sources, this work contains authentic facts and figures. I am deeply beholden to all the scholars whose writings are cited or substantially made use of in the present work. I am also thankful to Anmol Publications Pvt. Ltd. for undertaking publication of this encyclopaedia. I am solely responsible for shortcomings in presentation of matter.

Encyclopaedic in nature, this will prove a dependable reference work for scholars and academics besides those appearing for different competitive examinations.

**—Satish Tiwari**

# Preface

# 1

# Introduction

The Ministry of Petroleum and Natural Gas is concerned with exploration and production of oil and natural gas, and the refining, distribution and marketing, import, export and conservation of petroleum products.

Shri K. Ramamurthy held the charge as Minister and Shri Santosh Kumar Gangwar as Minister of State in the Ministry of Petroleum & Natural Gas.

**Principal achievements**

Crude oil production in the country during 1997-98 was 33.86 Million Tonnes per annum (MMT) against a target of 34.01 MMT. The target for the year 1998-99 is 34.72 MMT. Government had appointed a Committee of experts headed by Dr. K. Narayanan to examine reasons for shortfall in crude production and suggest remedial measures. The Committee has submitted its report covering Mumbai High. A monitorable action plan for implementing the recommendations of the Narayanan Committee has been drawn up by the Expert Group.

Measures taken by the Government to intensify exploration and enhance hydrocarbon reserves included

— development of new fields,

— additional development of existing fields,

— implementation of Enhanced Oil Recovery Schemes,

- — recourse to specialised technology,
- — enlisting the services of international experts,
- — encouraging participation of private and joint venture companies in the exploration programme,
- — activisation of the New Exploration Licensing Policy (NELP).

Under NELP, 48 exploration blocks were identified for offer. Of these, 26 are offshore upto 400 metre isobath, 12 are deep offshore of the East Coast of India beyond 400 metre isobath and 10 are onland blocks. The notice inviting offers was issued in January, 1999. The closing date is 18th May, 1999.

*Coal bed methane*

Government has announced a new policy on the exploitation of a new energy resource, Coal Bed Methane (CBM), reservoirs of which are estimated at 1000 billion cubic metres. 9 CBM blocks have been delineated in the States of Bihar, West Bengal and Madhya Pradesh. One block in West Bengal has been allotted to ONGC on nomination. Documents for offer of other blocks through international competitive bidding have been finalised,

*Imports and exports*

The import of crude oil between April and November, 1998 was 26.322 MMT and worth Rs. 10038 crore and of other petroleum products upto 12.991 MMT valued at Rs.6855 crore. Exports upto November, 1998 were of 1.005 MMT and worth Rs.612 crore.

*Refining*

The Refining sector was delicensed in June, 1998. Also, the public sector oil companies may establish refineries in the joint sector with the equity participation of 26%. The refining capacity of PSUs by the end of March, 1999 will be 67.55 MMTPA and is expected to increase to about 131 MMTPA (excluding production by 100% EOUs) by the end of IX Plan. The estimated demand for products is then likely to be 112 MMTPA. The refineries achieved a throughput of 50.13 MMT, against the target 'of 49.94 MMT upto December, 1998.

***Oil pool account***

To cancel the Oil Pool Deficit, it was decided that part of the liabilities to the Oil companies would be cleared by the Govt. through issue of special one time Govt. Bonds. The Oil Companies were required simultaneously to invest these amounts in Special Govt. Bonds issued by RBI. Under this expedient "10.5% Oil Companies (Nontransferable) Special Govt. Bonds 2005" totaling Rs. 12,984 crore were issued by the Govt. to the Oil Companies on 2.3.98.

***Prime Minister's self employment scheme***

On the eve of Republic Day, 1999, Government announced a scheme to be known as "Prime Minister's Self-Employment Scheme of Oil Companies." Under this Scheme about 10,000 SKO dealerships for Superior Kerosene Oil (SKO) are to be allotted, one at each Block Headquarters. SKO would be sold at normal rates without subsidy and without insistence on ration card.

***LPG supply to rural areas***

To meet the demand for LPG in rural areas of the country, Government propose to arrange about 1900 LPG distributorships in the next two years. Villages having a population of 10,000, small towns having a population of 10,000 and above and villages around cities having population of 1 lakh will be covered under the scheme.

The number of LPG customers of the Public Sector Oil companies in the country was about 353 lakh as on 1. 1.99. Government approved the release of 35 lakhs new LPG connections and 25 lakhs DBCs during 1998-99. LPG is an environment friendly and clean fuel. It has been, therefore, decided that the waiting list for LPG connections in all the North-Eastern States and hilly areas of altitude 2000 ft. and above, in the States of Jammu & Kashmir, Himachal Pradesh and in all the Union Territories should be cleared by 31.3.1999.

**Measures to combat adulteration**

Government has issued the Kerosene (Restriction, Use and Fixation of Ceiling Price) (Amendment) Order, 1998 and Motor Spirit and High Speed Diesel (Regulation of Supply and Distribution and Prevention of Malpractices) Order, 1998 to curb adulteration and malpractices.

Government has banned the supply of loose 2T Oil at petrol pumps and service garages in NCT of Delhi w.e.f. 31.12.1998. Also, in accordance with orders of the Supreme Court only unleaded petrol is being sold in NCT of Delhi from 1.9.98. Unleaded petrol has also been introduced in all State capitals and Union Territories and major towns. It would be available throughout the country by 1999-2000.

***Facilitation***

A Facilitation Counter has been operationalised in the Ministry of Petroleum & Natural Gas, in furtherance of the objective of the Government of promoting effective, responsive and citizen -friendly administration. It attends to enquiries and redressal of grievances. It is equipped with a computer network and postal/ electronic reply.

***Plan outlay***

The Revised Plan outlay of the Ministry of Petroleum & Natural Gas for the year 1998-99 is Rs. 12381.84 crore and Budget Estimate for the year 1999-00 Rs. 12123.80 crore. These outlays will be met from the Internal, and Extra Budgetary Resources of the Public Sector Undertakings. However, Biecco Lawrie has been granted an aid of Rs. 34

lakh from the National Renewal Fund towards its Voluntary Retirement Scheme.

*Earning of public sector undertakings*

The profit before tax earned by the Public Sector Undertakings, under the administrative control of the Ministry, during the year 1997-98 was about Rs. 9408 crore. The profit after tax was Rs. 7497 crore. The figures for 1998-99 are anticipated to be Rs. 10516 crore and Rs. 8299 crore.

*Conservation of petroleum products*

Measures initiated to conserve petroleum products include, accent on fuel efficiency, training programmes in the transport sector, modernisation of boilers, replacement of ill designed heat apparatus equipment, standardisation of irrigation pumpsets, rectification of existing and introduction of fuel efficient stoves. The Petroleum Conservation Research Association (PCRA) and oil companies foster these initiatives.

# 2

# Exploration and Production

ONGC & OIL are the two national oil companies engaged in the exploration and production of oil and natural gas in the country. Crude oil production during the year 1997-98 was 33.86 MMT though the target was 34.01 MMT. ONGC and OIL had achieved the targets set out in the MOU concluded with the Government. The private and Joint Venture fields fell short somewhat, Crude oil production target during the year 1998-99 is 34.72 MMT.

Government had appointed a Committee of experts headed by Dr. K. Narayanan to look into reasons for shortfall in crude production during 1996-97 and to suggest remedial measures. The Committee has submitted its interim report covering Mumbai High. A monitorable Action Plan for implementing the recommendations of the Narayanan Committee has been drawn up and its implementation is monitored

Several measures were taken by the Government to enhance hydrocarbon reserves and its production in the country. These include:

i) Development of new fields and additional development of the existing fields.

ii) Scaling up and Implementation of Enhanced Oil Recovery (EOR) Schemes.

iii) Recourse to extended reach horizontal and drain hole drilling.

iv) Indenting on the services of international experts of repute.

v) Improved maintenance of reservoir health.

vi) Conduct of 3D seismic surveys for precise reservoir delineation

vii) Application and optimisation of artificial lift operations.

viii) Stimulation of wells

ix) Optimisation and redistribution of water injection.

x) Infill drilling, mostly in the unswept areas of the reservoirs.

The highlights of liberalisation in the petroleum sector has been the participation of foreign and Indian companies in the exploration and development activities to supplement the efforts of National Oil Companies through production sharing contracts.

**New exploration licensing policy**

Altogether 48 exploration blocks, 26 offshore upto 400 metre isobath, 12 deep offshore off the East coast of India beyond 400 metre isobath and 10 onland blocks were identified for offer under the New Exploration Licensing Policy (NELP). Basin information dockets and data packages, Model Production Sharing Contract, Petroleum Tax Guide and other bidding documents were finalised and the Notice inviting offers, with bid closing date as 18-5-99, was issued in January 1999. Promotional presentations were held in Delhi, London, Houston, Calgary and Singapore.

*Coal bed methane*

In all 9 blocks have been delineated in the States of Bihar, West Bengal and Madhya Pradesh. One block in West Bengal has been given to ONGC on nomination basis. Various documents necessary for offer of blocks through international competitive bidding have been finalised. Bids are expected to be invited shortly.

*Oil and natural gas corporation limited (Ongc)*

During the year 1998-99, ONGC struck hydrocarbons at the following places:

| Name | Basin | Oil/Gas |
|---|---|---|
| 1. Anklav | Cambay | oil |
| 2. Gokarnapuram | Krishna Godavari | Gas |
| 3. Kesavadasapalem | Krishna Godavari | Gas |
| 4. Kali | Cauvery | Oil |

*Surveys*

Onland, against a target of 2996 Ground Line Kilometre (GLK) of 2D and 5204 GLK of 3D seismic survey for the year, 1799 GLK of 2D and 6752 GLK of 3D survey was completed upto September 1998. Offshore, against a target of 50,225 Line Kilometre (LKM). seismic survey, the performance was 21737 LKM.

*Drilling*

179.489 thousand metres of exploratory drilling has been carried out against the annual target of 331.579 thousand metres. Development upto November 1998 drilling achievement in this period was 191.873 thousand metres against the target of 332.841 thousand metres. Against the annual target of 140 exploratory and 171 development wells, the achievement during period upto November 1998 has been 81 and 98.

***Production***

ONGC has produced 20.114 million tonnes of crude oil upto December 1998 against the MOU target of 28.100 million tonnes for the year. The natural gas supplied during this period was 14112.55 million cubic metres against the annual target of 18543 million cubic metres.

***Financial performance***

(Rs./Crore)

| | Annual Target 1998-99 (B.E.) | Actual Achievement 1998-99 upto Dec. 1999 | Anticipated Annual Achievement 1998-99 (R.E.) |
|---|---|---|---|
| Plan Outlay | 4765.51 | 3263.11 | 4600.00 |
| Total Income | 14764.12 | 11212.91 | 15489.99 |
| Net Profit | 2195.45 | 1879.51 | 2441.38 |
| Internal Resources | 4541.21 | 4127.58 | 4582.69 |

The figure of physical and financial achievement are provisional.

***Other achievements***

Some of the major achievements of the ONGC have been:

— Under deep-water exploration programme, the drilling of second deep water well G-I-AD in KG Basin, Eastern offshore, has been taken up with ONGC's own, drillship Sagar Vijay. The well has been drilled to a depth of 1800m against 2500m to be intended. The first exploratory well was drilled at location CDWOI in Cauvery basin by the same rig.

— ONGC bagged three drilling service contracts, two in Bangladesh and one in Oman. Two rigs are in operation in Bangladesh and one rig is being mobilised. In Oman under JAPEX contract, the first well has been completed and the second is in progress.

— ONGC's Well Control School at Institute of Drilling Technology, Dehradun has been certified by the International Association of Drilling Contractors (IADC) for WELL CAP as a fully accredited institute.

— Two new structures Adavipalem and GS-23 in Krishna Godavari Project, Southern region were put on production.

— A new process complex HRC (part of Heera Phase-III development project) was hooked up with Heera Process Complex on 8.7.98, ten months ahead of schedule.

— Engineering & construction activities in B-55 project were completed ahead of schedule.

— Major construction activities of the Booster — ompressor platform project have been completed with installation of both BCP-A and BCP-B platforms.

— Two Enhanced Oil Recovery (EOR) commercialization schemes of Insitu combustion at Balol and Santhal fields of North Gujarat are in advance stage of completion.

— Quality Assurance Departments at Mumbai and Sibsagar (for Diesel Shop) were accredited with ISO 9002 certification.

**ONGC videsh limited**

ONGC Videsh Ltd. (OVL) is a wholly owned subsidiary company of ONGC. It is engaged exclusively in Corporation's foreign ventures including acreage/

property acquisition and E&P operations. The brief of activities of OVL in different projects is as under:

- OVL along with British Petroleum and Statoil has discovered natural gas in the offshore Lan Tay and Lan Do fields in Vietnam. Presently gas pricing and other commercial terms are being negotiated with Petrovietnam.
- Opportunities are being pursued by OVL in Iraq and Kazakhastan.
- Formalities for opening an office in Baku in Azerbaizan, and Moscow have been completed.
- Invitation for participation in exploration and development in a few projects in Sakhalin area of Russia was received from Roseneft and are being pursued.
- A proposal received, for exploration in Astrakhan region is under evaluation.
- Yet another proposal to participate in the Russian Sector of Caspian Sea is being negotiated with Lukoil.

**Oil India Limited (OIL)**

Recently hydrocarbons were discovered by OIL at the following structures in upper Assam :-

1. North Balijan
2. Mohanbari
3. South Kathaloni
4. Kamkhat
5. Khagorijan
6. Moran South

**Surveys**

During the year against a target of 1700 Straight Line

Kilometre/ Ground Line Kilometre of 2-D and 150 SQKM of 3-D upto December-1998, Oil India Limited completed 661.47 SLKM/GLKM of 2D and 62 89 SQKM of 3D seismic surveys.

**Drilling**

Against the annual target of 62.95 thousand metres of exploratory drilling, achievement upto December 1998, is 33.051 thousand metres.

OIL also completed 36.533 thousand metres of development drilling during same period, against the annual target of a total of 60.00 thousand metres.

**Production**

OIL has produced 2.475 MMT of crude oil upto December 1998 against a target of 3.20 MMT for the entire year. The total natural gas sales during this period were 828.99 MMSCM against a target of 1150 MMSCM and LPG 40443 MT against a target of 53000 MT.

**Financial Performance**

(Rs./Crore)

| | *Annual Target 1998-99 (B.E.)* | *Actual Achievement for 1998-99 upto Dec. 1999* | *Anticipated Annual Achievement 1998-99 (R.E.)* |
|---|---|---|---|
| Plan Outlay | 570.00 | 287.53 | 500.44 |
| Total Income | 1347.28 | 1029.32 | 1353.16 |
| Net Profit | 281.28 | 156.74 | 216.16 |
| Internal Resources | 493.31 | 292.99 | 402.09 |

The figure of physical and financial achievement are provisional.

**Other Achievements**

Some of the major achievements of the OIL are as under:

- The crude oil production is expected to be around 3.25 MMT as against the MOU target of 3.20 MMT in 1998-99. The previous year's production was 3.094 MMT.
- OIL started its exploratory drilling work in the Ganga Valley basin in Uttar Pradesh during the year.
- OIL entered into farm-out agreement with foreign company TOTAL for an exploration block in the Sultanate of Oman. OIL will have 20 % participation in the block.

**Gas autority of India Ltd. (GAIL)**

Gas Authority of India Limited (GAIL) was formed in 1984. It is a Navaratna and one among the top ten companies in India. It has secured the ISO 9002 certification for its pipelines and plants and ISO 14001 certification for environment.

The company recorded a turnover of Rs.5736 Cr. in 1997-98 and earned a profit after tax of Rs.1020 Cr. The dividend declared was Rs. 186 Cr. The volume of gas sold was 19.9 BCM. Production of liquid hydrocarbons was 6.34 lakh MT. GAIL now is supplying 60 million standard cubic metre per day (MMSCMD) gas as compared to 55 MMSCMD in 1997-98. Over 80% of gas sales today is to power and fertiliser sectors. GAIL produces 18% of the LPG in the country. GAIL's fuel generates 4500 MW of power.

The carrying capacity of GAIL's HBJ pipeline has been upgraded in July 1998 from 18.2 MMSCMD to 33.4 MMSCMD at a cost of Rs. 2376 crore. Additional facilities consisting of 4 compressor stations & a loop of 505 Kms have been provided. GAIL is to shortly commission a Rs. 2590 crore gas based Petrochemical project at Pata in Uttar Pradesh. The plant will produce 300,000 TPA of ethylene,

12,000 TPA of propylene, 1,60,000 TPA of linear low density polyethylene (LLDPE) one processing plant and 100,000 TPA of HDPE in another.

GAIL extracts LPG and other hydrocarbons from rich gas to augment value of products. The company has four LPG plants with a total installed capacity of 7,03,000 TPA of which the plants at Usar in Maharashtra and at Lakwa in Assam have been successfully commissioned recently. Besides, it has installed facilities for fractionating natural gas for production of Special Boiling Point (SBP), Pentane and Propane. In response to anticipated increases in market demand for LPG, GAIL is establishing another LPG recovery plant in Auraiya in U.P. of capacity 2,58,000 TPA to be completed by April, 2000 at an estimated cost of Rs.440 Cr. GAIL has also proposed establishing a gas processing complex at Gandhar in Gujarat at a cost of Rs. 333 crore which will have a LPG production capacity of 2,07,000 TPA.

GAIL is laying a pipeline of approximately 1,250 km to transport LPG from Kandla and Jamnagar in western India to Loni in northern India with capacity of 1.7 million TPA. The Rs. 1230 Cr. project is scheduled for completion by February, 2001.

As one of the pollution control measures to save Taj Mahal, gas to the Mathura Refinery and to industries in the Agra-Ferozabad region is supplied as fuel. 182 contracts have been signed so far for supply of gas to the industries.

GAIL has successfully completed a pilot project for domestic gas supply in the city of Delhi to over 1000 consumers in Kaka. Nagar, Bapa Nagar and Pandara Park. The company has introduced compressed natural gas for use in vehicles as an alternate more eco-friendly fuel. Over 1300 petrol cars have been converted to run on CNG. 9 distribution outlets have been opened in Delhi. The Delhi city gas distribution project, which will cater to 2,31,000 households, besides certain commercial consumers and 20,000 vehicles, will be implemented by Indraprastha Gas Limited, a joint venture company of GAIL &, BPCL. A similar project had been earlier undertaken in Greater Mumbai through Mahanagar Gas Limited, a joint venture company of GAIL and M/s British Gas, U.K. to supply of gas to about 6.26 lakh domestic consumers and to commercial, industrial and transport sectors. The joint venture has already extended supply to about 30,000 domestic consumers in the eastern suburban areas of Mumbai and provided CNG to 9,000 vehicles and 10 buses. During 1997-98, GAIL signed a gas sale/purchase contract wit Joint Venture Ravva Oil Field GAIL has strengthened its Petrochemicals marketing network with the appointment of stockists & with the setting up of regional offices in all the major cities of the country. It has completed its market seeding programme. Response to its products is encouraging.

Performance of GAIL at a glance for the year 1995-96, 1996-97, 1997-98 & 1998-99 (Prov. till December, 1998) is given below:

**Generation**

GAIL is one of the 108 Public Sector Enterprise that had signed MOU with the Government during 1997-98. It stood fourth in performance compared to 14th in the previous year.

**Performance at a glance**

**Physical:**

| *Description* | *Unit* | *Actual* | | | *Provisional* |
|---|---|---|---|---|---|
| | | *1995-96* | *1996-97* | *1997-98* | *Apr. 98 to Dec. 98* |
| Gas sales | MMSCM | 17,017 | 17,367 | 20,053 | 16,002 |

| LPG/SBP/ other production | ('000MT) | 588.22 | 621.87 | 634.97 | 499.79 |
|---|---|---|---|---|---|

**Financial:**

FINANCIAL:

| Description | Unit | Actual | | | Provisional |
|---|---|---|---|---|---|
| | | 1995-96 | 1996-97 | 1997-98 | Apr. 98 to Dec. 98 |
| Profits Gross | Rs. Crore | 516 | 620 | 1020 | 599 |
| Interenal | Rs. Crore | 724 | 854 | 1269 | 856 |

**Projects commissioned during the year**

1. Gas Rehabilitation & Expansion Project

   The mega project has been commissioned successfully by installation of four compressor stations at Hazira, Vaghodia, Jhabua and Khera to upgrade the HBJ pipeline to handle 39 MMSCMD of gas.

2. LPG Recovery Project, Usar

   Commercial production started on 16th August, 1998.

3. LPG Recovery Project, Lakwa

   The project was commissioned on 19th October, 1998.

4. Construction of City Gate Station at Agra & Ferozabad was completed in June '98.

5. Pipeline and terminal for supply of Natural Gas to M/s Global Steels was commissioned on 11-12-98.

**Major projects under implementation**

1. LPG Pipeline Project Installation of 1246 Kms pipeline from Kandla, Loni to Delhi at an estimated cost of Rs. 1229 crore.

2. LPG Plant at Auraiya at an estimated cost of Rs.439 crore to produce 2,58,250 TPA of propane.

**Future plans**

(i) GAIL is participating through Petronet LNG & other agencies in Liquefied Natural Gas (LNG) import projects. These would involve the establishment of LNG terminals at several locations on the east & west coasts of India.

(ii) GAIL has signed a "Principles of Agreement" with M/s Brown & Root, USA for developing a project for import, of gas from Myanmar & Bangladesh to India. Two more international companies viz. Cairn Energy & Shell are also being associated in the venture.

(iii) In a bid to explore gas from coal bed methane, the company intends to participate in the bidding round to be announced.

GAIL is also studying the feasibility of enhancing domestic availability of gas through gasification of underground coal & lignite available in Rajasthan, Tamil Nadu & Gujarat.. An MOU has been signed with the Govt. of Rajasthan for undertaking further work in the sphere of insitu gasification of lignite.

(iv) GAIL would be participating in the exploration bidding rounds under NELP.

(v) GAIL in association with other organisations, is implementing a National Gas Hydrate Programme which is concerned with developing technology for extraction of methane from oceanic gas hydrates. This is a collaborative R & D programme which if successful, would help meet the energy needs of India to a very large extent from hydrates.

GAIL has also signed a joint collaboration agreement with Indian Oil Corporation Ltd., Indian Institute of Petroleum & Amoco, USA on 20.7.98 for developing Di-Methyl Ether (DME) as an alternative fuel for power plants as well as an alternative to diesel & LPG.

(vii) GAIL is examining the business opportunities in power sector. It is equipped to integrate its gas infrastructure with the gas based power plants efficiently. It has submitted a proposal for setting up a 400-500 MW power project jointly with M/s BSES.

# 3

# Refining

## Refining capacity and throughout

There are 15 refineries in the country with a capacity of 67.55 MMTPA. Seven are owned by M/s. Indian Oil Corporation Limited, two by Hindustan Petroleum Corporation Ltd. and one by Bharat Petroleum Corporation Ltd. The other refineries stand alone. These are Madras Refineries Ltd. at Manali & Nagapattinam, Cochin Refineries Ltd., Bongaigaon Refinery and Petrochemicals Ltd. and Mangalore Refinery and Petrochemicals Ltd. The cumulative refining throughput from April-December, 1998 was 50.13 MMT as against the planned production of 49.94 MMT.

A number of new grass-root refineries and expansion of existing refineries will enhance the refining capacity to about 131 MMTPA (excluding export oriented units) by the end of the 9th Plan. The estimated demand of products would then be about 112 MMTPA. By the end of the 10th Plan, the refining capacity is likely to be 170 MMTPA and the product demand 156 MMTPA.

## Import of crude oil and petroleum products during 1998-99

### *Gross imports*

***Crude oil:*** In the year 1997-98, about 34.494 MMT of crude oil was imported valued at Rs. 15897 crore. Import of crude upto November, 1998 was 26.322 MMT valued at Rs. 10038 crore.

***Petroleum products:*** During 199798, 19.530 MMT of products was imported at a cost of Rs. 12432 crore. During the current year upto November, 1998 the import of petroleum products was 12.991 MMT valued at Rs. 6855 crore.

**Exports**

***Crude oil:*** Since 1988-89 no crude has been exported.

***Petroleum products:*** During 1997-98, the export of petroleum products was 2.929 million tonnes for a value of Rs. 1820 crore. The export of petroleum products during April-November, 1998 was 1.005 MMT valued at Rs.612 crore. This includes supplies of POL to Nepal upto September, 1998.

**Position of the oil pool account**

A comprehensive package was evolved by Government to erase the oil pool deficit. It provided for greater transparency in subsidies and movement of Prices towards the economic cost. Thus producers would benefit and simultaneously economically weaker sections of the society would be protected. Potential investors could expect a transparent and predictably reliable system, in line with the practice followed in the developed countries. The package included:

I. A modest increase in the prices of LPG, Diesel and Petrol but no increase in the price of SKO. The prices of Naphtha, FO and LSHS were revised on the basis of import parity.

II. Providing industrial intermediates at import parity prices. Petroleum products such as FO, LSHS, Naphtha and Bitumen were to be made available to end-users at import parity prices.

III. Fixing the consumer prices of Diesel (HSD) on the principle of import parity.

IV. Transferring the subsidy on fertiliser inputs to the Budget.

V. A loan to the oil companies by the Government to the extent of cumulative outstandings of oil companies. This loan amount would in turn be utilised by the oil companies to buy special bonds to be issued by the Government for the same. This would ensure,

   a) Improvement of the balance sheets of the oil companies by replacing their receivables as investment in Government securities; and

   b) Leave the fiscal deficit unaffected.

VI. Providing immediate liquidity to the Oil companies by making Rs.5000 crore of the above bonds eligible as collateral for loans.

VII. Dismantling the APM in a phased manner in accordance with the recommendations of the "R" Group.

VIII. Review of Excise duty on Diesel cars to discourage avoidable Diesel consumption by luxury vehicles.

IX. Restructuring of excise and customs duty, cess, etc. on petroleum products.

X. Revision of Natural gas prices suitably.

- In line with the above decision, the price of HSD has been revised effective November 7,1997, December 25, 1997, March 1, 1998, April 4, 1998, May 20, 1998, January 9, 1999 and mid night of 27/28th February, 1999.

**Phased dismantling of APM**

Based on the recommendation of the 'R' Group and the

Expert Technical Group (ETG), the Government in November, 1997 approved a time table for phased dismantling of APM over a period of four years, commencing from 1.4.1998.

a) The Cost-plus formula for Public Sector Oil Producers (PSOPs) has been withdrawn from 1.4.1998. They are now paid instead a percentage of the weighted average FOB price of actual imports of crude oil for indigenous production. However, a floor price of Rs 1991 / MT has been fixed.

b) In the transition period, producers of crude oil shall retain a pre-announced increasing share of free on board (FOB) cost of crude oil, while refineries will have to pay the import parity price for crude. The differential will accrue to the Oil Pool Account to discharge the Oil Bonds. Indigenous oil producers will pay oil cess of Rs.900/MT and royalty out of their own proceeds as in the past.

c) Cost plus formula for shipping of crude oil has been done away with and market determined rates to be paid.

d) Effective 1.4.1998 onwards, Refinery Gate prices of controlled products viz. MS, HSD, SKO, LPG and ATF are being fixed on the principle of import parity. However, existing refineries will contribute towards servicing of oil bonds through adjustment during the transition period. Other products of the refineries like Naphtha, FO, LSHS, Wax, Bitumen, etc., can be sold by them at market driven prices.

e) The ex-storage point prices of only MS, HSD, Kerosene (PDS), LPG (Domestic), ATF and NGL continue to be determined by the Government.

f) Private and Joint sector refineries have been permitted to import crude oil freely for actual use effective 13.7.1998.

g) Customs duty on crude oil has been reduced from 27% to 22% effective 2.6.1998.

h) Furnace oil has been decanalised effective 13.7.1998 under the provisions of the EXIM Policy. Naphtha exports have been decanalised effective 22.7.1998.

i) Refining sector has been delicensed with effect from 8.6.1998.

j) Freight under-recoveries on HSD (difference between actual railway freight and notional railway freight) to the extent of 20% have been passed on in the selling prices effective 9.1.1999.

k) The ex-storage point price of LPG Packed (Domestic) has been revised effective 1.2.1999 and thereafter on midnight of 27/28th Feb., 1999.

The process of deregulation and liberalisation will be continued during the transition period. Phased reduction in subsidies on transport, on Kerosene (PDS) and on LPG (Domestic) are proposed. The incidence will be transferred to the Budget at the end of the transition period. Marketing rights will be extended for transportation fuels viz. MS, HSD and ATF, subject to an investment of Rs. 2000 crore on owning and operating refineries or production of at least three million tonnes of crude oil annually. A regulatory framework is under consideration for the Hydrocarbon sector.

**Numaligarh Refinery Limited (NRL)**

Numaligarh Refinery is a grassroot Refinery at Numaligarh in the District of Golaghat (Assam) being set up in fulfilment of the "Assam Accord" of August 15,

1985. The project was approved in July, 1992 and the company incorporated on 22nd April, 1993. BPCL, IBP and Govt. of Assam have equity participation of 32%, 19% and 10% respectively, in the company. 39% of equity will be offered to Public. The project cost is Rs.2724 crore. Rs.908 crore will be raised as equity and Rs. 1816 crore as loan. The authorised capital of the company is Rs. 1000 crore.

Expenditure of Rs. 1875 crore on the project upto 31.12.1998 has been met out of equity contribution from promoters, loans from 011313, HUDCO and from Govt. of India. The Company has so far received Rs. 1333 crore from OIDB (including Rs.373 crore during 1998-99).

The project is scheduled to be commissioned by April 1999. The overall physical progress now achieved is 95% on the Refinery and 87% on the Marketing Terminal.

**Cochin Refineries Limited (CRL)**

The Refinery's initial installed capacity in September, 1966 was 2.5 MMTPA. It was raised to 3.3 MMTPA in 1973 to 4.5 MMTPA in 1984 and to 7.5 MMTPA in December, 1994.

*Physical performance*

During the year 1997-98, the Refinery processed 7.74 MMT of crude oil. The capacity utilisation was 103.15% and this was the tenth consecutive year when the Refinery achieved capacity utilisation of over 100%. CRL also set a record in crude throughput, production of Liquefied Petroleum Gas, Kerosene, Aviation Turbine Fuel, Bitumen and Special Boiling Point Spirit.

The anticipated crude oil throughput for 1998-99 is 7.55 MMTPA. Crude oil processed till 21.1.1999 was 6.13 MMT.

The company has augmented its Captive Power generating capacity by installing a 17.8 MW Steam Turbine Generator along with 80 TPH Boiler.

***Safety & environmental protection***

The company has initiated necessary action for implementing environmental management system in accordance with ISO 14001 Standard.

***Financial performance***

*Turnover and profits*

CRL achieved a record turnover of Rs.4,374.15 crore during the year 1997-98. The 1996-97 turnover was Rs. 3,917.75 crore. The Profit Before Tax (PBT) for the year was Rs. 291.91 crore including updation arrears amounting to Rs. 145.96 crore received during the year. In the previous year PBT was Rs. 108.93 crore.

It contributed Rs.1237.29 crore to the Exchequer by way of taxes, duties etc. During the year, the figure in 96-97 being Rs. 1113.82 crore. The dividend was 32%.

***MOU targets***

The company achieved an "EXCELLENT" rating for the seventh consecutive year.

***Project under implementation***

*Diesel hydro desulphurisation project*

The Rs. 852 crore Project approved in June 1997 aims at reducing sulphur content in diesel to 0.25% by wt. from the present level of 1.0% by wt. It is expected to be commissioned by December 1999.

*Stand alone water supply scheme*

The company is implementing a project costing about Rs.94.94 crore for drawing water by December 1999 for its industrial needs from the Periyar River. The Water Supply project will ensure the availability of 6.3 MGD of water by Dec., 1999 for the company's immediate requirement, and also an ultimate demand of 16.5 MGD in the future catering to capacity expansion to 13.5 MMTPA, and a- proposed 500 MW Power Generation project as well.

***Projects under consideration***

*Capacity expansion project*

A Detailed Feasibility Report (DFR) for the expansion of the crude oil refining capacity from 7.5 MMTPA to 13.5 MMTPA at an estimated cost of Rs.3993.26 crore has been submitted.

*Power generation project*

This Project based on heavy residues is proposed to be implemented as a Joint Venture with Cochin Ambalamugal Energy Company (CAEC), Larsen &, Tubro (L&T) and Kerala State Electricity Board (KSEB) as Partners. The estimated cost of the Project, as of 1998 is Rs.2,995 crore.

**Madras Refineries Limited (MRL)**

*Introduction*

Madras Refineries Limited (MRL) was formed on 30.12.1965 as a Joint Venture of the Government of India (GOI), Amoco India Inc. U.S.A. and National Iranian Oil Company (NIOC), Iran with initial equity contribution in the ratio of 74:13:13.

MRL's Refinery was originally designed for processing 2.5 MMTPA (Million Metric Tonnes per Annum) of imported crude from Iran supplied by NIOC. The Refinery was commissioned in the year 1969 and has been making profits from the second year of its operations.

MRL's Manali refining capacity was increased from 2. 5 MMTPA to 2.8 MMTPA in 1980, to 5.6 MMTPA in

1984-85 at a cost of Rs. 170 Crore and further to 6.5 MMTPA in March, 1993. MRL's Cauvery Basin Refinery at Nagapattinam was commissioned in 1993, thus increasing the total refining capacity to 7.0 MMTPA. Amoco Inc. disinvested its equity holding in favour of GOI in 1985. After a successful premium equity issue in 1994, the Government of India continues to remain as a major shareholder of the Company.

***Important achievements***

*Crude thruput*

During the year 1997-98, the total crude processed was 7.52 Million Metric Tonnes (MMT), an all time high figure, as against 6.97 MMT during the previous year. This production surpassed the MOU target of 6.75 MMT. The actual crude throughput upto December 1998 was 4.9 Million Tonnes and the throughput for the year 1998-99 is expected to be about 6.8 Million Tonnes.

***Major projects completed***

The following projects have beer completed :

*(i) Wax-deoiling plant*

The project to increase the existing Wax-Deoiling plant capacity from 20,000 TPA to 30,000 TPA at a cost of Rs. 41.32 Crore has been commissioned. The pelletiser unit has been installed and commissioned successfully.

*(ii) Wax hydrofinishing unit*

The project to install Wax Hydrofinishing Unit in place of the existing Clay Contacting Unit has been commissioned within the estimated cost of about Rs. 23.50 Crore.

*(iii) Fuel oil storage tanks*

Two Fuel Oil. storage tanks of 10,000 KL capacity each have been commissioned, thus augmenting the fuel oil storage capacity of the company and avoiding sullage problems.

***Projects under implementation***

*(i) Diesel Hydro Desulphurisation (DHDS) project*

The Diesel Hydro Desulphurisation (DHDS) project to reduce sulphur to 0.25% in diesel is scheduled to be completed by 31.03.1999.

*(ii) Multigrade bitumen despatch facilities*

In order to augment the storage and despatch facilities of Multigrade Bitumen, additional tanks/ pumping facilities and loading arms are being provided at a cost of Rs.720 Lakhs.

*(iii) Lube vacuum column revamp*

Modification of existing lube vacuum column to improve lube base oil quality, is being taken up at a cost of Rs.450 Lakh during Refinery shutdown planned this year.

*(iv) Water spray system on LPG spheres/sheds/bullets*

A scheme for augmenting the number of automatic sprinklers in LPG sheds is nearing completion.

*(v) Insitu stack monitors*

Provision for common In-situ Stack Gas Monitors for various heaters on an experimental basis to monitor and control the pollutants is under progress.

***Major projects approved***

MRL has obtained the first stage clearance from the Government of India to expand its refining capacity at Manali by another 3 MMTPA. A Detailed Feasibility Report for the project has since been submitted.

***Policy initiatives undertaken by MRL***

(i) MRL has signed a Memorandum of Understanding (MOU) with the Ministry for the year 1998-99.

(ii) The refinery proposes to install a 250 MW Power Plant, as a joint venture, near its existing Refinery at Manali based heavy residue. The estimated cost of the project is about Rs. 1600 crore.

(iii) MRL is planning to set up a permanent Jetty facility at Nagapattinam for receiving crude oil for its Cauvery Basin Refinery. The Jetty facility would also facilitate transshipment of petroleum products. Oceanographic studies have already been commissioned. The cost of the project is estimated to be Rs. 55 crore.

***Control of pollution and other environmental initiatives taken by MRL***

The Refineries are provided with dedicated Effluent Treatment Plants using the latest state-of-art technology. The Refinery used LSHS fuel throughout the year for controlling the sulphur emissions in the ambient air.

A Green Belt within the Refinery with the technical assistance from State Forestry Department was also developed at Manali and in the Cauvery Basin Refinery.

Cauvery Basin Refinery is gearing UP to get ISO 14000 accreditation.

**Bongaigaon Refinery and Petrochemicals Ltd. (BRPL)**

***Introduction***

BRPL was incorporated on February 20, 1974, to install a Refinery of I MMTPA and a Petrochemical Complex consisting of Xylene, Dimethyl Terephthalate (DMT) and Polyester Staple Fibre (P.S.F) Units. The crude processing capacity of the Refinery has since been enhanced to 2.35 MTPA in 1995-96.

The authorised equity capital of the company is Rs.200 crore. The paid up capital as on date is Rs. 199.82 crore. Government of India has so far disinvested 25.54% of the issued capital.

While the POL products from the Refinery are marketed by Indian Oil Corporation, the Petrochemical products and petroleum coke are marketed by BRPL itself.

***Physical performance***

The Performance highlight of the Refinery as well as Petrochemical units for 1998-99 has been as follows:

*(All figures in MT)*

| | *Item* | *1998-99* | |
|---|---|---|---|
| | | *Actuals till Dec. '98* | *1998-99 Anticipated* |
| a) | Crude throughput (million tonnes) | 1.14 | 1.65 |
| b) | Production of Major Petrochemical Products (tonnes) | | |
| | – Para xylene | 11,666 | 17,500 |
| | – Ortho xylene | 1,033 | 1,500 |
| | – DMT | 16,696 | 25,000 |
| | – PSF | 9,055 | 15,000 |

The lower processing of crude vis-a-vis capacity is due to lower crude availability. Production of petrochemicals is lower due to depressed markets.

***Financial performance***

The Profit before depreciation, interest and tax for the year 1998-99 till Dec. '98 was Rs. 50 crore and net profit after tax was Rs.20 crore. The net profit after tax for the year 1998-99 is expected to be Rs.45 crore.

The plan expenditure during 1998-99 will be Rs.40 crore. During the year, a Hydrotreatment of Coker LGO Project was approved for implementation at an estimated cost of Rs. 67 crore.

***Join venture projects***

Public sector companies have been allowed to set up refineries in joint venture participating 26%. The JVCs in this category are:

*(i) Bharat Oman refinery limited*

BPCL is setting up a 6.0 MMTPA Refinery in Bina, MP, as a joint venture with Oman oil Company. The proposal was approved in December 1995.

*(ii) West coast refinery*

The project was proposed as a joint venture between HPCL and Oman Oil Company in Deogarh in Maharashtra with a capacity of 6.0 MMTPA. Oman Oil Company is reviewing its participation in the venture.

*(iii) East coast refinery*

The Refinery is proposed to be set up by IOC as a joint venture with Kuwait Petroleum Corporation with a capacity of 9.0 MMTPA and was approved in July 1998.

*(iv) BPCL-shell joint venture refinery*

Government issued an LOI on 3.4.1996 for this Refinery to be set up as a joint venture between BPCL and Shell an International Company with a capacity of 7 MMTPA in up. The Detailed Feasibility Report (DFR) has been submitted by BPCL to the Government. The proposal is under examination.

*(v) HPCL joint venture refinery in Punjab*

Government has approved the proposal of HPCL in November, 1998 to set up a 9 MMTPA Grassroot Refinery, at Bhatinda in Punjab, at an estimated cost of Rs.9806 crore through a Joint Venture Company.

***Investment in refinery sector***

Government of India has encouraged private investments including foreign investment in the refining sector following liberalization of Industrial policy. In pursuance of this policy Letters of Intent have been granted to 10 companies for setting up of refineries in the private sector in the domestic Tariff Area for about 51 MMTPA of capacity. In addition 19 parties are holding LOI for setting up 100% EOU Refineries for a total capacity 37.1 MMTPA.

***Product pipelines***

Government has, on 10th April, 1996, approved the formation of a Holding Company (Non Govt.) with equity participation of oil companies, namely, IOC, HPCL, BPCL and IBP with equity contribution of 50% (IOC, BPCL, HPCL 16 each and IBP 2 %) and the balance 50% equity to be offered to private companies, Financial institutions, etc., for the purpose of implementation of the petroleum products pipeline. The pipeline Holding Company in the name, "Petronet India Limited" was incorporated on 26.05.1997 with its registered office at Mumbai.

***Diesel quality improvement***

With a view to improve the quality of HSD and to reduce pollution Desulphurisation (DHDS) projects are being established in nine Refineries in the country at a total cost of Rs. 5568.31 crore. The project will reduce sulphur content in HSD to 0.25%. Government have guideline, for setting up power plants by refineries utilising heavy bottom oils like Fuel Oil, LSHS, HPS and other heavy ends.

# 4

# Marketing and Distribution

**Prime Minister's self-employment scheme of oil companies**
The salient features of the Scheme are as under:

- There will be one dealership at each Block Headquarters. SKO would be sold at normal rates unsubsidised, freely without need for a ration card.
- The maximum age limit for 'Open' and 'SC/ST' category candidates will be 35 years and for categories of Defence, PH, PMP and Outstanding Sportspersons 45 years.
- Reservation is as follows:

| *Category* | *Percentage* |
|---|---|
| *SC/ST* | *As per Statewise SC/ST percentage Prescribed by the Government of India for reservation in employment.* |
| PH | 6 |
| DEF | 8 |
| PMP | 8 |
| OSP | 3 |
| OPEN | balance |

33% in each of the above categories will be reserved for women. Except SC/ST, in all other categories, reservation of 27% will be made for OBCs.

- All the dealerships will be given on partnership only to a maximum of 3 partners, all from the same specified category.
- The retail selling price of kerosene under the Scheme will be cost price plus normal reasonable margin.
- The dealer's commission will be Rs. 0.50 per litre.

**LPG marketing by PSUs**

To spread the rural use of LPG, Government plans to commission about 1900 rural LPG distributorships. Villages and small towns having a population of 10,000, and villages adjoining cities having a population of 1 lakh will be catered to by these dealers.

The customer population of LPG with PSU Oil Companies in the country was about 353 lakhs as on 1.1.1999. Government has approved the release of 35 lakh new LPG connections/ 25 lakh DBCs during 1998-99. 14.4 lakh new LPG connections were given upto December, 1998. Besides, 3 lakh connections will be given additionally during the year exclusively for Delhi against surrender of matching kerosene quota.

LPG is an environment friendly and clean fuel. It has been decided to clear the waiting list in all the North-Eastern States, hilly areas having an altitude of 2000 ft. and above, the States of J&K, H.P. and all the Union Territories by 31-3-1999. Thereafter Oil Companies will endeavour to release LPG connections in these areas across the counter. Having regard to environment in the TaJ Trapezium, LPG connections are released therein on demand. Innovative methods like use of Mobile LPG filling Truck and skid mounted vehicle have been introduced to market LPG in rural areas of Tamil Nadu, Gujarat,, U.P. and Punjab. Government has also proposed the use of LPG as automotive fuel. During April-December/98 the production and import of LPG was about 2.64 MMT (prov.) and 0.989 MMT (prov.) respectively.

**Parallel marketing of LPG and SKO**

In February 1993, Govt. introduced the parallel marketing of LPG and kerosene by private parties in the interest of the common man. The PSU Oil Companies were advised to facilitate private importers without jeopardising their own imports/ plans. Upto 31-12-1998, 117 parties for SKO and 18 parties for LPG had signed MOUs for importing these products utilising the Oil Companies' port facilities. 1070 TMT of SKO and 137 TMT of LPG had been imported under PMS upto Dec., 98. 104 private parties have imported about 4085 TMT of SKO and 19 parties have imported about 481 TMT of LPG. M/s Reliance Petroleum is marketing LPG produced from its Naphtha Cracker at Hazira effective April 1997 and has sold about 83 TMT during 1997-98 and 80 TMT till Dec., 1998. East India Petroleum Ltd. has commissioned its own LPG import facilities at Visakhapatnam on 5-9-1998 with a parcel of about 1229 MT of LPG imported by M/s SHV Energy India Limited. With this 9 parties have commissioned their own LPG import facility.

**Dealer selection boards**

A fair, transparent and objective procedure has been put in place for selection of dealers of petroleum products. Selection of dealers/ distributors had been pending in more than 5000 locations. Government decided to increase the number of Dealer Selection Boards from 14 to 52. It was decided to appoint Retired District Judges as Chairman of the Boards which are now constituted as under:-

(i) Retired Judge of High Court or retired District Judge.

– Chairman

(ii) An Officer not below the rank of Chief Manager of one/ concerned Oil Company.

– Member

(iii) An Officer of the rank of Chief Manager of another Oil Company.

– Member

Most of the Boards are in position and selection has commenced.

**Bharat Petroleum Corporation Limited (BPCL)**

Bharat Petroleum Corporation Limited (BPCL) was established as a Government Company on the 24th January, 1976.

The authorised and paid up share capital of BPCL are Rs.200 crore and Rs. 150 crore respectively. The share holding of Government of India in the Corporation is 66.2%. It is a Navratna.

During the year 1997-98 the Corporation achieved a Refinery throughput of 7.94 MMT compared with 7.59 MMT in the previous year. The total sale of petroleum products was 16.37 MMT and higher than 15.76 MMT achieved in 1996-97. The sales turnover increased to Rs.20,918.7 crore from Rs. 18,156.4 crore in the previous year and the net profit after tax Rs. 533 crore from Rs.433 crore. The Corporation declared a dividend of Rs.75 crore, equivalent to 50% for the year that ended on 31.3.98.

The Corporation has entered into a Joint Venture agreement with Oman Oil Company Limited for establishing a 6 MMTPA grassroot Refinery at Bina in

Madhya Pradesh. Another Joint Venture Company, Bharat Shell Limited, has been formed with Shell Overseas Investment B.V. Netherlands for marketing Shell's lubricants in the country. BPCL is a major promoter in the Refinery at Numaligarh, Assam. It is one of the promoter of Petronet India Limited, a company formed for developing and laying a network of petroleum product pipelines in the country. It is establishing a Joint Venture with GAIL for Gas Distribution in Delhi.

The following projects of importance have been commissioned or are under implementation.

- Diesel Hydro Desulphurisation project facilities at its Mumbai refinery at an estimated cost of Rs.622 crore will be completed by March, 1999.
- Mumbai-Manmad Product Pipeline was completed in March 1998.
- A new Jetty alongwith Coastal Installation of Jawahar Lal Nehru Port Trust.
- Additional Product Tankages of 4,85,000 kl has been commissioned.
- LPG Bottling Plants were commissioned at Sultanpur and Uluberia.
- 4 Bottling Plants are expected to be commissioned during 1998-99.
- New Black Oil Facilities were commissioned at Vizag and Sweree.
- Dockliness were commissioned at Kandla, Tondiarpet and Vizag.

During April-December, 1998, 3 new Retail Outlets (ROs) have been commissioned. During the remaining part of the year 1998-99, 17 new ROs and 5 SKO/LDO dealerships are expected to be commissioned.

The Corporation duly implements Govt. Policy of reservation for Scheduled Castes/ Tribes. It has adopted villages under SC component & Tribal Sub Plan to promote various welfare schemes. BPCL also continued to support other public welfare activities and rehabilitation schemes for disabled/ handicapped.

The Corporation lays stress on Human Resources Development and training and has constituted an Employees Satisfaction Enhancement Department.

**Hindustan Petroleum Corporation Limited (HPCL)**

Hindustan Petroleum Corporation Limited (HPCL) was established as a Government Company in March, 1974. The authorised and paid-up share capital of the Corporation as on March 3 1, 1998, were Rs.250 crore and Rs.221 crore respectively. The Govt. of India holding in HPCL is 51.06%. It is one of the Navratna companies.

During the year 1997-98 the two refineries of the Corporation at Mumbai and Visakhapatnam achieved a combined crude thruput of 8.84 million tonnes whereas they had achieved 11.39 million tonnes in the previous year. The total sale of petroleum products during 1997-98 was 16.00 million tonnes compared with 15.46 million tonnes in 1996-97, representing a growth of 3.5%. The sales turnover was Rs.20512.91 crore in 1997-98, and in 1996-97 Rs. 18089.00 crore. The net profit was Rs.701.16 crore for 1997-98 being an improvement on Rs.612.22 crore for the previous year. The Corporation has declared a dividend of 50% in 1997-98 outstripping 40% declared in the previous year.

During the year, 17 new retail outlets, 6 kerosene dealerships and 17 LPG distributorships were commissioned bringing the total numbers to 4327,1622 and 1463 respectively. The Corporation enrolled 10.35 lakh new customers and released 9.92 lakhs DBC during the year.

HPCL's Joint Venture Refinery, namely, Mangalore Refinery and Petrochemicals Limited (MRPL) achieved a crude thruput of 3.953 MMT in the year 1997-98. MRPL is currently expanding its Refinery capacity from 3 MMTPA to 9 MMTPA. The project is scheduled to be commissioned by November, 1999.

***Major projects completed/commissioned***

- Visakhapatnam-Vijaywada product pipeline of 350 km length at a cost of Rs.521.61 crore.
- Black Oil pipeline from Mumbai Refinery to Vashi Terminal at a cost of Rs.44.15 crore.
- LPG horton (1400 MT) spheres at Visakhapatnam at a cost of Rs.41.55 crore. Bottling plant capacity was augmented at Paharpur and Khapri LPG plants at a cost of Rs.28 crore.
- A new Terminal at Kakinada with 30,000 kl Tankage and allied facilities at a cost of Rs. 15.06 crore.
- New POL Depots at Desur, Panipat and Karari.

***Major Project under Implementation***

- A low cost expansion of Visakhapatnam Refinery from 4.5 MMTPA to 7.5 MMTPA at a cost of Rs.1138.02 crore.
- CDU-I/CTU project at Visakhapatnam Refinery at an estimated cost of Rs.24.59 crore.
- A project to maximise M.S. at a cost of Rs.45.27 crore at Mumbai Refinery.
- Hydro-desulphurisation of Diesel project at Mumbai and Visakhapatnam Refinery at an estimated cost of Rs. 1552 crore.

- Additional product tankage and allied facilities at an estimated cost of Rs.80 crore.
- LPG Plants at Chennai, Usar, Pampore, Madurai and Mangalore.

***Major projects under consideration and development***

- New Terminal at Uran including Jetty facilities.
- Dock line between Jetties and Terminals at Kandla.
- LPG bottling plants at 30 locations.
- Visakhapatnam-Vijayawada pipeline extension at Secunderabad.

**Indian Oil Corporation Limited (IOCL)**

IOC has six operating refineries at Guwahati, Barauni, Gujarat, Haldia, Mathura and Digboi. It has recently commissioned a 6 million tonnes capacity refinery at Panipat. The refineries of IOC achieved a crude throughput of 27.50 million tonnes during 199798 and 22.50 million tonnes during the current yeai. IOC's pipelines achieved a throughput of 31.03 million tonnes during 1997-98 and 24.86 million tonnes during April-December 1998 against the MOU target of 32.12 million tonnes for the year 1998-99.

The Corporation sold 43.41 MMT of petroleum products during 1997-98 registering an increase of 1.44 MMT over previous year. During April-December 1998, it has sold 33.861 MMT of petroleum products with a market participation of 54.30% at the end of December, 1998.

The Corporation achieved a turnover, of Rs. 59,176 crore in 1997-98 as against Rs. 55,389 crore in the previous year. The profit before tax was Rs. 1964 crore for the year 1997-98 and the profit after tax was Rs. 1706 crore. The corresponding figure in the previous year was

Rs. 1766 crore and Rs. 1408 crore respectively. The Corporation declared a dividend of 50% amounting to Rs. 195 crore. The cumulative dividend declared by the Corporation amounts to Rs. 1050 crore. It is a Navratna company.

The Corporation commissioned 63 retail outlets and 36 LPG distributorships so far during the current year. The number of retail outlets and LPG distributorships of the company as on 31.12.1998 was 6841 and 2936 respectively. During the period April-December, 1998, the company released 7.00 lakh new LPG connections. The number of LPG customers as on 31.12.1998 was 177.40 lakh.

The following projects have been completed during the year 1998-99 :

- Catalytic Reformer at Mathura Refinery.
- Production of Paraffin wax at Barauni Refinery.
- Marketing terminal at Panipat Phase-II.
- Lighterage terminal at Paradip.

***Major projects under implementation***

1. Grassroot Refinery at Panipat of 6 MMTPA capacity.
2. Haldia-Barauni Crude Oil Pipeline (4.2 MMTPA capacity).
3. Hydrofinishing of Waxes at Digboi Refinery.
4. New Delayed Coker Unit at Digboi Refinery.
5. Expansion of Gujarat Refinery by 3.0 MMTPA alongwith augmentation of FCCU Capacity.
6. Matching Secondary Processing Facilities at Mathura Refinery.

7. Diesel Hydro-Desulphurisation Units at Haldia, Mathura, Gujarat & Panipat Refineries.
8. Augmentation of Salaya-Viramgam (SV) & Viramgam-Koyali (VK) Section of SMPL (Salaya-Mathura Pipeline) for Gujarat Refinery Expansion.
9. Tap Off Point (TOP) at Manmad in Mumbai-Manmad Pipeline.
10. New Marketing Terminal at JNPT.

*New projects planned*

1. Expansion of Panipat Refinery, by 3 MMT and Augmentation of pipeline capacity for additional crude oil to refinery for this purpose.
2. Low cost expansion of Barauni Refinery to 6 MMTPA and related Augmentation of Haldia-Barauni crude oil pipeline capacity.
3. Marketing complex for Eastern India Refinery Project.
4. Production of PTA/ Paraxylene at Panipat Refinery.
5. LPG Import facilities at Haldia in a Joint Venture.
6. Improvement of Lube Oil Quality by Catalytic Iso-Dewaxing at Haldia.
7. Crude oil pipeline from Pipavov to Koyali.
8. Hydrotreater at Digboi.
9. Fluid Catalytic Cracking Unit (FCCU) at Haldia Refinery.

**Indian Oil Blending Limited (IOBL)**

The Indian Oil Blending Limited is a 100% subsidiary of the Indian Oil Corporation Limited engaged in the manufacturing of lubricants and greases. During 1997-98, IOBL produced 3.05 lakh KLs of lubes and earned a net profit of Rs.7.58 crore as against Rs.6.51 crore in the previous year. A dividend of 25% has been declared for the year 1997-98.

# 5

# Other Undertakings/Organisations

## Engineers India Limited (EIL)

*Introduction*

Engineers India Limited is a leading engineering and consultancy company in India situated at New Delhi. It has been serving petroleum, petro–chemical and other process industries, and the metallurgical sector since the mid sixties. EIL provides a complete range of project services, including process design, engineering, procurement, construction management, project management and supervisory assistance for commissioning & plant start–up. It has set up a large number of process plants in India and abroad.

EIL's quality management system conforms to ISO–900 1. The company has Regional Engineering Offices in Chennai and Vadodara, Overseas Engineering Office in Doha(Qatar), Branch Offices in Calcutta and Mumbai, Inspection/ Procurement Offices at various locations in India, in London and Tokyo and Construction Offices at different project sites in India and abroad. The number of employees of the company is 3730.

*Important assignments*

The Company continued to keep its order book healthy inspite of the stiff competition.

Major assignments secured by EIL during the year, were:–

- AVU Project for Yield and Energy Improvement Project at Mathura Refinery of IOC,
- FCCU including related utilities and offsites facilities at Haldia. of 10C,
- Revamp of Bitumen Blowing Unit at Mahul of BPCL,
- Enhancement of LPG production/ unit at Cochin Refineries,
- Second VDU Project at Haldia Refinery of IOC,
- Preparation of Detailed Feasibility Report for the expansion Cochin, Madras and Barauni refineries,
- Installation of additional Steam Boiler at Hazira,
- Detailed Feasibility Report for Para–Xylene Project,
- Additional jobs for Uran Plant such as Food Grade Hexane Project, Bid package for Zero Flaring System, Thai–Uran Gas Line laying Phase–I & II and Slug Catcher Revamp of ONGC,
- The 280 km Cochin–CoimbatoreûKarur multiproducts pipeline of BPCL/Petronet,
- 380 km multiproducts MangaloreûBangalore pipeline of HPCL/ Petronet,
- Expansion of NALCO smelter from 230,000 tonnes/annum to 345,000 tonnes/annum.
- Detailed Feasibility Report for Expansion of INDAL's Hirakud Smelter Project,
- Updation of DFR for Utkal Alumina project,
- Setting up of Gallium (upto 5N Purity level) Plant at Damanjodi of NALCO,

- Coordination–cum monitoring of PMN programme of Department of Ocean Development, and
- Time and cost monitoring system for Expansion of NALCO's Aluminium Smelter and Captive Power Plant.

The company is now turning to LNG and Power sectors. It secured assignments in the sectors connected with Basic Engineering Package (BEP) for LNG Terminal and Marine Facilities at Kochi, preparation of LSTK bids for LNG Import Terminal at Dahej and, site selection study for LNG Terminal at Kandla of GAIL. The company was awarded the process feasibility study for Andhra Pradesh Gas Power Corporation for improvement of Natural Gas quality & quantity and amendment of DPR for Integrated Solar Combined Cycle Power Plant of Rajasthan State Power Corporation. It has secured a number of assignments in Environment engineering, Specialised Maintenance, Risk Analysis and systems engineering.

EIL won contract for Gasoline Production facilities in the Jabel Ali Free Zone, Dubai. The Company has also subsequently been entrusted additional work for carrying out the Environment Impact Assessment, Hazop study and Risk Analysis of the project.

It secured assignment from the Saudi Basic Industries Corporation (SABIC) for engineering services at AI–Jubail, Saudi Arabia. EIL also secured an assignment for providing technical services for NODCO Refinery in design and detailed engineering services to MANCO Contracting Co., Qatar for Feed and Fuel Stock Supply to QAFAC, Qatar, detailed engineering services for Ras Abu Aboud Jetty Strengthening and Fendering Upgradation project of QGPC, Qatar and training services for Hazop Chemical and Fertilizer Company in Saudi Arabia.

***Policy initiatives undertaken by EIL during 1998–99***

The major policy initiative taken by EIL include:

*(i) Strategic alliances*

Alliances are being developed with organisations for LNG Projects, Refinery residue based power plants, Deep Water technology and LSTK bids.

*(ii) Implementation of major recommendations of system Review to reduce customer response time*

Following the Customer Satisfaction Survey in 1995–96, a System Review was carried out in 1996–97 to identify ways and means of reducing customer response time. Major recommendations of the system Review in the areas of engineering and procurement were implemented in 1997–98. A structured review of the implementation of the major findings of the Customer Satisfaction has been done in 1998–99.

*(iii) Turnkey assignments*

Bidding for turnkey projects was taken up. One Turnkey project–The Offsite Automation Project at Mathura Refinery of Indian Oil has been secured during 1998–99.

*(iv) Technology development*

Three R&D Development Projects were identified in the MOU for completion in 1998–99.

*(v) Information technology services*

Information Technology Services have been identified as a thrust area for future.

**Lubrizol India Limited (LIL)**

Lubrizol India Limited (LIL), a Public Sector Undertaking, was incorporated in 1966 in collaboration with the Lubrizol Corporation, U.S.A., under the Companies Act, in pursuance of an agreement between the Government of India and the Lubrizol Corporation, U.S.A. in December 1965. Government of India holds

60% of the subscribed equity capital of the Company and the Lubrizol Corporation, U.S.A., 40% thereof. The manufacturing unit is situated at Village Turbhe, Thane–Belapur Industrial Complex, adjacent to New Bombay. The Company has a second unit for manufacture of Extreme Pressure speciality chemicals and Additives at Aloja, Dist. Raigad. LIL develops, manufactures and markets additives systems for automotive and industrial lubricants and catering to the needs of the Petroleum Industry. The Authorised, Issued and Subscribed share capital of the company is Rs. 1920 lakhs.

The Company has earned Profit Before Tax (PBT) of Rs.46.14 Crore in 1997–98, For the year 1998–99, the projected PBT in Revised Estimate is Rs.38.50 crore. Projected Profit for 1998–99 is lower than the previous year by approximately 16.6% due to higher cost on account of fluctuations in exchange rate, increase in import duty, intensive competition, etc.

The Company paid a dividend of 40% on the Paid up share Capital of Rs. 1920 lakhs for the year 199798 as against 35% during the previous year. The contribution made by the company to the exchequer by way of duties and taxes during the year 1997–98 was Rs.130.38 crore as compared to Rs. 128.09 crore during the–previous year.

The Company achieved a sales volume of 38490 MT and income of Rs.363.12 crore in 1997–98. The projection for 1998–99 are 38,100 MT and Rs.380.05 crore.

The production of Chemical Additive Packages upto 31st December, 1998 has been 29,421 MT.

**Indian additives limited**

***Introduction***

Indian Additives Limited (IAL) is a joint venture company promoted by Madras Refineries Limited (MRL) and Chevron Chemical Company (Chevron) in the year 1989. It has manufacturing facilities including a blending unit for lubricant additive packages. The joint venture agreement between MRL and Chevron provides for their participation in the capital of IAL in the ratio of 60:40. Chevron is the technical collaborator and has provided formulation technology and technical know–how for the project.

IAL, being a subsidiary of MRL, is a Government Company functioning under the administrative control of the Ministry of Petroleum & Natural Gas, Government of India.

IAL, has an authorised capital of Rs.30 crore divided into 30 lakh equity shares of Rs. 100 / – each. The subscribed capital as at March 3 1, 1998 is Rs. 19.72 crore, which is held in the ratio of 60:40 between MRL and Chevron.

***Physical performance highlights***

| *Major Products* | *Installed capacity* | *Actuals – 1997–98* |
|---|---|---|
| Blending Units | 15000 MT | 12625 MT |
| Ashless Dispersant | 6300 MT | 4231 MT |
| Metallic Detergents (Phenate and Sulphonate) | 3000 MT | 4068 MT |
| Dispersant Base Stock | 4200 MT | 3708 MT |

***Financial performance highlights***

| *Particulars* | *Actuals–1997–98 In Rs. Lakhs* |
|---|---|
| Sale of Additives | 13255 MT |
| Sales Turnover | 13992.18 |

| | |
|---|---|
| Earnings before Depreciation, Interest and Tax | 2965.03 |
| Financing charges | 853.65 |
| Earnings before Tax | 1559.12 |
| Taxes | 164.71 |
| Profit after Tax | 1394.41 |
| Dividend | 7.50% |
| Share Capital | 1972.34 |
| Capital Employed | 5974.62 |

***Policy initiatives undertaken by IAL***

It is the first Additive Company in India to obtain ISO Certification. It presented latest global developments on Automotive Engine Oil, Passenger Car Motor Oil, 2–T / 4–T and Natural Gas Engine Oil product lines to Indian customers along with overseas participants.

***Environment and safety***

IAL has received Certificate of Merit from the Tamilnadu Chapter of National Safety Council of India during November 1997 in recognition of its contribution in the promotion of Safety, Health and Environment.

The Plant meets the effluent and emission norms set by the Tamilnadu Pollution Control Board, on a continuous basis.

**IBP company limited**

IBP Co. Limited was incorporated in 1909. It became a subsidiary of IOC in 1970. Thereafter it became an independent Government Company in 1972. Government shareholding in IBP Co. Limited is 59.58 percent. Balmer Lawrie & Co. Limited is a subsidiary of IBP– The Company has participated in four Joint Venture Companies. These are Numaligarh Refinery, IBP–Caltex Limited, Indian Oiltanking Limited and Petro India Limited. Over the years, the Company has diversified into other activities, such as Industrial Explosives and Cryocontainers. It has now three distinct business groups, namely Business Group (Petroleum), Business Group (Chemicals) and Business Group (Engineering). During the year 1996–97, two depots were commissioned at Rewari in Haryana and at Meerut in Uttar Pradesh. Panipat Depot was commissioned March, 1998

Following up on its entry into LPG marketing, the Company is in the process of taking steps to operationalise the distributor network for full–scale launch under the LPG Marketing Plan 1996–98 adopted by the Government. The Company is actively pursuing the project for setting up of Terminalling facilities in India through the Joint Venture Company, Indian Oiltanking Limited.

The physical performance of the Company during 1997–98 in regard to sale of petroleum products is 5523905 KL representing a 6.78% growth from the previous year. The volume is anticipated to be 5898393 KL in 1998–99. The sale of Lubricants and Greases in 1997–98 was 27091 KL marking a 21.05% growth from the previous year. It is anticipated to be 32794 KL in 1998–99. The company is the largest manufacturer of explosives in India and is the only manufacturer of explosives within the country to have been accredited with the prestigious ISO 9002 Certification.

The anticipated turnover of the Company for the Year 1998–99 is Rs. 5235.00 crore. The turnover in 1997–98 was Rs.4960.38 crores. Profit after tax in the current year is expected to be Rs.60.00 crores compared with Rs.31.56 crore in 1997–98.

**Balmer lawrie & co limited**

Balmer Lawrie & Co. Ltd. became a subsidiary of IBP Co. Ltd. in August 1972. The authorised capital of the company was Rs. 30 crore and paid up capital was Rs.

16.29 crore as on 31–3–1998 The reserves & surplus of the company as on 31–3–1998 was Rs. 13374 lakhs.

The company is a diversified medium sized company with operations in India and Overseas. The current operations of the Company are classified into groups namely :–(i) Industrial & Packaging (ii) Greases &. Lubes (iii) Containerisation (iv) Performance Chemicals(v) Travel, Tours & 'Cargo (vi) Tea Exports & International Trading (vii) Project Engineering & Consultancy (viii) Research & Development.

During the year 1998–99, the company is expected to manufacture 26.00 lakhs barrels/drums against 24.56 lakhs in 1997–98. The Company is expected to produce 0.35 MT/Lakhs tonnes of greases and lubricants during 1998–99 as against 0.30 MT/Lakhs in 1997–98. It also anticipates a decrease in the number of marine freight containers & special containers for export from 4079 in 1997–98 to 3000 in 1998–99.

The total turnover of the company is anticipated to increase from 668.43 crore in 1997–98 to Rs. 700.00 crore in 1998–99. While the company has achieved a Profit After Tax of Rs. 16.41 crore during 1997–98, the anticipated profit after tax for the year 1998–99 is Rs. 13.40 crore. The Foreign exchange earning of the company is expected to be Rs. 110 crore in 1998–99.

**Biecco lawrie limited**

Biecco Lawrie Limited a Government of India Enterprise under administrative control of Ministry of Petroleum and Natural Gas and established in 1919, is a Calcutta based medium size Engineering Company having two factories at Calcutta.

The authorised Capital and the issued and subscribed capital of the company during 1997–98 was Rs. 50.00 cores, and Rs. 42.00 crore respectively. The total sales turnover of the company for 1997–98 was Rs. 80.54 crore against Rs. 115.60 crore in 1996–97. This was mainly due to de–control of Paraffin Wax business by the Government of India. As a result the sale of Paraffin Wax decreased.

The physical performance of the company upto December, 1998 in regard to sale of switchgear panels and switchgear spares and others was Rs. 1932 lakhs. It has done electrical repair jobs amounting to Rs. 137 lakhs upto December, 1998. It has been updating its manufacturing technology by introducing latest state–of–the art plant and machinery. Shop layouts have been changed and modern machinery installed.

**Oil industry safety directorate**

OISD assists Safety Council of the Ministry of Petroleum and Natural Gas (MOP&NG) which is headed by Secretary, MOP&NG as Chairman and includes the Joint Secretaries, Advisors in the MOP&NG, Chief Executives of all the Public Sector Undertakings (PSUs) under the Ministry, Chief Controller of Explosives (CCE), Adviser (Fire) of the Govt. of India and the Director General of Factory Advice Service & Labour Institute as members.

Standardisation is one of the major activities of the Safety Directorate, standardisation is required to keep, abreast of the latest design and operating practices in the areas of safety and fire fighting in the hydrocarbon processing industry in the developed countries, so as to develop standards and codes that would be suitable for the conditions in India. The areas where standards/ recommended practices/ guidelines need to be developed are identified by analysing the incident data–base developed at OISD. The standardisation work is then taken up by the Functional Committees nominated by the Steering Committee. As a continuous exercise, new areas standardisation are identified. During the period under review, 7 new Standards were cleared by Safety Council and three old standards were amended. As of December, 1998 overall status of Standardisation is as follows:

***Total standards recommended practices guidelines identified : 79***

| | | |
|---|---|---|
| (i) | Published & Distributed | : 58 |
| (ii) | Approved by Safety Council & are under Printing | : 07 |
| (iii) | New Standards under various stages of preparation | : 14 |

***Accident data base and dissemination of safety information***

This is a continuous activity of OISD wherein report on fires, accidents and near misses occurring in the installations of the entire industry are received on a quarterly basis and stored in a computerised data base. After analysis, the information showing statistical trends, areas of concern, major recommendations etc. is disseminated to industry through Steering Committee Meetings, workshops and OISD journal PETROSAFE.

***Sale of OISD Standards to Private Parties***

Safety Council had approved the sale of OISD standards to private marketers/ contractors/ consultants @ Rs.500 per standard. 328 Standards have been sold during April–December, 1998.

**Centre for high technology (CHT)**

The Centre for High Technology (CHT), is a Registered Society functioning under the Ministry of Petroleum & Natural Gas, Govt. of India. It acts as a focal point for the oil industry to coordinate and fund research in refining and marketing and for the exchange of information. It assesses technology requirements and prospects of developing these indigenously. It renders advice on scientific and technological programmes and recommends measures to modernise and improve the performance of refineries. It is the technological think tank of the Ministry. It publishes a quarterly journal on Hydro Carbons Technology.

***CHT projects completed and expected to be completed during 1998–99***

The major R&D projects under the aegis of CHT are:

(i) Development of Sheet Metal Structured Packing (PARLPAK): Phase–II by EIL (R&D)

(ii) Studies on application of Modern Packings for liquid –liquid extraction : Phase–I by EIL (R&D)

(iii) Optimisation of the dewaxing/ deoiling operation in Lube Oil Base Stock (LOBS) manufacturing with / without dewaxing aids by IIP, Dehradun

(iv) Diesel fuel quality requirement for meeting the future emission standards by IIP, Dehradun

(v) Hydrocracker Pilot Plant / Laboratory project by IOC (R&D)

(vi) Research facility in the area of Advanced Control by IIT-Kanpur & EIL(R&D)

(vii) Etherification of C5 olefins and FCC gasoline by IIP, Dehradun

(viii) Development of cooling tower technology by EIL(R&D)

(ix) Cold Flow Model studies in FCC area by EIL (R&D)

***Centralised assistance from abroad***

CHT had entered into Technical Services Agreements with M/s B P International Limited, UK and M/s Caltex, USA, in 1996 for a period of 2 years. The agreements expired in July/August 1998. Under these agreements,

Indian refineries received technical assistance in various areas of oil Refinery such as operation, maintenance, safety, environment protection, plant reliability, quality control, risk management etc.

**Petroleum India International (PII)**

Petroleum India International (PII) is a consortium of ten India Public Sector Companies operation in the Petroleum and Petrochemical sectors. PII was established in 198 with the objective of mobilising individual capabilities of member companies into a joint endeavour for providing resource support to oil companies abroad and thereby export technology and services. The consortium members are :–

- Bharat Petroleum Corporation Limited
- Bongaigaon Refinery & Petrochemicals Limited
- Cochin Refineries Limited
- Engineers India Limited
- Hindustan Petroleum Corporation Limited
- IBP Co. Limited
- Indian Oil Corporation Limited
- Indian Petrochemicals Corporation Limited.
- Madras Refineries Limited
- Oil & Natural Gas Corporation Limited

PII has provided services to well known companies abroad, such as:

1. Nigerian National Petroleum Corporation (N.NPC).
2. Kuwait National Petroleum Company (KNPC), Kuwait.

3. Technip ESIA at Khaleej Joint Venture (TPJV), France.
4. Abu Dhabi National Oil Company (ADNOC), UAE.
5. Jeddah Oil Refinery Company (JORC) Saudi Arabia.
6. Kellog Plant Services Inc., Kuwait.

Revenue generated and the profit made by PII during the last two years and estimates for the 1998–99 and 1999–2000 are given below:

*(Rs. in lakh)*

| *Particulars* | *Audited* | | *Projected* | |
|---|---|---|---|---|
| | *1996–97* | *1997–98* | *1998–99* | *1999–2000* |
| Project income | 2074 | 2271 | 3015 | 3310 |
| Profit before tax | 1416 | 1353 | 1198 | 1280 |
| Profit after tax | 1014 | 988 | 810 | 832 |

**Oil Co-ordination Committee (OCC)**

The Oil Co–ordination Committee (OCC) was born on 14.7.75, with the Secretary (Petroleum & Natural Gas) acts as its Chairman, while the Additional Secretary, Joint Secretary & Financial Adviser, Joint Secretary (Refineries), Chief Executives of the Oil Companies and ED, Oil Industry Safety Directorate are members of the OCC Apex Body. The day to day functions are handled by the OCC Secretariat under the Executive Director who is also the Member Secretary of the Committee. The Committee has its offices at Delhi and Mumbai.

The main functions of OCC are as under:

i) Co–ordination of various activities of the Industry.

ii) Co–ordination of supply of crude oil to the refineries.

iii) Operation & Maintenance of pool accounts.

iv) Preparing short term estimates for supply/ demand and import plans.

v) Monitoring the performance of oil industry to achieve optimality.

vi) Co–ordination of Marketing functions.

Monthly industry coordination meetings and supply plan meetings are held to resolve problems and work out supply plans and maximise product yields.

OCC has prescribed targets for the industry in regard to provision of infrastructure handling, storage and transportation. It monitors the progress in realisation of these targets.

**Oil Industry Development Board (OIDB)**

*Functions of the board*

The Oil Industry Development Board(OIDB) was set up in January 1975 under the Oil Industry (Development) Act, 1974 to provide such financial and other assistance as is conducive for the development of oil industry. The financial assistance is extended by way of loans and grants for activities like prospecting, refining, processing, transportation, storage, handling land marketing of mineral oil , production and marketing of oil products etc.

*Resources of the board*

The funds for various activities envisaged under the Act are made available by the Central Government, to the Board, after due appropriation by Parliament from out of the proceeds of cess levied and collected on the indigenous crude oil. These are supplemented by the internal resources generated by the Board as interest ion loans etc. Out of about Rs. 31,000 crore collected as cess by the Government, a sum of Rs. 902 crore has been made available to the Board. Together with the internal generation of funds, a sum of Rs.4728 crore has accrued to the fund, as on 31st March, 1998. During 1997–98, Rs.510.66 crore was internal resource generation of the Board.

***Assistance to Oil Industry***

The Board has extended financial assistance by way of long–term loans (including loans at concessional rates of interest for priority activities etc.) to the oil industrial concerns for meeting expenditure, mostly on approved plan projects. Out of a sum of Rs. 9841 given as loan till 31.12.1998, a sum of Rs. 4593.37 crore was outstanding from Oil companies to the Board as on that date. Board has also given grants–in–aid amounting to Rs. 256.68 crore till 31.12.1998. During 1998–99, availability of funds with the Board will be approximately Rs. 855 crore. Out of this, loans amounting to Rs. 715.70 crore and grants amounting to Rs. 27.46 crore have already been released upto 31st. December, 1998. During 1999–2000, approximately Rs. 900 crore will be available to the Board for investment/ disbursement as loans/ grants.

Financial assistance is extended by way of loans and grants.

***Deployments of funds***

The OIDB, on cumulative basis upto 31.12.1998, has given following financial assistance to the oil industry.

***Financial assistance since 1975***

| | *Rs./Crore* |
|---|---|
| Loans | 9841.08 |
| Grants | 256.68 |
| | 10097.76 |

A major portion of the loan assistance has gone towards meeting capital outlay on Plan projects approved by the Ministry of Petroleum and Natural Gas in consultation with the Planning Commission and the Ministry of Finance. The loan outstanding from oil companies to OIDB, as on 31.12.1998 is Rs. 4593.37 crore Loans and grants given during the year 1997–98 were Rs. 1513.65 crore and Rs. 37.80 crore respectively. The availability of funds with OIDB during the year 1998–99 and 1999–2000 will be Rs. 885 crore and Rs. 900 crore (approx.) respectively.

***Disbursement of loans during the year 1998–99 (upto 31.12.98)***

*(Rs. in Crore)*

| *S. No.* | *Organisation* | *Allocation as per BE/RE 1998–99 of MOP&NG* | *Funds released upto 31.12.98* |
|---|---|---|---|
| 1. | Balmer Lawrie | 41.00 | 24.00 |
| 2. | BRPL | 10.00 | 1.30 |
| 3. | IBP Co. | 111.23 | 66.52 |
| 4. | MRL | 111.00 | 111.00 |
| 5. | NRL | 373.00 | 373.00 |
| 6. | BPCL | 200.00 | – |
| 7. | CRL | 200.00 | 139.88 |
| | Total | 1046.23 | 715.70 |

***Disbursement of grants during the year 1998–99 (upto 31.12.98)***

*(Rs. in Crore)*

| *S. No.* | *Organisation* | *Allocation as per BE/RE 1998–99 of MOP&NG* | *Funds released upto 31.12.98* |
|---|---|---|---|
| 1. | CHT | 23.23 | 5.70 |
| 2. | DGH | 25.00 | 13.36 |

| | | | |
|---|---|---|---|
| 3. | IPCL (PPOT) | 0.18 | – |
| 4. | IIP, Dehradun | 0.21 | – |
| 5. | GAIL | 0.50 | – |
| 6. | OISD | 3.22 | 1.70 |
| 7. | ONGC | 1.43 | 0.30 |
| 8. | TERI | 0.02 | – |
| 9. | PCRA | 11.74 | 5.23 |
| 10. | IIPM | 0.03 | 0.03 |
| 11. | CIPET | 2.50 | – |
| 12. | Delta Studies Institute of Andhra University | 2.90 | 1.00 |
| 13. | RRL Jorhat | 0.55 | – |
| 14. | PDS | 0.18 | 0.10 |
| 15. | R&D Projects approved by the OID Board/Central Government | 20.00 | 0.04 |
| 16. | Anna University | 0.03 | – |
| | Total | 91.72 | 27.46 |

**Directorate general of hydrocarbons (DGH)**

Directorate General of Hydrocarbons (DGH) was established by a Government Resolution in 1993 under the administrative control of Ministry of Petroleum & Natural Gas. The objective of DGH is to promote sound management of the Indian petroleum and natural gas resources having a balanced regard for environment, safety, technological and economic aspects of the petroleum activity. Details of some of the main activities undertaken by DGH during the year 1998–99 are as under:–

**Opening up of new areas for exploration**

In order to upgrade the information in respect of poorly explored and virgin areas various types of geo–scientific surveys are being conducted. During the period, processing and interpretation of the data acquired earlier in the East Coast and Andaman Sea under joint venture Speculative Seismic Survey Programme was completed. Data acquired from magneto–Telluric (MT) survey in Nagpur–Wardha area and along a regional profile in Nagpur – Belgaum was also processed, and interpreted. Interpretation of data of reconnitory JV Speculative Seismic Survey in the Vindhyan basin and Ganga Valley areas is in progress.

Based on the earlier satellite gravity surveys carried out in Western, Eastern, and Andaman offshore areas covering 1.642 million sq.kms. areas, Bouguer gravity maps have been prepared over the entire offshore areas of India. These maps will provide basis for planning further reconnitory surveys in offshore areas.

***National E&P data and management system***

A feasibility study to establish a national E&P database and archive in India, which started in October, 1997 through ADB grant was completed in August 1998. Another study to suggest the design of information flow system for upstream sector under a grant from Untied State Trade Development Agency (USTDA) was also completed in August 1998. Implementation of consultant's recommendations in both projects are under progress.

# 6

# Oil and Natural Gas

Research and development activities by Oil and Natural Gas Commission (ONGC) and Oil India LImited (OIL) and Gas Authority of India Limited (GAIL) in the field of crude oil and natural gas exploration and production, processing and marketing sectors are carried out at their respective R and D centers. ONGC has established eight institutes, viz., Kishav Dev Malviya Institute of Petroleum Exploration (KDMIPE), Dehra Dun; Institute of Reservoir Studies (IRS), Ahmadabad; Institute of Engineering and Ocean Technology (IEOT), Bombay; Institute of Oil Gas Production Technology (IOGPT), Bombay; Geophysical Data Processing and Interpretation Centre (GEOPIG), Dehradun; Institute of Petroleum Safety and Environment Management (IPSEM), Goa; Institute of Biotechnology and Geotectonics (INBIGS), Jrhat; and Institute of Drilling Technology (IDT), Dehra Dun.

The main objective of the KDMIPE is to provide back-up services to exploration efforts of ONGC. IRS provides R and D back-up for preparation of development plans of ONGC"s oil and gas fields and application of enhanced oil recovery methods with a view to improve their oil and gas recovery. IDT attends to the development of techniques for drilling difficult wells in high pressure/high temperature regime as well as super deep wells in technically complex areas. IEOT carries out design review for all offshore platforms, deep water production systems. * IOGPT had been set up to provide continuous back-up to situation specific production problems and long term application of appropriate techniques and technologies. GEOPIC is ONGC's premier seismic, gravity, magnetic, logging and geochemical data processing and interpretation center. IPSEM aims at creating awareness for improved safety and environment management and minimize the pollution accidents and loss of life caused by petroleum exploration and production operations. INBIGS, when fully operational, will be able to provide genetic probes for direct detection of hydrocarbons. Additionally, ONGC has set up a joint ONGC-Schlumverger Wireline Research Center at Delhi to meet the long term need of high technology requirement for wireline logging and related fields. OIL has its R&D center at Duliajan, mainly dealing with exploration, oil field chemicals, EOR and production engineering related matters. GAIL is also developing in-house R&D facilities mainly in the area of gas processing storage, distribution and utilisation.

Production of natural gas in 1994-95 was 19.38 BCM as compared to 18.33 BCM in the year 1993-94. The utilisation in 1994-95 was 17.35 BCM as compared to 16.41 BCM in 1993-94. The balance recoverable reserves as on 1 April 1994 were around 700 BCM.

Gas Authority of India Limited (GAIL) was incorporated i 1984 for the transportation, processing and marketing of natural gas and was assigned the priority task of setting up the cross country HBJ pipeline. Presently GAIL is the largest company in India for marketing natural gas. It operates over 3,000 km of pipelines in the country and supplies gas to power plants for the generation of 6,000 mw of power to the fertilizer sector for the production of 10 MTPA of urea and to about 150 industrial units.

GAIL is operating on the plants LPG at Bijaipur (Madhya Pradesh) and Vaghodia (Gujarat). It is putting up two more LPG plants at Lakwa (Assam) and Usar (Maharashtra), a petro-chemical complex at Auraiya (Uttar Pradesh) and proposes to put up a gas processing complex at Gandhar. GAIL has formed a joint venture company with British Gas to implement the Bombay City Gas Distribution Project. It is also upgrading the HBJ pipeline capacity from 18.2 MMSCMD to 33.4 MMSCMD.

The Government of India has been inviting offers from Indian and foreign companies for development of discovered oil fields as well as for exploration of oil and gas in various blocks in India. Against the offer of discovered oil field made in August 1992, contracts for development of five medium sized fields and 12 small sized fields have been signed. The medium sized fields * are MId and South Tapti, Mukta and Panna (Bombay offshore); Ravva (Krishna-Godavari offshore) and Kharsang (Arunachal Pradesh). The small fields are Hazira, Cambay, Bhandut, Matar, Sabarmati, Indora, Bakrol, Lohar, Dholka, Wavel, Baola and Asjol in Gujarat.

The medium-sized fields would be developed through joint ventures between Oil and Natural Gas Commission (ONGC) Oil India Ltd. (OIL) on the one hand and private companies on the other. These joint ventures could be either incorporated or unincorporated ventures. Where they are incorporated, ONGC/OIL would have a 49 per cent share in the equity of the venture. In unincorporated ventures, ONGC/OIL would take a 40 per cent share in the venture.

The small-sized fields would be developed by commmpanies on their own, with no participation by ONGC/OIL, under production sharing contracts to be signed by the companies with the Government of India. In both cases, companies would also be required to bear their share of statutory levies like royalty, cess, etc. Foreign companies would be levied income-tax at a fixed rate of 50 per cent, while Indian companies would be governed by the relevant provisions of the Income Tax. The Government has the first right of refusal in respect of the contractor's share of oil, with international price being payable. Companies have also been exempted from payment of customs duty on goods imported for use in petroleum operations.

In addition to the above, the Government has signed production sharing contracts for exploration of oil and gas in four blocks under the fourth round of bidding. These blocks are: (i) in Pranhita-Godavari (Gondwana) onshore basin; (ii) Krishna-Godavari offshore basin; (iii) Rajasthan basin and (iv) Cauvery offshore basin.

Government is actively encouraging the acquisition of acreages overseas to enhance the flow of equity oil into the country. As part of this policy, ONGC Videsh Ltd. (OVL) has been aggressively pursuing opportunities overseas to acquire exploration and producing acreages.

OVL entered into a production sharing contract in 1988 with Petro-Vietnam for exploratiion for hydrocarbons in blocks 6,12E and 19 in offshore Vietnam. Subsequently, in 1992. OVL assigned 45 per cent of its interest in the blocks to the alliance of British Petroleum (BP), UK and Statoil, Norway.

The OVL-BP-Statoil consortium carried out further survey and drilling work during the second phase of exploration between May 1992 and November 1994, leading to a discovery of about two trillion cubic feet (TCF) of gas in the Lan Tay and Lan Do structures in block 6. Techno-economic appraisal of the gas discovery with a view to its development is currently in progress. OVL has so far spent about US dollar 30 million on this venture.

OVL signed an agreement with British Gas, UK, in June 1995 for taking a 50 per cent participating interest in the North Zaafarana concession in Egypt. Under this agreement, OVL is scheduled to drill an exploratory well with and expenditure of about US dollar 7 million. It has also signed an agreement with Command Petroleum, Australia in July 1995 for taking a 40 per cent participating interest in the Fejaj permit in Tunisia. Drilling of an exploratory well is currently in progress.

In addition to the above, OVL is also engaged in negotiations with British Gas for taking a participating interest in offshore block in Yemen. It is also actively evaluating exploration and production opportunities in a number of other countries in order to enhance its reserves in overseas acreages so that a significant contribution to the equity oil accruing to the country from overseas ventures can be made.

The total refining capacity in the country as on 1 April 1994 was 53.40 MMTPA spread over 13 refineries. The actual crude processed was 54.30 MMTPA year 1993-94 representing a capacity utilisation of 101.7 per cent. The cumulative refinery production from April-August 1995 was 24.12 thousand tonnes as against the *pro-rata* installed capacity * While making projections for the Eighth Five Year Plan, it has been estimated that the demand of petroleum products will be around 79 MMTPA in the terminal year of Eighth Plan and around 102 MMTPA by the end of Nineth Plan *i.e.* in the year 2001-20002. To meet the consumption levels, Government approved proposals to set up the following new refineries in addition to implementation/expansion/ debottlenecking of existing refineries: (i) Mangalore Refinery (JV)-Three MMTPA; (ii) Numaligarh Refinery-Three MMTPA and (iii) Panipat Refinery-Six MMTPA. With the modernisation of Digboi Refinery, its capacity would be increased from 0.5 to 0.65 MMTPA. Further expansion of Bongaigaon Refinery and Petrochemicals Limited (BRPL) from 1.35 MMTPA to 2.35 MMTPA has already been implemented. Haldia and Vizak refineries plans have been also approved for expansion by one and three MMTPA respectively. Besides, the Government had decided in July 1992 for setting up of three new grass-root refineries during the Eighth/Ninth Plan, each with a capacity of six MMTPA as joint ventures with suitable private parties from India or abroad.

The Government of India has welcomed proposals for private investment including foreign investment in the refining sector following liberalisation of industrial policy. In pursuance of this policy, Letters of Intent have been granted to 11 companies for setting up refineries in the private sector including EOU refineries to the extent ofabout 60 MMTPA. In case all the approved refineries are implemented by the end of century, India will be mot self-sufficient in the refining capacity but also export some products.

Lubrizol India Limited (LIL), a public sector undertaking was incorporated in 1966 in collaboration with the lubrizol Corporation, USA under the Companies Act. The authorised and paid-up share capital of the company is Rs. 19.20 crore. The Government of India holds 60 per cent of the subscribed equity capital of the company and the Lubrizol Corporation, USA 40 per cent thereof. LIL develops, manufactures and markets additive systems for autommotive and industrial lubricants and also develops other speciality chemicals for catering to the needs of the petroleum industry. The company has one manufacturing unit and the second unit for manufacturing of extreme pressure additives at Taloja, district Raigad, was commissioned on 30 March 1995.

The Engineers India Limited (EIL) was established in 1965 in collaboration with the Bechtel Corporation,

USA mainly to indigenise engineering and project management capabilities in the petroleum sector. In 1967, the shareholding of Bechtel was taken over the Government of India and since then the company has been a fully-owned public sector undertaking. The authorised and paid up capital of EIL is Rs. two crore as on 31 March 1994. The reserves and surplus of the company have grown to Rs. 197.90 crore as on 31 MArch 1994 and its net worth on that date was Rs. 199.90 crore.

EIL today provides a complete range of project services in the fields of petroleum refining, petrochemicals, oil and gas processing pipelines, ocean engineering, ports and harbours, fertilizer and non-ferrous metallurgy, cement, paper, etc., and has emerged as South Asia's leading design and engineering company. In order to increase its global competitiveness, EIL has adopted a three-pronged strategy, *i.e.* setting up of joit ventures, formation of strategic alliances and stand alone ventures. The company has formed a joint venture company in the name of AMEC Engineers India Limited (AEIL) in 50:50 partnership with M/s AMEC Process and Energy International, in UK.

The EIL has also formed a wholly-owned subsidiary in India under the name Certification Engineers International Limited (CEIL) in order to provide certification, recertification and third party inspection services to the Indian as well as overseas clients. The company is also in process of establishing a wholly-owned subsidiary company in Malaysia under the name EIL, ASIA PACIFIC SDN BHD. It has diverse consultancy assignments in Iran, Algeria, Qatar, Abu Dhabi and Malaysia.

The growing demand for petroleum products has been casting a heavy burden on the economy. Hence a very high priority is being attached to the conservation of petroleum products. A variety of measures taken by the Petroleum Conservation Research Association * (PCRA), a registered society under the Ministry of Petroleum and Natural Gas, to promote conservation of petroleum products cover transport, industrial, agricultural, household and oil sectors which account for the PCRA are creation of mass awareness on the need for the conservation of petroleum prosucts, promotion of measures to curb wasteful practices, and improve the oil use efficiency of equipment, devices and vehicles and research and development for improving oil use efficiency in various end uses. As a result of these efforts it has been possible to achieve quantifiable savings of about Rs. 491 crore during 1994-95 including recurring saving of Rs. 417 crore achieved as a result of efforts made by and through the PCRA.

In addition, new areas or the inadequately covered areas are also being taken up including promotion of inter-seul subsititution. As part of a programme for inter-fuel substitution, CNG was introduced as an alternate fuel in the road transport sector. In all 1,677 petrol driven vehicles have been converted for CNG operation.

Marketing and distribution network of the Indian pteroleum industry is widespread and, by and large, under the control of the public sector oil companies. Apart from over 2,736 km of product pipeline, the industry has a network of about 16,023 MS/HSD retail outlets, 6156-light diesel oil/kerosene dealers and over 4,673 LPG distributors up to April 1995. Fair distribution of products all over the country at stipulated prices is generally ensured.

A major landmark development in the petroleum marketing has been the decanalisation of kerosene, LPG and LSHS and the introduction of parallel marketing of these products to augment their domestic availability. As a result of this liberalisation, the private entrepreneurs can now undertake import of these commodities and sell them at market determined prices. As on 31 July 1995, about 73.5 TMT of LPG and 817.3 TMT of kerosene has been imported. The private sector has also been allowed to invest in the development of infrastructure for petroleum marketing. Private investment has been invited for setting up and operation of depots, tank farms, import facilities, product and crude pipeline and manufacture of railway tank wagons for use by the oil industry. Several products like naptha, hexane, toluene, petroleum coke, carbon black feed stock, lube oil base stock, etc., have been decanalised for better availability of these products.

In order to inform and educate the public about the credentials and credibility of parallel marketers, a system of rating has been introduced in June 1995, by which every parallel marketer is required to obtain a rating certificate from one of the approved rating agencies.

Several joint ventures have been set up in the petroleum sector by both the public and private enterprises. Six joint ventures have been set up by the public sector oil marketing companies with reputed international companies for manufacture and marketing of lubricants, bitumen emulsions, and insfractructure for LPG. Several private sector companies have also entered into joint venture agreements with transnational companies. These are expected to bring in foreign investment as well as help in upgrading the indigenous technologies.

Indian Oil Corporation (IOC) was set up in September 1964, by amalgamating Indian Refineries Limited with Indian Oil Company Limited. The Corporation has three division, namely, (i) Marketing Division with headquarters at Bombay. (ii) Refineries and

Pipelines Division with headquarters at Delhi; and (iii) Assam Oil Division with headquarters at Digboi. IOC has a Research and Development Centre at Faridabad in Haryana. The Centre provides technical service to customers and is engaged in development of sophisticated lubrication oils. It is actively working on possibilities of production and utilisation of viable substitute fuels. IOC is also having a wholly-owned subsidiary called Indian Oil Blending Limited (IOBL) which is engaged in blending lubricants.

The market share of the Corporation was 55.76 per cent of the total oil industry's sales in April 1995. The Corporation had in existence 2,295 cooking gas (LPG) distributorships, 6,277 retail outlet (petrol/diesel) dealerships and 3,283 kerosene/light diesel oil dealerships in the country.

Following government's acquisition of two Burmah-Shell companies in January 1976, name of Burmah-Shell Refineries Limited was changed to Bharat Refineries Limited from 12 February 1976. Being an integrated refining and marketing company, name of the company was changed to Bharat Petroleum Corporation Limited (BPCL) from 1 August 1977.

The company is engaged in processing of crude oil in its refinery at Bombay and storage, distribution and marketing of petroleum products in country. In addition, it is in the process of diversifying into ptero-chemicals using certain refinery streams as feed stock. Market share of BPCL in 1994-95 was 20.01 per cent of total oil industry's sales. As on 1 April 1995, the company had a total of 948 cooking gas (LPG) distributorships, 4,204 petrol/diesel retail outlets and 937 kerosene oil/light diesel oil dealership.

Hindustan Petroleum Corporation Limited (HPCL)

was set up on 15 July 1974 by acquiring assets in India of ESSO Eastern Inc. USA and became a wholly government-owned company. On 21 December 1976, Government acquired Caltex Oil Refining (India) and merged it with HPCL. The main activities of HPCL are refining of crude oil, manufacturing lubricating base oil, manufacturing and blending of lubricants, grease and petroleum products and related automative accessories all over the country and marketing of petroleum products including LPG. Market share of HPCL in 1994-95 was 19.54 per cent of total oil industry's sales. As on 1 April 1995, the company had a total of 1307 cooking gas (LPG) distributorships, 4154 retail outlets (petrol/diesel) and 1,580 kerosene/light diesel oil dealerships.

IBP Company Limited has three divisions, namely, oil, chemicals and engineering. Oil division has a country-wide retail network marketing petroleum products which it obtains from other oil companies in the absence of its own refining facility at present. The Company had in existence 1388 retail outlets (petrol/diesel) dealerships and 356 kerosene/light diesel oil dealership in the country.

As India is one of the lowest cost refiners in the world, experts believe that it might become a net exporter of petroleum products in the coming century and a "swing producer" to stabilise global product markets. Though the first oil well in India was completed late in the last century—drilling for the oil well at Digboi in Assam was begun in September 1889 and completed in November 1890—the search for oil in a big way started only after the country gained Independence. The first well at Digboi was drilled by the Assam Railway and Trading Company. Later the Assam Oil Company (AOC) came into existence, which sold its rights to the Burmah Oil Company.

These were the beginnings of Oil India Limited, which became a fully-owned Government company in the early eighties. Thus at the time of Independence, indigenous production of crude oil was confined to Assam. Since this was hardly enough to meet the country's needs for petroleum products, the Government of India took a conscious decision to develop the country's oil resources, both onshore and offshore.

Creating a Petroleum Division within the Geological Survey of India in October 1955, exclusively for country-wide oil exploration, was the first step. It did not take much time for GSI's Petroleum Division to grow into the Directorate of Oil and Natural Gas, and subsequently into an autonomous Oil & Natural Gas Commisssion through an act of Parliament in October 1959. Now, of course, the Commission is known as Oil & Natural Gas Corporation Limited.

The real fillip to the development of the indigenous petroleum industry was given by the late Keshav Deo Malaviya, who gave ONGC the necessary push and was also responsible for the creation of Indian Oil Corporation, India's first national refining and marketing corporation.

Later, of course, the refineries and marketing companies owned by Burmah-Shell, Esso and Caltex (not to talk of the small Digboirefinery owned by Burmah Oil Company) were nationalised giving birth to two more national oil companies, i.e. Bharat Petroleum and Hindustan Petroleum. Today there are 14 refineries (including the two mentioned above)—13 in the public sector and one in the joint sector. The Gas Authority of India Limited (GALL) was set up in 1984 for planned utilisation of gas reserves and was given the responsibility to set up the HBJ pipeline.

These are briefly the main operators in the oil and

natural gas sector, which is basically a public sector monopoly now. While Oil India's operations, in the initial stages, were confined to the north-eastern region, ONGC's initial successes came in the western region. The first discovery of oil and gas made by ONGC was in 1958 in the Cambay onshore basin in Gujarat. Also in Gujarat, the first giant oilfield was discovered at Ankleshwar in 1960.

In what was termed as "Samudra Manthan" in the early sixties, ONGC decided to step up its offshore exploration activity in earnest. Seismic surveys helped in the discovery of the Aliabet structure at the mouth of the Narmada and later in "Bombay High". A big debate raged in the late sixties whether we should develop "Bombay High" on our own or entrust the job to foreign compaines. The first option was chosen and ONGC acquired its first jack-up type rig "Sagar Samrat" (built for the Commission in Japan) in 1973. "Sagar Samrat" started drilling in "Bombay High" in January 1974 and about a month later oil was discovered at the very first well it drilled in this oilfield, which has met part of the country's crude needs for the past 15 years or so.

This writer was fortunate enough to be among the group of reporters who were on board the "Sagar Samrat" in early 1974 to witness the drilling for the first well. By the time we returned to shore and about to report this first experiment in offshore drilling, news arrived that oil has been found. February 1974 will thus be a landmark in the development of offshore oil production in India.

ONGC has travelled quite far in the 22 years since oil was established in "Bombay High". Crude oil production from offshore areas (which is solely from ONGC) has risen from five million tonnes in 1980-81 to a high of 21.2 million tonnes in 1990-91. It was around 20.2

million tonnes 1994-95. Total crude production both from onshore and offshore areas (i.e. the total output of OIL and ONGC) was around 35.2 million tonnes in 1995-96.

But the country's requirements of petroleum products have grown at a rapid rate, from 30 million tonnes in 1980-81 to almost 75 million tonnes in 1995-96. Current estimates indicate that it would reach a level of about 113 million tonnes by 2001-02.

Looked at from a different perspective. India's domestic oil production vis-a-vis petroleum product consumption indicate that the percentage of slef-sufficiency has declined from 55.6 per cent in 1990-91 to 43.7 per cent in 1995-96 and is estimated to decline further to 23.5 per cent by 2006-7. In other words, the percentage of self-sufficiency in another 10 years (which is not far away) will be half of what it was in 1990-91.

While of course it is true that it is the Centre's responsibility to find adequate funds to develop the oil and gas industry, the above figures only highlight the need to let the oil and gas industry generate more internal resources to finance its future development. It is an open secret that the Government of India's finances are none too rosy and there are too many competing claims on the limited kitty available with the Centre.

All the more reason for immediate reforms in the hydrocarbons sector. Though it is difficult to quantify in monetary terms the benefits of reforms, the R Group has estimated that the net present value of the reforms it has suggested would amount to around Rs. 100,000 crore. And that is a lot of money.

The controversy that is raging at the moment over raising the prices of some of the heavily subsidised petroleum products only serve to highlight the problems that arise in opening up the oil and gas sector in line with the changes that are taking place in other sectors of the economy.

For instance, it is widely admitted (even in official publicity material) that a level playing field should be given to national oil companies "particularly by paying them international market price of oil". This will help them to raise more revenue, but this good intention still remains on paper only.

"If discovered fields are offered in future for improving economic viabiloity, the national oil companies, who have discovered the fields, should be reimbursed the past costs incurred by them", says an official note explaining the short-term measures to be taken for development of the oil sector. This is another contentious issue on which there is more noise than action.

The Government has allowed entry of private sector in a major way into the oil refining sector (proposals, including export-oriented refineries, adding up to 70 million tonnes per annum have been cleared so far). Similarly, parallel marketing in gas has been allowed (though this has yet to pick up) and with the approval in principle for the Southern Gas Grid, several policy decisions with regard to the natural gas sector have also to be taken. For instance, natural gas is underpriced and there is a recommendation that it should be raised.

Development of the natural gas sector (which will, as per present indications, will be largely based on imported gas) means heavy investment in pipelines, port and storage facililties, etc. It takes years to set up these. Here again, to facilitate and encourage investment, a rational pricing policy must be in place, the sooner the better.

Since the country has mastered the art and science of

setting up refineries as well as running them, experts believe that india might become a net exporter of petroleum products in the coming century and a "swing producer" to stabilise global product markets. This expectation is based on the fact that India is one of the lowest cost refiners in the world.

But, to quote Dr. Kelkar again, "our present administered prices regime is non-transparent and certainly not efficency compatible. Further, our current tariffs provide negative rate of protection for the refining sector and as such it discourages provate investors to bring in new investments". Hence, what is required is comprehensive reforms of pricing and tariff policy as that alone can promote adequate infusion of capital and efficient use of these resources, he argues.

Now, that prescription applies not only to the refining sector, but to the entire oil and natural gas sector. This is not the place to go into specific details, but a visionary approach is needed similar tot he one shown by many of those who have helped paying the foundation for the oil and gas industry.

The great institutional base built up within the country over the past several decades in exploration, production and refining should be strengthened further, along with the entry of a range of new actors. Major investments are taking place in sectors like automobiles, but these can become infructuous if the main engine of growth (here one means both industrial and agricultural growth) i.e. the oil and gas sector, is not properly taken care of. It is time we put this sector on a faster track.

Both at the central and state level, the Government has initiated and supports many efforts towards capacity-building. The major thrust of development is on the implementation of sectoral programmes, particularly those related to agriculture and allied sectors.

Programmes such as the National Rural Employment Programmes (NREP), Rural Landless Employment Guarantee Programme * (IRDP) aim to alleviate rural poverty. Programmes such as Hill Area Development are designed to tackle hostile environmental factors which affect development of certain areas. In the Drought-Prone Areas Programme (DPAP) and Desert Development Programme (DDP), the emphasis is on water and moisture conservation.

India has sovereign rights and jurisdiction in the economic zone extending 200 nautical miles from the coastline. The Government has established a wide-ranging network of legislative and institutional frameworks for protecting and preserving the marine environment.

The programme of the Department of Ocean Development and associated organizations include Development of Coastal Zones and Islands, Monitoring and modelling of the Marine Environment, Control of Marine Pollution, Wave Power Generation, Ocean Modelling, Sea Level Monitoring and Modelling, and Coastal Mapping.

Marine Satellite Information Secvice centres and a multi-institutional Marine Pollution Coastal Ocean Monitoring and Predictive System have been established.

The National Environmental Awareness Campaign (NEAC), which began in 1986, is a major programme of the Ministry of Environment and forests. The programme seeks to increase environmental awareness through the involvement of governmental and non-governmental organizations. Activities under the NEAC include seminars, workshops, rallies, teacher training, eco-clubs, environmental campus etc.

The Ministry of Environment and Forests set up the

Environmental Information System (ENVIS) in 1982 as a decentralized system using a network of databases to ensure integration of national efforts in collecting information related to environment.

ENVIS has ten centres working in diverse areas such as pollution control, coastal ecology, environmentally sound and appropriate technology etc. It has a documentation service and processes queries from national and international useres. A quarterly abstracting journal Paryavaran Abstracts is published after scanning nearly five hundred scientific journals. ENVIS maintians a close liaison with other national information systems like National Information System on Science and Technology (NISSAT) and Biotechnology Information System (BTIS).

The Central Arid Zone Research Institute (CAZRI) was set up at Jodhpur in Rajasthan by the Government of India to undertake studies on land, soil water and vegetation resources of arid and semi-arid areas. The Institute carries out studies on precipitation, the regional dynamics of the landscape and the impact of climatic conditions and man-animal activities on it in order to determind the optimal natural plant community of major environments, and to optimize the use of water and land. CAZRI is also involved in transfer of technology, publicity and extension work to create awareness about the desertification process, and to achieve public participation in the development programmes of arid and semi-arid regions.

In the area of formal education, the National Policy on Education (1986) stresses the paramount need to create consciousness about the environment. This must permeate all ages and sections of the society, beginning with the child. The Policy gives unqualified priority to universalization of elementary eduction and substantial improvement in the quality of education. Detailed school mapping exercises have been planned under a master plan for universal provision of facilities for environment education. The National Council of Educational Research and Training (NCERT) has been assigned the responsibility of developing model syllabi and instructional packages in ten core cureicular ares, of which protection of environment is one.

The Ministry of Human Resource Development (MHRD) has taken a major initiative in the field of environment education through the launching of the Environment Orientation to School Education scheme. Under this scheme special cells have been created in the state departments of education. Support is also extended to NGOs to facilitate the development of locale-specific programmes and materials.

The Ministry of Environment and Forests supports two centres of excellence in the area of environmental educationl. These are the Centre for Environment Education, Ahmedabad, and the CPR Environmental Education Centre, Madras. The Centre for Environment Education, Ahmedabad, is involved in developing innovative programmes and materials to increase awareness about the environment.

The National Museum of Natural History (NMNH), New Delhi, is a unique facility which provides people an opportunity to acquire a direct understanding of the world of nature, the inter relationships among plants, animals, and the environment, and the need to develop a new approach and ethic towards the natural environment. NMNH also has centres at Mysore, Bhubaneshwar and Bhopal.

The Government of India supports research projects for the study of ecosystems and the causes of their degradation. In this regard, two committees—the Environmental Research Committee (ERC) and Man and the Biosphere (MAB) Research Committee function as advisory bodies under the Ministry of Environment and Forests. The research is followed up by formulation of action plans for optimal utilistion of resources leading to sustainable development.

Man and the Biosphere programme is an inter-disciplinary programme of research and training which emphasized and ecological approach to the study of inter-relationships between humans and their environment. The programme aims to provide scientific basis to solve practical problems of resource management through understanding the environmental problems in the ecosystem context.

The Environmental Research Committee addresses problems of chemical, engineering and technological aspects of environmental management, and promotes research in all subjexts concerned with the human environment that are not covered by the MAB programme. ERCs thrust areas include environmental aspects of rural and urban settlemens, resource management, environmental degradation, planning, training and education. It promotes integrated action-oriented programmes which deal not only with research but also its demonstration and extension. Such action-oriented research has been taken up in the Himalayan region, and in the Western and Eastern Ghats, besides multinational project of integrated studies on the Kaveri river.

The Ministry of Environment and Forests has so far supported about 500 environmental research projects in different parts of the country. Of these, about 300 had been completed by March 1990. The findings of the research projects are published in a departmental publication and also in scientific journals and the popular press. Some of the findings have direct applicability while others contribute to the data base for environmental planning and management.

Various other research organizations set up by the Government and other agencies are concerned with different aspects of evnironment. The physical Research Laboratory (PRL) Ahmedabad, is a premier national centre for research in space and allied sciences; the Indian Institute of Remote Sensing (IIRS), Hyderabad, imparts training in remote sensing techniques and promotes research in areas like thematic mapping of land.

The functions of the Council of Scientific and Industrial Research (CSIR) include institutional financing, awarding fellowships, collecting and disseminating information on research and industrial matters. It has a chain of 39 laboratories and about 80 field centres. From aeronautical products to oceanography, and from drugs to salt and marine chemicals research, CSIR is involved in helping the country enter frontier areas of research.

Its centres include the Central Drug Research Institute, Lucknow; National Environmental Engineering Research Institute, Nagpur; Indian National Scientific Documentation Centre, New Delhi; National Chemical laboratory, Pune; Central Institute of Medicinal and Aromatic Plants, Lucknow; Industrial Toxicology Research Centre, Lucknow; Indian Institute of Chemical Technology, Hyderabad; and Central Food Technology Research Institute, Mysore.

Council for Advencement of People's Action and Rural Technology (CAPART), set up in 1986 is the central agency for funding rural development projects of voluntary agencies. It assists voluntary efforts which aim to implement locale-specific rural development projects. Funding for projects coming under several government programmes like the Drought Prone Area programme, Integrated Rural Development Programme etc., are disbursed through CAPART.

CAPART gives financial assistance to registered voluntary organization. Up to 80 per cent of the project expenditure is made available and the remaining has to be raised by the organization for other sources.

The Department of Science and Technology, Government of India, is involved in research and development related to several environmental issues throuhg its institutions.

The Indian Institute of Tropical Meteorology, Pune, is involved in studies of atmospheric ozone, effect of aerosols on climate change, effect of stratospheric changes and anthropogenic activities on climate change, carbon dioxide studies etc.

The Birbal Sahni Institute of Paleobotany, Lucknow, is engaged in paleobotanical research which aims to build up an evlutionary sequence charting the history of modern vegetation. It is also involved in investigating past climates.

The Wadia Institute of Himalayan Geology, Dehra Dun, has been studying various aspects of the chemistry of Himalayan glaciers. It has also conducted studies on the impact of growing human population on the Himalayan ecology.

The Indian institute of Astrophysics, Bangalore, studies solar activity while the Indian Institute of Geomagnetism, Bombay, has a programme for the study of atmospheric and solar terrestrial weather relationships.

The Survey of India, Dehra Dun, is responsible,

among other things, for tide gauge observations along the Indian coastline and for the study of anticipated problems of sea-level rise and impact on coastal environment.

The Centre for Atmospheric Studies at the Indian Institute of Technology, New Delhi, studies the effect of aerosols on climate change, air pollution over India, and other related issues.

The Department of Science and Technology is also actively involved in the national efforts of the International Geosphere-Biosphere programme.

The practice of scientific forestry in India dates back to over 120 years. Systamatic research and trainign in foresting commenced nearly 70 years ago. Research and forestry education now come under the purview of the Indian Council of Forestry Research and Education, which conducts its programmes through six regional institutions and a number of universitites and other organizations. Its six regional institutions, including the Forest Research Institute at Dehra Dun which is a premier institution in forestry, carry out extensive field and laboratory research. The Indian Institute of Forest Management (IIFM) Bhopal, was established in 1982 to meet the growing need for managerial expertise in forestry and allied sectors. The institute also runs management development programmes for in—service managers of forest departments, forest development corporations, forest based industries, financial institutions and voluntary organizations. In addition, the Institute is involved in applied research and provides consultancy service.

Forest management in the field is planned and implemented by the Indian Forest Service (IFS). Two year postgraduate training in forestry is imparted to IFS officers at the Indira Gandhi National Forest Academy, Dehra Dun. There are also three regional State Forest Service colleges and numerous rangers' colleges for training middle level and field professionals.

NGOs in India have played a vital role in raising awareness about the issues related to environment and development, and in mobilizing people to take action. They have employed a variety of techniques and media. The Kerala Sastra Sahitya Parishat, which was the catelytic agency involved in mobilizing public opinion agaisnt the Silent Valley hydroelectric project, uses traditional and folk media to communicate its messages. The Centre for Science and Environment (CSE), New Delhi, has brought out three widely circulated volumes on the state of India's environment, in addition to several other publication. CSE has also played a key role in bringing in the South perspective in International discussions of environment and development issues. Eklavya, Bhopal, develops innovative and relevant school programmes and material. The Assam Science Society which has a membership of professional and students, attempts to enhance science education.

The Narmada Bachao Andolan has brought together scattered voices of protest against the damming of the river Narmada and has raised awarness not only in the affected area and in the rest of India, but alos among the international community. The Vivekanand Kendra, Tamil Nadu, trains hundreds of workers in the fields of health, education and development.

A major focus of its activities is in Arunachal Pradesh where it runs 14 residential schools for tribal children. The People's Commission on Environment and Development, New Delhi, is a forum creatd to bring together and articulate citizen's concerns to put before the UNCED. Kalpavriksh, New Delhi, organizes awareness programmes and carries out campaigns on specific issues by lobbying, holding demonstrations and fighting legal cases.

The Ministry of Environment and Forests has instituted a number of awards to recognize outstanding contributions of individuals and organizations in various environment related endeavours.

National Awards for Prevention and Control of Pollution have been instituted to recognize the achievements of industries for their contribution in the prevention and control of pollution.

Indira Priyadarshini Vrikshmitra Awards are given to individuals and organizations for outstanding work in the field of afforestation and wastelands development.

Indira Gandhi Paryavaran Puraskar is awarded to either an individual or organization for contribution in the field of environment.

Pitamber Pant National Fellowship recognizes excellence in research in any branch of environmental science.

The Centre for Mining Environment at Dhanbad (Bihar) was establised in 1987 by the Ministry of environment and Forests to generate scientific data for sustainable mining in the country. The Centre conducts postgraduate and doctoral level courses, as well as training programmes for in service professionals. Research areas include land use management, noise and vibration problems in mining areas, air pollution in fire areas and its effects on health.

Remote sensing for survey of resources is carried out by India's earth observation satellite system, the IRS series of satellites. Projections of crop yields, land-use mapping, monitorin of forest cover and biomass, identification of agro-climatic zones are today possible, and provide a basis for micro-level planning. Drought monitoring on a real time basis is also becoming possible, as is the use of remote sensing for mitigating damage due to floods. Detailed remote sensing surveys have also helped to considerably narrow down areas for groundwater exploration. Satellite based glacier inventory of the Himalayan states has been found promising for planning and operating mini and micro hydroelectric stations.

Fishers prospect charts, derived from satellite monitoring of sea surface temperature anamolies, are in regular use. Remote sensing has also been used extensively for forest mapping, in India. It is through this that a correct picture of the extent of forest cover and the relative changes in it have been obtained.

The National Natural Resource Management System of the Ministry of Environment and Forests involves utilization of remote sensing technology for accurate inventory of resources such as land, water, forests, minerals, ocean, etc., and to utilize this information for monitoring changes in ecological systems.

The objective of all development is to add to the economic well-being of the people so that their standard of living can be improved. Development projects are, therefore, taken up to convert the natural resources into goods and services. It is imperative to incorporate environmental aspects into the development projects right at the inception stage to prevent the erosion of the resouces base itself. Impact assessment is a handy tool to assess the environmental compatibility of the projects in terms of their location, suitability of technology, efficiency in resource utilisation and recycling etc. Impact assessment was introduced in 1978 and now covers almost all major projects.

At present environmental impact assessment is being done for the following types of project: (a) (i) river valley; (ii) thermal power; (iii) mining; (iv) industries; (v) atomic power; (vi) rail, road, highways, bridges; (vii) ports and harbours; (viii) airport; (iv) new towns and (x) communication projects, (b) projects which require approval of the Public Investment Board/Planning Commission/Central Electricity Authority; (c) projects referred to the Ministry of Environment and Forests by other ministries; (d) projects which are sensitive and located in environmentally degraded areas; (e) public sector undertakings of the Centre where the project cost is more than Rs. 50 crore. A notification has been issued in January 1994 which makes Environmental Impact Assessement statutory for 29 categories of developmental projects under various sectors such as industrial, mining, irrigation, power, transport, tourism, communication, etc. The notification contains details aimed at rationalising and standarding the procedure for environmental clearance. Extensive delegations to the stae governments are also provided in this notification. An amendment to this notification stipulates inter alia that all applications complete in every material aspect have to be examined and decision conveyed to the applicants within 30 days in the case of site clearances and 120 days in the case of environmental clearnce of projects. Once an application has been submitted by project authority the preliminary scrutiny of the project is done by the respective technical divisions and the overall appraisal of the projects is undertaken by specially constituted environmental appraisal committees of experts. In addition, special groups/committees and task forces are constituted as and when needed for expert inputs on major projects. After a detailed scrutiny and assessment, the appraisal committee makes its recommendation for approval or rejection of the projects. Depending on the nature of the project, certain safeguards are recommended. For monitoring and timely implementation of safeguards suggested, six regional centres have been set up by the Ministry at Shillong, Bhubaneswar, Chandigarh, Bangalore, Lucknow and Bhopal.

Under the Forests (Conservation) Act, 1980 diversion of forest land for non-forest purpose requires prior approval from the Central Government. While proposals involving forest land less than 20 hectare can be decided by the state forest departments, proposals involving more than that are appriased by the Advisory Committee of the Ministry, constituted under the Forests (Conservation) Act, 1980 as amended in 1988.

When a project requires both environemental and forest clearance, the proposals are simultaneously processed under the Single Window Celearance Scheme. All cases with complete environmental data and action plans are decided within three months. In the case of diversion of forest land, the decision is taken within six months

Major environmental impacts of river vally projects which need consideration are: (i) degradation of catchment areas; (ii) command area development; (iii) rehabilitation of those affected; (iv) incresed incidence of water-borne diseases; (v) reservoir induced seismicity; and (vi) deforestation and loss of flora and fauna including gene-pool reserves.

Major environmental impacts of mining operations are: (i) degradation of land; (ii) pollution of surface and ground water resources; (iii) pollution of air; (iv) deforestation including loss of flora and fauna; (v) rehabilitation of affected populationincluding tribals; and (vi) impact on historical monuments and religious places. A major component of the mining operations in India is the opencast mining which severely affects land use pattern. Mining operations have serious adverse impact on the growth of vegetation and general landscape. Minerals extracted interact with surface and ground water thus polluting the water resources. Loss of top-soil due to deforestation also depletes ground water resources and results in drying up of perennial sources like springs and streams especially in hill areas.

Major environmental impacts of thermal power projects include; (a) air pollution; (b) water pollution; (c) deforestation; (d) rehabilitation; and (e) land degradation. Flue gases emerging from stacks containing sulphur dioxide, oxides of nitrogen, carbon monoxide, etc., are detrimental to human beings and vegetation. Water pollution from thermal stations can due to release of slurry which is a mixture of flyash and water. Thermal pollution is due to release of cooling water which can affect acquatic life. Solution to disposal of ash problem is in its recycling by converting it into building blocks and its use in other construction works. Another step which helps in abating pollution cuased by ash is stabilisation of ash dumps through suitable vegetation.

Major environmenal impacts of industrial projects include (i) are pollution; (ii) water pollution; and (iii) disposal and utilisation of solid waste. Impacts of projects in specific areas are examined in great detail and suitable control measures suggested. Linkages of project requirements to utilisation of resources in an optimal way is an essential pre-requisite. Concept of recycling, reuse and adoption of clean technologies is increasingly becoming predominant.

Projects considered under the transport sector include laying of railway lines, roads and bridge construction, airport construction and establishing of ports and harbours. The environmental parameters affected by the transport projects have been classified into (i) natural physical resources; (ii) natural ecological resources; (iii) human/economic development resources; and (iv) quality of life values including aesthetic and cultural values. Adverse impacts on above environmental parameters are to be identified and mitigation measures provided for to offset such impacts.

Under the Environment (Protection) Act, 1986, a notification on Coastal Zone Regulation has been issued declaring coastal stretches of seas, bays, estuaries, creaks, rivers and backwater within 500 meter of High Tide line as Coastal Regulation Zones. Setting up of new industries or expansion of existing industies except those directly related to waterfront, manufacturing, handling, storage or disposal of hazardous substances and setting up and expansion of units/mechanisms for disposal of wastes and effluents etc., are prohibited in these Costal Regulation Zone. All the seven coastal states are required to prepare coastal management plans which would provide protection to ecologically fragile coastal areas rich in biological diversity and provide for land use zoning. The Coastal Regulation Zone notification, 1991, has been amended.

In nuclear power plants, safety from radiation during the operation of the plants and after, and disposal of nuclear wastes are of prime concern. Major environmental impacts of nuclear power projects which need consideration are; (i) radio-active contamination of air, water and soil; (ii) thermal pollution due to discharge of cooling water; (iii) deforestation and loss of flora and fauna; (iv) rehabilitation; and (v) radio-active waste disposal. Exposure to radio-active radiations in excess of the prescribed limits are detrimental to human beings, aquatic life, flora and fauna. The long half life periods for radio-active decay necessitate sealing of the reactor vessel and components for a dormant period of about 30 years after decommissioning of the plant.

Afforestation of wastelands through proper financial assitance by various agencies would provide income and employment opportunities to the poor and improve the quality of the environment. The government can play a facilitating role by removing obstacles and simplifying procedures. The lack of ground-level data has affected the afforestation programme. The afforestation of wastelands has now emerged as an important feature in the present socio-economic and political scenario in India, which aims at solving the problems of scarcity of timber, firewood, fodder and other forest produce as well as reclamation of wastelands and degraded forests. India has vast tracts of wastelands, and these lands are mostly owned by government and village Panchayats and are highly degraded. Tree plantation is the socially optimum and ecologically-sound use of such lands. It may not be economically desirable for a farmer to plant trees on good lands which have a very high opportunity cost in terms of value of agricultural production forgone. However, tree planting may be profitable for a farmer in region prone to recurring drought and having unproductive soil which is not fit for growing agricultural crops.

Although the practice of planting trees is as old as cultivation of other crops, the need for government intervation to promote afforestation was articulated by the National Commission on Agriculture (NCA) in 1976. The government of India accepted the NCA's recommendation and subsequently various afforestation programmes like farm forestry, rehabilitation/ reforestation of degraded lands, formation of community woodlots and strip plantation were started in some States in the late seventies. Recent evidences from various parts of the country indicate that the success of afforestation programmes has been remarkable. In India, there is still a vast scope for implementing afforestation programmes in regions which are not yet brought within the fold of tree plantation schemes and in which there is acute shortage of firewood, timber and other forest produce.

In conjunction with technical guidance and financing, availability of wastelands for afforestation is the other crucial component of the wastelands development and afforestation programmes determing their success. There are many constraints which are hampering the implementation of afforestation programmes in various parts of the country. The non-availability of wastelands for afforestation programmes is one of them. In the absence of a comprehensive survey of land use, several estimates have been made about the extent of wastelands in India. One of the estimates of wastelands indicate that about 175 million hectares of (m ha) land fall in this category (Sigh et al, 1981). The other estimate by the Society for the Promotion of Wastelands Development (SPWD) puts it at 129 m ha-93 m ha in non-forest area and 36 m ha in forest area (SPWD, 1984). The National Wastelands Development Board (NWDB, 1989) estimates wastelands to the extent of 120 m ha with 40 m ha in forest lands and 80 m a in agricultural lands. According to Singh (1994), more than half of the geographical area of India consists of degraded lands. The estimates for wastelands range between 38.4 m ha (11.7% of total geographical area of the country, Directorate of Economics & Statistics, GOI, New Delhi 1978-79) to 175 m ha (53.2% of total geographical area of the country, Ministry of Agriculture & Co-operation, New Delhi, 1982) (Gautam and Narayan, 1988:96). However, Bentley (1984) has estimated that 200 m ha of land in India are partially degraded in terms of short-term productivity. According to Khan (1987), the wastelands which may ultimately be available for development would not be more than 80 m ha, bulk of which is degraded forests and marginal agriculatural lands. There are many other estimates of wastelands in India.

The information needed for assessing the potential of non-forest and cultivated lands, like ownership, extent and type of degradation, and present and future uses, has never been collected on a systematic basis for the entire country (Romm, 1981). Recently, some initiatives have been taken to improve the availability of grass roots level data for this purpose. The Government of India has already implemented a National Wastelands Identification Project to identify the extent and type of wastelands in 146 districts in 19 States.

One of the most serious problems threatening the country today is its population growth. Although the foodgrain production in the last few years has kept pace with the population increase, the daunting task of feeding each and everyone in the next century is the biggest challenge before us. In our attempts to meet such increasing demands, the improper and over—use of chemical inputs had deteriorated the agro—ecosystems to a considerable extent. Moreover, the pressure due to growing human and cattle population on the land has added to the deterioration of land status of the country. The increasing deterioration of land due to soil—erosion, injudicious use of chemical fertilizers, water logging, salinity/alkalinity, shifting cultivation, etc. necessitates a more scientific approach towards the utilisation of these lands, often termed as degraded or waste—lands. The growing awareness world over on the environment conservation and the emphasis on the concept of 'sustainability' has focussed on the area of 'wasteland utilization' as an important component of 'sustainable development.'

There are various aerial estimates of wastelands in

the country varying from one—third to one half of the country's total area. The primary reason of the variation in such estimates could be ascribed to the fact that until recently, wastelands had neither been systematically defined nor identified. The first comprehensive attempt to map out such areas and categories them, was done by the National Commission on Agriculture (1976), which estimated different types of wastelands and suggested guidelines for reclaiming and developing such land. The Commission had estimated the extent of wastelands in the country to be 175 million hectares which is more than half the total geographical area in he country. However, this estimate was not based on scientific data. As per an estimate by the Society for Promotion of Wastelands Development (1993), the area under wastelands is around 129 million hectares or about one—third of country's total geographical area.

According to the statistics presented, the state with the greatest expanse of wastelands in the country is Madhya Pradesh with 20.14 million ha very closely followed by Rajasthan with 19.93 million ha. The states with over 10 million ha of wastelands each are Andhra Pradesh and Maharashtra. Gujarat, Karnataka and Uttar Pradesh have each approximately 9 million ha of wastelands.

To a layman, wasteland is a piece of land which is lying uninhabited or uncultivated. These lands are also commonly perceived to produce much less than their potential. Despleted of the green cover and productivity, such lands are often in a critical condition.

Boradly, wastelands may be defined as land where the production of biomass is less than its opotimum productivity. Wasteland also refers to lands which are economically unproductive, ecologically unstable and subject to environmental deterioration.

According to the Technical Task Group, constituted by the Planning Commisison and NWDB (National Wastelands Development Board), wasteland is defined as that land which is degraded and is presently lying unutilised except as current fallows due to different constraints.

Wastelands have been classified by NWDB into culturable and unculturable wastelands.

*Culturable Wastelands:* Land which is capable of or has the potential for the development of vegetative cover and is not being used due to different constraints of varying degree is termed as culturable wasteland. The culturable wastelands comprise the following categories:

— Gullied and/or ravinous land;

— Undulating upland with or without scrub;

— Surface–waterlogged lands and marsh;

— Salt–affected land;

— Shifting—cultivation area;

— Degraded forest—lands;

— Degraded pastures/grazing—lands;

— Degraded non forest–-plantation land;

— Strip—land;

— Sands; and

— Mining/industrial wastelands.

*Unculturable Wastelands:* Lands, which can not be developed for vegetative cover, are defined as unculturable wastelands. The unculturable wastelands comprise the following categories:

— Baren rocky/Stony wastes/Sheet–rock area;

— Steep–sloping area; and

— Snow–covered and/or glacial area.

Besides the above categories of wastelands, the following could also be included:

— Over cultivated soils leading to depletion of micro–nutrients;

— Acidic soils; and

— Land overgrown with aggressive weeds.

The major causes of land being rendered waste include—deforestation, overgrazing, faulty water management practices, extensive mining activities, etc. Deforestation and overgrazing distinctly hastens the process of soil erosion and land degradation. Faulty water managemnt practices lead to problems such as water logging, soil salinity/alkalinity, etc. Deforestation has often been described as the most primary reason of land degradation and the factors in deforestation are—conversion of forest land into agricultural land, the urban and industrial demand for forest products, indiscriminate quarrying for mineral resources, etc. Besides the above mentioned casuses, the environmental factors like slope, intensity of rainfall and the pedogenic characteristics of a particular area interact to increase the formation of wastelands.

Our forest cover has dwindled notwithstanding three successive National Forest Policies. A scientific land use policy alone can ensure sustained production, ecological balance and environmental benefits. It is time that the Forest Policy is reviewed and a new strategy adopted keeping in view that conservation includes preservation, maintenance, sustainable utilization, restoration and enrichment of the environment.

Man depends on natural resources from his forest environment for all his basic needs. No doubt, the majority in the industrialized countries is no longer dependent on the natural living resources but the bulk of the rural and a section of the urban population in India and the rest of the developing world continue this dependence, especially for their fuel, fodder and timber needs. The forest serves many valuable functions as has been reflected in the national forest policies. Moreover, forest plays an active role as a storehouse of living organisms of potential use and as a regulator of rainfall, soil and water regime, source of many basic needs of the weaker sections of the rural population. The relationship between land, climate and forest is such that if the soil is allowed to deteriorate or lost, degradation of both land and vegetation becomes inevitable. Unfortunately, in the developing countries like India, biotic pressures are intense.

The situation is worsening in spite of the lofty aims propagated by the three successive national forest policies. In India, although the first policy is nearly a century old, the present forest cover is worse than when it was originally proposed. The failure of the national forest policies is perhaps due to their focus on government forests rather than to the land and soil in general. There has been a lack, of scientific land use policy having legal backing and public support. For these reasons, the definition of 'forest' has come to imply land area constituted as reserve forests and not general tree cover.

Biotic Pressure: The tremendous increase in human population, the resultant poverty nd the heavy dependence on agriculture have resulted in the use of wood as the main fuel. India's ecology is today no better with the deficit of firewood at 145 million $m^3$ and 43 million ha of land brought under the plough between 1951 and 1976 for the extension of agriculture. The loss of forest area for various purposes during 1951-76 was substantial.

The situation has still remained the same and the condition has not changed as is evident from the cases of some of the States. The problem has worsened due to excessive grazing coupled with forest fire. About 52 per cent of India's forests are incapable of regenration largely due to the combined effects of biotic pressures.

In a developing country like India, forests have suffered badly because of the failure in land management practices. To what extent can we put the blame on forest policies? Are the policies wrong or inconsistent or is it that the policies have remained merely ceremonial documents devoid of the will to implement or people's support? An analysis cf the forest policies of India would reveal that the main cause of failure has been, perhaps, viewing forests in isolation rather than taking into consideration the country's soil as a whole. It is after all the soil which supports all kinds of plant life in the biosphere.

Forests are a renewable source and contribute substantially to economic development. They play major role in enhancing the quality of environment. The country has an area of 752.3 lakh hectare notified as forests, of which 406.1 lakh hectare is classified as reserved and 215.1 lakh hectare as protected. Unclassified forest area is spread over 131.1 lakh hectare. About 19.47 per cent of the total geographical area of the country is under actual forest cover.

India is one of the few countries which ahs a forest policy since 1894. It was revised in 1952 and again in 1988. Main plank of the revised forest policy of 1988 is protection, conservation and development of forests. Its aims are: (i) maintenance of environmental stability through preservation and restoration of ecological balance; (ii) conservation of natural heritage; (iii) check on soil erosion and denudation in catchment area of rivers, lakes and reservoirs; (iv) check on extension of sand dunes in desert areas of Rajasthan and along coastal tracts; (v) substantial increase in forest/tree cover through massive afforestation and social forestry programmes; (vi) steps to meet requirements of fuel wood, fodder, minor forest produce and soil timber of rural and tribal populations; (vii) increase in productivity of forest to meet the national needs; (viii) encouragement of efficient utilisation of forest produce and optimum substitution of wood, and (ix) steps to create massive people's movement with involvement of women to achieve the objectives and minimise pressure on existing forests.

The entire gamut of forest activities are being given a new orientation in the light of the National Forest Policy of 1988. Some of the important areas for immediate and effective protection of forests include afforestation and development of wastelands, reforestation and replantation in existing forests, settlement, restriction on grazing, encouragement for wood substitutes and supply of other kinds of fuel, elimation of forest contractors, discouragement of monoculture practice etc.

Increasing destruction and degradation of forests and treelands especially in the Himalayas and other hilly areas, is contributing to heavy erosion of top soil, erratic rainfall and recurring floods. It is also causing acute shortage of firewood and loos of productivity due to eroded and degraded lands. The Forest (Conservation) Act, 1980 enacted to check indiscriminate deforestation/ diversion of forest lands for non-forestry purpose was amended in 1988 to make it more stringent by prescribing punishment for violations.

Another area of concern has been degradation of forests due to biotic pressure. Guidelines have been framed for preparation of working plans and felling in forests. Some of the salient features are: (i) working plans shoudl be up-to-date and stress conservation; (ii) preliminary working plan should have multi-disciplinary approach; (iii) tribal rights and concessions should be highlighted and with control mechanisms; (iv) grazing should be studied in detail and specific prescriptions should cover fodder propagation; (v) shifting cultivation and encroachments need to be controlled; (vi) clear-felling with artificial regeneration should be avoided as far as possible and clear felling blocks should not exceed 10 hectare in hills and 25 hectare area in plains, and (vii) banning all felling above 1,000 metre altitude for a few years should be considered to allow these areas to recover. Critical areas in hills and catchment areas prone to landslides, erosion etc., should be totally protected and quickly afforested.

Guidelines have been issued in June 1990 to state governments for involving village communities and voluntary agencies for regeneration of degraded forest lands on usufruct shraing basis. As a follow up of these guidelines, 14 states have issued appropriate orders. These states are: West Bengal, Orissa, Bihar, Madhya Pradesh, Rajasthan, Gujarat, Maharashtra, Tripura, Himachal Pradesh, Haryana, Jammu and Kashmir, Andhra Pradesh, Karnataka and Tamil Nadu. Other states are being persuaded to issued such orders.

Firewood occupies a predominant place as an energy source in rural areas. As against the estimated requirement of about 15.7 crore tonnes of fuelwood per annum, recorded production is only 5.8 crore tonnes. Due to scarcity of firewood, considerable quantities of cowdung and agricultural residues are burnt as fuel leading to air pollution. It is expected that programmes of renewable energy sources and augmenting fuel growth in wastelands will help in closing the gap.

Fire is one of the major factors responsible for destruction of forests in the country. In India, most of the fires are man-made and are generally deliberate and on rare occasions accidental. The causes of deliberate fire incidences are grazing, mahua seed and flower collections, tendu leaf collection, poaching and shifting cultivation, etc. In order to reduce the incidents of fire in India, the following steps have been undertaken by the forest department: (i) development of firelines and (ii) establishment of watch towers besides employing fire watchers during fire seasons. In order to develop the techniques for detection, prevention and suppression of fire in the country, a UNDP assisted Modern Forests Fire Control Project was initiated in 1984 in Chandrapur, Maharashtra and Haldwani/Nainital, U.P. Techniques like development of better communication network and effective use of hand tools and other equipments developed under the projects have proved successful in reducing the fire damage. In addition, fire danger rating system, wireless network, fire reporting system and hand tools etc., were designed. This scheme is being continued in 11 states of the country.

The National Wildlife Action Plan adopted in 1983 provides the framework of strategy as well as programme for conservation of wildlife. At present the protected area network comprises 80 national parks and 441 sanctuaries covering 4.5 per cent of the total geographical area of the country. The Wildlife (Protection) Act, 1972 adopted by all states except Jammu and Kashmir (which has its own Act), governs wildlife conservation and protection of endangered species. The Act prohibits trade in rare and endangered species. India is also a signatory to the Convention on International Trade in Endangered Species of Wild Flora and Fauna. Under this, export or import of endangered species and their products is subject to strict control. Commercial exploitation of such species is prohibited.

The Centre provides finanacial and technical assistance to states for: (i) development and improved management of national parks (ii) protection of wildlife and control of poaching and illegal trade in wildlife products; (iii) eco-development in areas around national parks and sanctuaries; (iv) conservation of elephant and its habitat; and (v) conservation of rhinos in Assam. The Wildlife (Protection) Act, 1972 has been amended to make the provisions more effective.

Endangered species of plants and animals have been brought under the purview of the Act. A Central Zoo Authority has been set up to look after the management of zoological parks in the country. The Authority has since notified rules for recognition of zoos which stipulates the standards for upkeep, maintenance and veterinary care of animals. It coordinates the activities of over 200 existing zoos and also supervises the exchange of animals on a scientific basis. Project Tiger, one of the premeir conservation efforts of the country has completed 20 years in April 1993. Under this scheme 21 Tiger Reserves have been set up all over the country. A Global Tiger Forum has been set up for Tiger Range countries and an interim secretariat has been set up at New Delhi. A Tiger Crisis Cell has been set up to obtain all the information essential for conservation of the tiger.

The Animal Welfare Board of India, established in 1962 under the provisions of the Prevention of Cruelty to Animals Act, 1960 is an autonomous organisation of the Ministry of Environment and Forests working for the cause of animal welfare in the country. A series of camps for training the members of SPCAs and Animal Welfare

Organisations are being held all over the country, in collaboration with the Royal Society for Prevention of Cruelty to Animals, London. The Board also celebrates Animal Welfare Fortnight from 14 January every year.

At the time of India's Independence, our priority was the provision of the basic human needs of food, fuel, shelter, health, employment, etc., to our vast population. As such the focus of our Five Year Plans was on agriculture, health, family welfare etc. In the Fourth Five Year Plan, problems related to environment received direct attention and a Committee was set up in 1972 to look into these problems and suggest a solution in consulation with experts and concerned minstries/ departments of the government. Another Committee was set up in January 1980, for reviewing the existing legislative measures and administrative machinery for ensuring environmental protection and for recommending ways to strengthen them. On the recommendation of this high-powered Committee, the Department of Environment was set up in 1980. Consequently in 1985, it was upgraded to a full-fledged Ministry of Environment and Forests to serve as the focal point in the administrative structure for the planning, promotion and coordination of environmental and forestry programmes.

Environmental problem in India can be classified into two broad categories: (a) those arising as negative effects of the very process of development and (b) those arising from conditions of poverty and under-development. The first category has to do with the impact of efforts to achieve rapid economic growth and development. Poorly planned developmental projects are usually environmentally destructive. The second category has to do with the impact on the health and integrity of our natural resources such as land, soil, water, forests, wildlife, space, etc., as a result of proverty.

There are about 30 major enactments related to protection of environment now being administered by the Central and state governments. Prominent among these are: Wildlife (Protection) Act, 1972; The Forest (Conservation) Act, 1980; The Water (Prevention and Control of Pollution) Act, 1974; The Air (Prevention and Control of Pollution) Act, 1981; The Water (Prevention and Control of Pollution) Cess Act, 1977; The Environment (Protection) Act, 1986; The Public Liability Insurance Act; 1991; The Motor Vehicle Act, 1938 as amended in 1988; The Factories Act and the Insecticides Act. These are implemented through several organisations like Central and state pollution control boards, chief inspectors of factories and insecticides inspectors of agriculture departments, etc.

The Environment (Protection) Act, 1986, brought into force from 19 November 1986 is a landmark legislation as it is an umbrella Act for the protection of environment and aims at plugging the loopholes in the other related Acts. The salient features of this Act are as follows: (a) conferring powers on the Central Government to; (i) take all necessary measures for protecting quality of environment; (ii) coordinate activities of states, officers and other authorities under the Act or under any other law related to the objects of this Act; (iii) Plan and execute a nationwide programme for prevention, control and abatement of environmental pollution; (iv) lay down standards for discharge of environmental pollutant; (v) empower any person to enter, inspect, take samples and test; (vi) establish or recognise environmental laboratories; (vii) appoint or recognise analysts; (viii) lay down standards for quality of environment; (ix) restrict areas in which industries, operations or process may not be carried out or shall be carried out subject to certain safeguards; (x) lay down safeguards for prevention of accidents and take remedial measures in case of such accidents; (xi) lay down procedures and safeguards for handling hazardous substances; (xii) constitute an authority or authorities for exercising powers; (xiii) issue directions to any person, officer or authority including the power direct closure, prohibition or regulation of any industry, operation or process or stoppage or regulations of supply of electricity, water or any other services; (xiv) require any person, officer, state government or authority to furnish any prescribed information; and (xv) delegate powers to any of a state or authority; (b) it confers powers on persons to complain to courts regarding any violation of the provisions of the Act, after a notice of 60 days to prescribed authorities; (c) the Act makes it obligatory for the person incharge of a place to inform the prescribed authorities regarding any accidental discharge or apprehended discharge of any pollutant in excess of prescribed standards. Authorities on receipt of such information or otherwise shall take remedial measures are recoverable with inerest from the pollute; (d) it prescribes penalties for violation of the provisions of the Act. No distinction is shown between government of the Act. These include issue of rules, notification of standards, action regarding environmental laboratories, strengthening of state departments of environment and pollution control boards, delegation of powers, identification of agencies for carrying out various activities for hazardous chemical management and setting up of environemtn protection councils in the states. The Water (Prevention and Control of Pollution) Act, 1974 and the Air (Prevention and Control of Pollution) Act, 1981, have been made more stringent. Steps have been taken to: (i) prevent pollution at source; (ii) encourage, develop and apply the best available practicable and technical solutions; (iii) ensure that the polluter pays for the pollution and control arrangements; (iv) focus protection on heavily polluted areas and river stretches; and (v) involve the public in decision-making.

The rapid increase in industrialisation and urbanisation has exerted extra pressure on the infrastructural facilities of human settlements manifesting in environment problems like increased incidence of air, water and noise pollution.

The ambient aire quality major towns and cities in the country is being monitored under the National Ambient Air Quality Monitoring (NAAQM) programme. The monitoring results indicate that Sulphur Dioxide and Nitrogen dioxide levels are mostly within the permissible limits whereas Suspended Particulate Matter (SPM) values are higher than the prescribed limits at some places due to vehicular and air pollution, burning of fossil fuel and natural dusty conditions.

The pollution caused by vehicles contributes significantly towards air pollution. The problem of suspended particulate matter is more acute during the summer due to local dusty conditions. During the winter months, lower ambient temperatures, lower mixing depth temperature inversion, higher traffic density, higher consumption of domestic fuels, aggravate the pollution problems.

The data on ambient water quality of rivers indicates that levels of coliform count and Biological Oxygen Demand (BOD) are generally high resulting in deterioration of water quality. This is primarily due to inadequate sanitation facilities and discharge of waste water into the surface water bodies without proper treatment.

Urban noise levels in major cities also indicate and incresing trend due to rise in human population, automobiles and industrial activities. Specific studies reveal that noise levels in industrial areas are generally within the prescribed limits but exceed the standards in respect of commercial, residential and silence zones during certain hours. The problem is more conspicuous near the traffic intersections and commercial centres.

The on-going initiatives of Government to improve environment include preventive as well as promotive measures. Fiscal incentives are provided by the Government to encourage the installation of appropriate pollution abatement equipment in the form of custom waive off and soft loans. While the industries are encouraged and the fiscal incentives are provided for installing equipment for control of pollution, punitive measures including legal action is taken against the defaulting units.

To achieve the goal pollution abatement, emission and effluent standards for air, water and noise have been notified. Regular monitoring is carried out and the enforcement efforts have been intensified. At present, a majority of identified units have already installed the requisite pollution control equipment. According to the data collected by the Central Pollution Control Board (CPCB) on September 30, 1996, out of 1,551 units belonging to 17 categories of highly polluting industries, 1,259 units had facilities to comply with the environmental standards, 112 were closed and 180 were not having adequate facilities. Show cause notices under Section 5 of the Environment (Protection) Act 1986 have been issued to all the defaulting units.

Apart from notifications of effluent and emission standards for the major categories of polluting industries, national ambient air quality standards including ambient noise standards have been notified. Industries have been directed to instal necessary pollution control equipment within a stipulated time frame. More stringent norms for vehicular emissions have been notified under the Central Motor Vehicles Rules which have come into effect from April, 1996. Supply of unleaded petrol in four metropolitan cities of Mumbai, Calcutta, Delhi and Chennal has been introduced with effect from April 1, 1995 for use in four wheel vehicles fitted with catalytic converters. The use of unleaded petrol will be gradually expanded to other cities in the country.

Twenty-four critically polluted areas in the country have been identified and action plans have been drawn up to improve the quality of environment in these areas. Adoption of clean technologies of production and formation of Waste Minimisation Circles is being encouraged to minimise environmental pollution. Under the World Bank aided Industrial Pollution Control Project, technical and financial assistance is provided for setting up Common Effluent Treatment Plants (CETPs) in clusters of small scale industrial units. An "Eco-Mark" scheme has been launched to certify various products of the industries which fulfil the prescribed pollution control standards to achieve the objective of environment-friendly production, packaging and waste disposal. To increase public awareness and participation, several public awareness campaigns on effects of pollution and measures to control it have been launched.

The Polity Statement for Abatement of Pollution indicates adoption of best available clean and practicable technologies, rather than end-of-the-pipe treatment, as the key elements for pollution prevention. As a part of this thrust, the Ministry of Environment & Forests has set up a Clean Technologies Division for identifying cleaner technologies that can be introduced in different development sectors. Techniques like coal beneficiation are being promoted. The programme envisages setting up a National Clearing House for cleaner technologies as the overall co-ordinating agency and sectoral centres in different areas of development to focus on their activities. Another initiative taken to motivate environmentally oriented technologies and practices is mandatory submission of Annual Environmental Statements which would be subsequently evolved into environmental audit.

Prior environmental clearance of development projects based on impact assessment is being increasingly emphasised. Such clearance has been made mandatory for 29 specified categories of development projects through a statutory notification issued in January, 1994. This has been done with a view to mitigating the adverse environmental effects of these projects and in integrating the environmental concerns into development. This mechanism is also of help in catalysing the process of inducing cleaner environment-friendly technologies into the developmental process.

The success of the Ganga Action Plan has encouraged its replication for water pollution abatement in tributaries of the Ganga (Yamuna, Gomati and Damodar) under Ganga Action Plan Phase-II. A wider scheme called the National River conservation Plan covering pollution abatement works for grossly polluted stretches in 18 major rivers in 10 States of the country has also been initiated. Further, a programme for conservation of selected lakes has also been formulated by the Ministry.

The National Environmental Tribunal Act, providing relief, compensation and restitution to victims of accidents while handling hazardous substances, and for environmental damages, came into force from 17 June, 1995. The Act provides (i) strict liabilitiy for damages arising out of any accident occurring while handling any hazardous substances and (ii) Establishment of National

Environmental Tribunal for effective and expenditious disposals of cases arising from such accidents with a view to give relief and compensation for damage to persons, property and the environment and (iii) matters connected therewith or incidental thereto.

The National Environment Appellate Authority (NEAA) has been set up by the Government in January 1997. Public hearings have now been built into the environment impact assessment. The machinary for hearing appeals against environment pollution impact assessment is also being set up. The measures are to ensure greater transparency and faster decision-making in matters concerning the environmental impact of industrial projects.

As per the Policy Statement of Abatement of Pollution announced in February 1992, the key elements for pollution prevention are adoption of the best available clean and praticable technologies rather than end of the pipe treatment. The focus is on source reduction and substitution of chemicals, with safe alternatives. The thrust has, therefore, been made for considering process changes which involve significant improvements in energy and water conservation. To follow up on the various issues covered in the Policy Statement for Abatement of Pollution, the National Conservation Strategy and the Forest Policy Statement, several new programmes and studies have been initiated and commissioned. An Environment Action Programme has been formulated covering a wide ambit of subjects such as clean and low-waste technologies, improvement of water quality, institutional and human resources development, forestry and natural resources accouning.

To integrate natural resource accounting into the national accounting process, collection and analysis of environmental data has been initiated. It is proposed to produce a computerised map of the critically polluted areas through digitisation, on a format based on Geographic Information System. Base thematic maps on 1.6 M scale have been prepared for the country on the following themes: (i) major river basins and drainage network; (ii) administrative divisions; (iii) designated best use classification of streams; (iv) location of water and air pollution monitoring stations; (v) location of critically polluted areas; and (vi) major cities of India (above one lakh population).

The gazette notification on environmental audit issued in 1992 has been amended and now applies to all units seeking environmental clearance, and such units are required to submit environmental statements for the period ending 31 March on or before 30 September every year beginning from 1993 To facilitate industries in preparing environmental statements, model environmental statement reports for six categories of industries have been prepared. A booklet titled "Environmental Statement as part of environmental audit" has also been prepared by the Ministry. A software package 'Paryavaran' along with a user manual, has been prepared for analysis of information submitted in these environmental statements and is being distributed to all the SPCBs.

An 'Eco-Mark' label has been introduced to label consumer products that are environment friendly. Sixteen products have been identified for labelling and standards for toilet soaps and detergents, paper, paints, architectural paints and laundry soaps have been notified for awarding this label. The procedure for granting consent to small scale industries has been simplified. A new format for the consent application and for authorisation required under the Environment (Protection) Act, 1986 has been developed and notified.

Under the scheme "Adoption of clean technology in the small scale industries and to extend necessary technical support", training and awareness programmes for personnel in small Industry Development Organisation and entrepreneurs are being organised. A manual "From Waste to Profits" giving guidelines for waste minimisation has been prepared.

The Central Pollution Control Board (CPCB) is the national apex body for assessment, monitoring and control of water and air pollution. The executive responsibilities for enforcement of the Acts for Prevention and Control of Pollution of Water (1974) and Air (1981) and also of the Water (Cess) Act, 1977 are carried out through are Board. Twenty three states and union territories have already adopted the Act and respective state pollution control boards have been constituted. These states are Andhra Pradesh, Assam, Bihar, Goa, Gujarat, Haryana, Himachal Pradesh, Jammu and Kashmir, Karnataka, Kerala, Madhya Pradesh, Maharashtra, Meghalaya, Mizoram, Orissa, Punjab, Rajasthan, Sikkim, Tamil Nadu, Tripura, Uttar Pradesh, West Bengal, Delhi and Pondicherry. Arunachal Pradesh has adopted the Act, but is yet to constitute the board. Enactment of the Enviornment (Protection) Act, 1986 has further extended the scope of the activities of the Board. Under the Environment (Protection) Act, 1986, effluent and emission standards in respect of 61 categories of industries have been notified. So far, 84 laboratories have been recognised as environmental laboratories. Minimum National Standards (MINAS) for effluents and emissions from specific industries have been formulated and control measures are being implemented in a phased manner. A notification consolidating all the environmental standards including general effluent, emission and noise standards has been issued. It also includes standards for waste water generation in respect of 11 categories of industries. Further mass emission norms which would come into effect from 1 April 1996 have also been issued for petrol and diesel driven vehicles under the Central Motor Vehicles Rules of the Ministry of Surface Transport. Unleaded petrol of Delhi, Bombay, Madras and Calcutta from 1 April 1995. Petrol with a maximum lead content of 0.15 g/l has been introduced at all the retail outlets of these four metro cities since June 1994.

Seventeen categories of heavily polluting industries have been identified namely, cement, thermal powre plants, distilleries, sugar, fertilizer, integrated iron and steel, oil refineries, pulp and paper, petrochemicals, pesticides, tanneries, basic drugs and pharmaceuticals, dye and dye intermediates, caustic soda, zinc smelter, copper smelter and aluminium smelter. Action is taken against the defaulting units in these categories on priority. On the basis of the designated best use of criteria CPCB has identified 13 grossly polluted stretches of Sabarmati, Subernarekha, Godavari, Krishna, Indus (tributaries), Sutlej, Ganga (tributaries), Yamuna, Hindon, Chambal, Damodar, Gomati, and Kali rivers to formulate short-term result oriented programmes. The CPCB, in consultation with SPCBs has identified 22 critically polluted areas in the country which need special attention for control of pollution. These are Vapi (Gujarat), Singrauli (U.P.), Korba, Ratlam, Nagoda (Madhya Pradesh), Digboi (Assam), Talcher (Orissa), Bhadravati (Karnataka), Howrah (West Bengal), Dhanbad (Bihar), Pali and * Pataucheru (Andhra Pradesh), Chembur (Maharashtra), Najafgarh (Delhi), Govindhgarh (Punjab), Udyog Mandal (Kerala) and Parwanoo and Kala Amb (HP). The progress in abatement of pollution in these areas is being reviewed. A Bill has been introduced in the Parliament for establishing a National Environment Tribunal.

There are a host of human interventions including development activities which have resulted in considerable environmental degration. Major human interventions in forests are deforestation, commercial logging, setting up protected area, partial closure of forests, etc which are described below:

— There is increasing deforestation due to commercial exploitation, building of dams, mining and construction activities. Of the world's estimated 8.4 billion hectares of forests in 1990, tropical forests covered 1.76 billion ha. During 1981-90, tropical forests were lost at the rate of 0.8 per cent (15.4 million ha) a year, as per estimates of the World Resources Institute. The net annual deforestation during 1981-90 exceeded two per cent in 10 tropical countries of Asia and Africa.

— Commercial logging for industrial activities is increasing rapidly. Eighty-four per cent of such logging took place in closed tropical broadleaf forests in primary (undisturbed forests) during the 1980s. Logging activity is a causal factor for forest degradation and is reflected in rough wood production which increased by 19 per cent between 1979-81 to 1989-91. Globally, almost 50 per cent of such rough wood is used for industrial purposes, the rest for heating and cooking.

— Setting up of protected areas for conservation purposes has led to complications and conflict-situation with indigenous communities and also denial of many of their rights and privileges.

— Closure of parts of forests for setting up of industries or agro-based activities for private, semi-private lands, construction of railways, roads and new settlements has led to shrinkage of forest cover and increased hardship for local communities in their day-to-day existence.

— Interventions for adhering to international agreements have also alienated many local communities and some of their practices, eg, tribal hunting of wild animals which goes against biodiversity agreements.

— Policies of economic liberalization, privatization and globalization have both, directly and indirectly, led to reduction of forest cover and cuts in subsidies and grants affecting food subsidies and other welfare schemes involving poor and marginalized communities.

The environmental research programme aims to develop strategies for sustainable resource management and create facilities and trained manpower to conduct research in priority areas. Research projects are supported under three main schemes: (a) Man and Biosphere Programme; (b) Environment Research Programme; and (c) Action-oriented research programme for Eastern and Western Ghats. A number of small, specific research projects are also beng supported. Expert committees and expert working groups make recommendations for undertaking research in priority areas, scrutinise proposals, evaluate progress and recommend suitable mechanisms for implementation of the research projects. Priority areas of research are identified in five fundamental elements viz., land, water, air, space and energy. To strengthen the environmental research and training base, the following Centres of Excellence have been set up: Ecological Research and Training Centre, Bangalore: Centre for Mining Environment, Dhanbad: Centre for Environmental Education, Ahmadabad: CPR Environment Education Centre, Madras and the Salim Ali Centre for Orinthology and Natural History, Coimbatore.

This Institute, established in 1988, is an autonomous organisation of the Ministry of Environment and Forests for developing strategies, technologies and knowledge base for ecologically sound developoment of the Himalayan region. Besides undertaking action-oriented research projects the Institute has also installed three weather monitoring stations for collecting and analysing climatic data for the Himalayan region. Units of the Institute are also located at UP, Sikkim, Nagaland and Himachal Pradesh.

Forestry research is the primary responsibility of the Indian Council of Forestry Research and Education. It has the following forestry research institutes and centres under it: (i) Forest Research Institute, Dehra Dun; (ii) Institute of Arid Zone Forestry Research, Jodhpur; (iii) Institute of Rain and Moist Deciduous Forests, Jorhat; (iv) Institute of Wood Science and Technology, Bangalore; (v) Tropical Forestry Research Institute, Jabalpur; (vi) Institute of Forest Genetics and Tree Breeding, Coimbatore; (vii) Temperate Forest Research Centre, Shimla (viii) Centre for Forest productivity, Ranchi and (ix) Centre for Social Forestry and Environment, Allahabad. In addition, the Indian Plywood Industries Research and Training Institute, Bangalore, has been transferred to the Ministry of Environment and Forests from the Ministry of Industry. Besides forestry research in wood panel products, this Institute imparts training to workers in optimum utilisation of timber.

Research programmes in wildlife are carried out by the Wildlife Institute of India, Dehra Dun and the Salim Ali Centre for Orinthology and Natural History, Coimbatore. Several projects on habitat evolution, elephant movement, ecology of gharial and turtles, status of endangered species behavioural ecology, bio-diversity, resource study, conservation, ecology and management of specific animals etc., are being carried out by both these institutes.

Priority is accorded by the Ministry of Environment and Forests to promote evironmental education, create environmental awareness among various age groups and to disseminate information through Environmental Information System (ENVIS) network to all concerned. Special emphasis is given to non-formal environmental education through seminars/symposia/workshops, training programmes, eco-camps, audio-visual shows etc. The Ministry has been organising a National Environment Awareness Campaign (NEAC) since July 1986. As a part of this Capaign, 19 Novmber to 18 December every year is observed as the National Environment Month. Students/youth, techers, women, tribals, administrators, professionals, legislators, industrial workers, Armed Forces and the general public are covered under this Campaign. During 1994-95 about 2,200 organisations have been granted financial assistance by the Ministry to organise various activities for creating environmental awareness. The Ministry also provides financial support for setting up eco-clubs at schools and for production on films on environment.

A new scheme "Paryavaran Vahini" has been launched during 1992-93 to create environmental awareness and to ensure active public participations by involving the local people in activities relating to environmental protection. Parayavaran Vahinis are proposed to be constituted in 183 selected districts all over the country which have high incidence of pollution and density of tribal and forest population. The Vahinis also play a watch dog role by reporting instances of environmental pollution, deforestation, poaching, etc. They function under the charge of District Collectors with active cooperation of the state/union territory governments. this scheme is entirely financed by the Ministry of Environment and Forests.

The National Museum of Natural History (NMNH) set up in New Delhi in 1978, is concerned with the promotion of non-formal education in the area of environment and conservation. Besides permanent exhibit galleries on various aspects of environment, the museum also conducts temporary exhibitions and a large number of educational programmes and activities for school children, college youth and the general public. A Regional Museum of Natural History has been established at Mysore and two more and planned at Bhopal and Bhubaneswar.

The Indian Council for Forestry Research and Education is the focal point for forestry education and extension developmnet in the country. Indira Gandhi National Forest Academy, Dehra Dun imparts in-service professional training to Indian Forest Service (IFS) professionals. State forest service colleges provide training to the officers of the State Forest Service (SFS). The Indian Plywood Industries Research and Training Institute, Bangalore organises short-term courses in the area of wood science.

The Indian Institute of Forest Management, Bhopal, also provides training in forest management and allied subjects to persons from the Indian Forest Service, forest development corporations and forest related industries to develop forestry management skills. The Wildlife Institute of India, Dehra Dun conducts various programmes to provide in-service training in wildlife management for forest officers, wildlife ecologists and other professionals.

Environmental Information System (ENVIS) has been set up by the Ministry in 1982 as a decentralised information system network for collection, storage, retrieval and dissemination of environmental information to decision makers, policy planners, scientists, engineers, environmentalists, research workers and the general public all over the country. Besides the Focal Point in the Ministry, the ENVIS network presently consists of 20 subject oriented centres known as ENVIS centres, set up in various institutions/organisations of the country on priority areas of environment such as environmentally sound and appropriate technology, bio-degradation of wastes, desertification, estuary, mangroves, corals and lagoons, media and environment, environmental education, solid wastes disposal, animal ecology, Himalayan ecology, etc. The Focal Point brings out a quarterly abstracting journal "Paryavaran Abstracts" containing information about environmental research in the Indian context.

ENVIS has been designated as National Focal Point (NFP) and Regional Service Centre (RSC) for South Asia sub-regional countries by INFORTERRA (an international referral system for sources of information on environment) of United Nations Environment Programme (UNEP). As NEP, ENVIS updated more than 250 Indian Potential Sources in the International Directory of UNEP for providing information in the field of environment and its related areas.

The Ministry functions as a nodal agency for United Nations Environment Programme (UNEP), South Asia Cooperation Environment Programme (SACEP) and International Centre for Integrated Mountain and Development (ICIMOD) and various international agencies, regional bodies and multilateral institutions. In coordinates all bilateral cooperation in the field of invironment. India has such cooperation programmes with the Netherlands, Norway, Sweden, Denmark, Great Britain, USA, the Russian Federation, Canada, Japan and

FRG in addition to forestry programmes with external assistance.

India is signatory to the following important international treaties/agreements in the field of environment: (i) International Convention for the regulation of Whaling; (ii) International Plant Protection Convention; (iii) The Antarctic Treaty; (iv) Conventon on Wetlands of internatonal importance especially as waterfowl habitat; (v) International Convention on international trade in endangered species of wild flora and fauna; (vi) Protocol of 1978 relating to the international convention for the prevention of pollution from ships, 1973; (vii) Vienna Convention for the protection of the ozone layer; (viii) Convention on Migratory Species; (ix) Basel Convention on trans-boundary movement of hazardous substances; (x) Framework Convention on climatic change; (xi) convention on conservation of bio-diversity; (xii) Montreal Protocol on the substances that deplete the ozone layer and (xiii) International Convention for Combating Desertification.

Instituted in 1987, the Indira Gandhi Prayavaran Puraskar, consisting of a cash component of rupees one lakh, a silver trophy and a citation, is awarded every year to an organisation and to an individual for significant contributions in the field of environment.

The Indira Priyadarshini Vrikshamitra Awards have been constituted by the Ministry of Environment and Forests in 1986 to recognise outstanding contributions of individuals and organisations in the field of afforestation and wastelands development. Ten awards are given every year to individuals, educational institutes, Panchayats, voluntary agencies and government agencies. Each award carries a medallion, a citation and a cash component of Rs. 50,000.

The Maha Vriksha Puraskar, instituted by the NAEB during 1993-94 will be given every year to individuals/ organisations for trees of notified species having the largest girth and height and in good health and vigour. These awards would consist of a cash prize of Rs. 25,000, a plaque and a citation.

Since 1991, national awards are being presented every year to eligible industries in recognition of their contributions to the prevention and control of evnvironmental pollution.

Human activities have pushed our planet to the brink of disaster necessitating a comprehensive global action to retrieve the situation. While exploring newer forms of renewable sources of energy to address the environmental malady, our planners and administrators need to address the most urgent task of improving energy efficiency. The rural areas should depend on minihydel projects and bioenergy as far as possible. A serious and lasting government commitment to the development and use of energy efficient and renewable technologies is the need of the hour. Like it or not, we find ourselves in a world where we are responsible for each other's well-being. In the last few years of this millennium, difficult questions of social equality, national sovereignty, and individual rights and responsibilities are emerging. A person may be able to afford a large, energy-consumptive automobile, but can the planet afford it? Indeed, the larger question boils down as to how many carbon-emitting automobilies can the planet tolerate without the habitability of the earth being disturbed. At a more mundane level, a couple may desire and be able to support several children, but can the planet afford several children per family? Does our generation have the right to extinguish plant and animal species that have evolved over millions of years? Do we not have the obligation to preserve our biological heritage for our future generations?

An affirmative answer to these questions depends on restoring and prserving the conditions that make the earth habitable, a place capable of supporting a diversity of life and modern civilization. Human activities have pushed the planet to the brink of disaster.

A comprehensive global action plan to remedy the situation should include: developing energy strategies that have climate protection as their cornerstone; expanding the earth's forest cover so as to prevent global warming; doubling the per capita grain production and lastly, breaking the momentum of population growth.

While these are the macro-level targets for making this globe a sustainable one in the forthcoming century, at the micro-level it amounts to a severe test on the capacity of world leaders as well as the local ones in their efforts in ecological economic betterment of the populations under their jurisdiction.

It is no wonder that the modes of energy production that are in vogue around the world are primarily responsible for the change in the earth's climate. The huge quantities of oil, coal and natural gas that fuel the global economy account for most of the carbon dioxide emissions responsible for global warming through the greenhouse effect. Producing less carbon dioxide requires using less fuel from among the traditional category. This in turn means exploring other non-conventional energy sources, enough to substitute the fossil sources.

Even though India is one of the few Third World countries which has constitutionalized protection and improvement of environment, the various enactment suffer from several lacunae including the non-recognition of the crucial role that PRIs can play in the endeavour.

The involvement of PRIs as the watch-dog of environmental protection at the grass roots level needs to be duty recognized. The Constitution (73rd Amendment) Act 1992 now provides these institutions an opportunity to play their legitimate role. Environment protection represents one of the more recent and yet one of the more profound aspects new public affairs dimension in public administration.

Environmental issues have aroused too much intellectual and academic interest both in developing and underdeveloped nations. They include envioronmental degradation, deforestation and desertification, atmospheric pollution and imbalances as well as disertifications in ecology resulting from the way natural resources—land, water, forests, minerals, etc are harnessed for fulfilment of human needs. The UN Conference on Human Environment in 1972 proclaimed that the defence and improvement of human environment both natural and man-made had become an imperative good for mankind, to be pursued together with fundamental goals of peace and worldwide economic and social development.

The achievement of these goals was the responsibility of citizens, communities, enterprises and institutions at every level. Later on, the World Conservation Strategy (1980) and the Brundthland Report also noted the irreversible destruction of ecosystems of the poor countries and the implicit threat to the world security and the consequent political instability and social problems. The problem of environmental crises of the developing countries is different from that of the developed countries. The establishment of viable community-based institutions for environment protection was suggested with full legal, administrative and technical support. These institutions should be empowered to plan, to work out the modality and to implement the various measures for environment protection and conservation. The Panchayati Raj as an institution of local rural government is the excellent model for it in rural India.

Among the developing countries, india is also facing environmental problems and crises. The enormous increase in population is the most potent cause for acceleration of the overutilization of productive resources and downgrading the quality of environment.

India has a domesticated animal population of nearly 500 million. Considering that only 3.5 per cent of the land area are under grass, the population is supported by the forest and agriculture residues which are thereby diverted from agricultural land. Out of the total cultivable land, 175 million ha are degraded needing special treatment to restore productivity. Of the 75 million ha designated as forest land, only 35 million ha are close forest. Despite all efforts, India has continued to lose forest cover. The deforestation causes loss in bivodiversity. Over 1,500 species of plants and animals are on the endangered list. Levels of air and water pollution are much beyond acceptable limits. These challenges disturb the environment equilibrium and the life of mankind.

The basic aim of our National Forest Policy must be to ensure environmental stability and maintenance of ecological balance including atmospheric which are vital for the sustenance of all forms of life—human, animal and plant. Rural India has different kinds of environmental crises compared to other countries. The rapid growth of rural population has placed inexorable burden on farm as well as on other land resources, on forests, on water resources and worsened the quality of life of the rural poor in respect of housing, health, ecological surroundings and other essentials.

The Un Declaration on Human Environment in 1972 signalled India to initiate positive steps in the direction towards environment improvement. The Constitution of India has conceptualized its thinking on environment in the form of the Directive Principles of State Policy in favour of protection and improvement of environment, and safeguarding of forests and wildlife (Article 48A), a fundamental duty to protect and improve the natural environment including forests, lakes, rivers and wildlife and to have compassion for living creatures [Article 51A(g)], and a subject in the Consurrent List in its Seventh Schedule (Item 17A and 17B). Both the Directive principles and Fundamental Duty are non-justiciable, but these provide the necessary constitutional sanction if the State intends to adopt a law in the matter.

The other component of the infrastructure for environment improvement and protection is provided by the existing legislation. There are 30 major enactments such as Water Cess Act, Forest Act, Forest Conservation Act, Wildlife Protection Act, Environment Protection Act, of Union and State Governments.

Administrative actions—regulatory, negotiational and persuasive—under these enactments are mainly taken by the Central and State administrative organizations—the Central Ministry of Environment and Forests, the Central Pollution Control Board and the State Departments of Environment and State Pollution Control Boards. Besides this, there also exist the other administrative mechanisms concerned with the implementation of policies on environment. The Panchayati Raj institutions have also become important instruments in rural India for environment protection and improvement.

There is no end to the debate on environment and development. However, instances of the preservationist approach is to be found in the local indigenous communities living in and around forests. In real life, such communities have been seriously affected as a result of both degradation of forest land and their reduced accessibility to forest resources on account of strict forest laws. Degradation of surrounding environment and rigid forestlaws have adversely affected food accessibility, livelihood options and quality of life of local indigenous communities. Such degradation has often caused periodic phases of hunger and malnutrition in the absence of supportive means of livelihood for acquiring basic essentials of life.

Forest plantations of eucalyptus and other species no longer provide the rich biodiversity available earlier in natural forests. Common property resources, in which groups of local people have co-equal use rights, such as community pastures, community forests, wastelands, village ponds, rivers, etc have declined at a rapid pace. Such phenomenon has led to a diminished role of local natural resources which have traditionally constituted invaluable asset-base for meeting basic needs and livelihood requirements of indigenous communities.

Such relatively undisturbed lands include forests, grasslands, wetlands, water bodies, etc which constitue habitat for indigenous communities, plants and animal species and thus contribute to maintenance of human and biological diversity. Such lands perform important environmental functions and also constitute essential means of livelihood. As far as fragility of such ecosystems is concerned, the indigenous communities have traditionally presented little threat to sensitive ecological zones, because their production systems have been sustainable, scattered over a large area, and they have traditionally kept encroachers, poachers and others out of the area.

The benefits provided by forests, trees and common property resources are basic to such communities and amongst direct benefits, the following are included:

— food such as nuts, wild fruits, vegetables, leaves, flowers, roots, stems honey, wild animals insects, etc;

— habitat and shelter;

— raw materials like bamboo, canes, fibres, oils, bhabbar grass, waxes, resins, gums, dyes and wood for furniture and capital equipment for agriculture, artisanship, etc;

— wood for building, fencing, tool making, etc;

— firewood;

— medicines and drugs;

— fodder such as grass, branches, twigs and leaves, grazing sites;

— means of livelihood, both seasonal and annual;

— shade;

— ornaments, religious items and cultural symbols; and

— drought relief.

Apart from direct benefits, forests, trees and common property resources also provide indirect benefits, such as preventing erosion, conserving moisture, conserving water, recycling nutrient, preventing drought or reducing its impact, providing leaf manure, fixing nitrogen by leguminous trees, regulating climate and rainfall, providing greenery and beauty and reducing pollution.

Forests as safety net: In short, forests, trees and common property resources provide safety nets to the local indigenous communities. In the presence of spiraling prices, reduced wages in real terms, unemployment, sickness, reduced productivity from land,

and recurring shortages, forests, trees and common property resources act as a kind of safety net for local communities, protecting them from the harshness of market forces. They come to the rescue by providing a safety net against food and livelihood insecurity, drought attacks, pest attacks, illness, pollution, high prices, high rents, etc. They play a dominant role in providing alternative sources of livelihood and in offering coping strategies to local communities.

The strategy for development of the Scheduled Tribes is based on the TSP (tribal sub-plan) approach which came into operation since 1974-75 (V Plan) in 16 States (now 18 States) and two Union territories. The main objective of the tribal sub-plan is to (i) raise the socio-economic condition of the tribal population and strengthen infrastructure in the tribal areas, and (ii) to protect and promote tribal interests through legal and administrative support.

The programmes are now being implemented through (i) 194 Integrated Tribal Development Projects (ITDPs) comprising generally blocks/tehsils with 50 per cent or more Scheduled Tribe population; (ii) 277 pockets of tribal concentration (Modified Area Development Approach Projects) having a total population of 10,000 or more, and Scheduled Tribe population of 50 per cent or more; and (iii) 90 primitive tribe projects or micro-projects.

The tribal sub-plan has a two-fold thrust, viz (i) socio-economic development of the tribal areas, and (ii) socio-economic development of the tribal families.

It was expected that during the Seventh Plan period, there would be cent per cent coverage of Scheduled Tribe population under the tribal sub-plan. Benefits were also proposed to be extended to the scattered Scheduled Tribe population which was not covered by any specific project through family-oriented programmes. It may be mentioned that the tribal population coverage during the Sixth Plan period was only 75 per cent. During the Seventh Plan, the following were the objectives under tribal sub-plan approach: (i) taking up family beneficiary programme through raising productivity-level of the beneficiary families in the field of .agriculture, horticulture, animal husbandry, small industry, etc. (ii) elimination of exploration of the tribals in the sphere of alienation of land, money-lending, debt bondage, forest, etc. (iii) human resource development through education and training programmes, (vi) infrastructure development, (v) development of vulnerable tribal areas and groups like, forest villagers, displaced tribes and tribal women; and (vi) upgradation of environment of tribal areas.

For the year 1985-86, the target of tribal families to be economically assisted was fixed at 8.35 lakh, and the achievement reported was 8.3 lakh families. For 1986-87, the target fixed was 8.35 lakh tribal families and for 1987-88, a tentative target of assisting 8.50 lakh tribal families had been kept.

Special Central Assistance: Under tribal development, Special Central Assistance (SCA) is an additive to the State Plan efforts for Scheduled Tribes. The Eighth Plan had a target to cover 46.50 lakh families. Against this, 28.69 lakh families were covered during the first three years of the Plan (8.88 lakh in 1992-93; 10.42 lakh in 1993-94; and 9.39 lakh in 1994-95). This constituted 61.7 per cent of the target. To improve the literacy rate among tribal women, a new scheme was introduced since 1992-93, and is being implemented through non-governmental organizations in 48 districts with tribal concentration where female population is less than two per cent.

Financing tribal sub-plan: There are four sources for financing tribal sub-plan programmes: (i) Special Central Assistance (SCA) administered by Ministry of Welfare, (ii) State Plan funds, (iii) centrally-sponsored schemes, and (vi) institutional finance.

Since the V Plan period, with the launching of the tribal sub-plan approach, special programmes for extremely backward tribe groups had been taken up. These were micro-projects or projects for primitive tribal groups. These primitive tribal groups had three criteria for their identification: (i) almost stagnant population, or extremely low growth rate facing the danger of extinction, (ii) having are pre-agricultural level of technology, and (iii) extremely low level of literacy.

Another important factor was the ecosystem in which they lived. There were also other factors which entered into the situation of each of these tribal groups calling for a sensitive and in-depth study of each, precedent to enforcement of any action plan.

The Planning Commission also mentioned that particular care need to be taken of the small primitive tribal groups, some of which were on the verge of extinction.

The Dhebar Commission (1961) alluded to them as the 'lowest layer}, and listed 50 tribes in various States which were in an extremely underdeveloped state. During the V Plan period, the Ministry of Home Affairs identified 52 tribal communities as primitive, their estimated population being 10 lakhs. During the VI Plan period, an additional 20 tribal groups were identified raising their total number to 72 with an estimated population of 14 lakhs. Now the clusters of tribal concentration have gone up to 90.

There had been emphasis since the V Plan period on

preparation of a project report for each of these groups relative to its situation. Nevertheless, there had been considerable neglect in this regard. Apart form the continued misery of conditions in which they lived, the risk of extinction of some of these tribes was also great.

One in every seven persons on this planet lives in India. With 16 per cent of the world's population and only 2.4 per cent of its land area, there is obviously a great demand on the natural resources including land. This is so in spite of the fact that an average Indian consumes a much lower quantum of resources than a person in the developed world. If an average person in the South were to consume as much as an average person in a developed country, the environmental crisis would be unimaginable. While, to a large extent, the lower per capita consumption is due to poverty, an important reason is also that a majority of the population in India follows a sustainable lifestyle which is based on environmentally sound practices evolved over thousands of years.

The environmental problem today is being precipitated partly because practices which were appropriate earlier, like shifting cultivation and unrestricted cattle grazing, are not so anymore. For instance, as a result of increasing population and decreasing availability of land, crop-fallow cycles in shifting cultivation have been reduced to a mere five years from a more sustainable 20-40 years in the past.

But just as there were learnings and difficulties with regard to traditional practices, so was the case with newly introduced technologies. Many measures, at one time seen as solutions, are today extracting an unanticipated price. The Green Revolution of the 1960s met India's growing demand for food. While it helped India to dramatically increase foodgrain production, what was not fully appreciated then was that the Green Revolution would on the one hand affect the country's natural resource capital, and on the other, create dependencies on inputs such as chemical fertilizers and pesticides. There are indications of soil health problems such as deficiency of micronutrients and organic matter, incidence of soil salinity and damage to the physical structure of the soil, apart from increasing dependence on chemical inputs, many of which are imported.

Today there is widespread realization that there can be no readymade solutions, that technology alone cannot solve problems, that we have to use all our ingenuity to find solutions which combine the best of the old practices with the benefits that modern science and technology can offer.

The challenges are staggering in number, scale and complexity. We need to develop and to modernize in less wasteful ways than is the current paradigm, but not lose our sound traditional values and practices. India will have to leap-frog over wasteful and polluting technologies and go for technologies which are the most environmentally sound, and are based on maximizing recycling and efficient use of resources practices which are inherent in India's traditions. It is when such development comes about that the population pressures will ease, as development brings down demographic growth rates.

The task is stupendous. For while the challenge of development might seem to be 'how to get there' the real challenges is 'how not to get there'. Urbanization, industrial growth, transportation systems, agriculture, housing... all have to stop imitating practices that are already being phased out in the developed world. With the North becoming more conscious about the condition of their own environment, 'dirty' factories are moving

South. To cite only one example, the production of harmful and toxic dyestuff intermediates such as H-acid, K-acid, gamma acid and metanilic acid taken up in the 60s stands at over 41,000 tonnes in the country today, with an estimated Rs. 6 billion worth for export to the developed countries.

The forces which are taking India, and much of the developing world, on the conventional and largely imitative and unimaginative development path are many. But this path is not sustainable—for India or for the world. As Mahatma Gandhi remarked over 60 years ago. "God forbid that India should ever take to industrialism after the manner of the West. The economic imperialism of a single, tiny kingdom is today keeping the world in chains. If an entire nation of 300 million took to similar economic exploitation, it would strip the world bare like locusts.

When the West developed, it did so perhaps in ignorance of the environmental impact of its activities. Today we know that such a path is neither practicable nor desirable for countries which are raising their standards of living. We, along with other developing countries, have to find alternative paths to an alternative goal.

A goal which ultimately is the true goal of development—an environmentaly sound and sustainable quality of life, which is socially just and equitable. A goal that must be common to all citizens of the planet. A goal that is perhaps as distant from the developing world as it is from the over-consuming, wasteful societies of what is currently referred to as the 'developed' world.

It is this goal of development that we seek together as people, as organizations and as governments at the United Nations Conference on Environment and Development. It is this intermeshing of environmental and developmental concerns that must form the goal of humankind.

The world is rapidly realizing that environmental issues such as global warming and ozone depletion, acid rain, marine pollution and the threat to biodiversity are global and not merely national issues. But in a world where per capita GNP varies from US $ 80 in Mozambique to US $ 29,880 in Switzerland; where life expectancy at birth varies from 42 years in Sierra Leone to 79 years in Japan; and where literacy rates vary from about 12 per cent in Somalia to over 95 per cent in the United States, what is not as explicitly understood is that development too is a global issue. And perhaps even less understood is the fact that a sustainable and viable planet requires that development be global. As Mrs. Indira Gandhi, then Prime Minister of India and the only visiting head of government to attend the UN Conference on the Human Environment in Stockholm in 1972, said, the removal of poverty is an integral part of the goal of an environmental strategy for the world.

Energy, an essential input for economic development, is consumed in a variety of forms in India. Fuelwood, animal waste and agricultural residues are traditional sources of energy that continue to meet the bulk of the energy requirement in the rural areas. These 'non-commercial fuels' are gradually getting replaced by 'commercial fuels' such as coal,l lignite, petroleum products, natural gas and electricity.

The Government has formulated an energy policy with the objectives of ensuring adequate energy supply at a minimum cost, achieving self-sufficiency in energy supplies and protecting environment form adverse impact of utilising energy resources in an unjudicial manner. The development and promotion of non-conventional/alternate/new and renewable sources of energy such as solar, wind and bio-energy, etc., are also getting sustained attention from the Department of Non-Conventional Energy Sources, created in september 1982. Nuclear energy to * contribute significantly to the overall energy avalalbility in the country.

Electricity is the most convenient and versatile form of energy. Demand for it, therefore, has been growing at the rate faster than other forms of energy. Power industry too has recorded a phenomenal rate of growth both in terms of its volume and technological sophistication over the last few decades. Electricity plays a crucial role in both industrial and agricultural sectors and, therefore, consumption of electricity in the country is an indicator of productivity and growth. In view of this, power development has been given high priority in development programme.

Studies have shown that while the demand for electricity in the entire economy has riisen at the rate of 9.73 per cent during 1986-87, the demand in the residential and agricultural sectors has been increasing at an alarming rate of 14.03 per cent and 14.58 per cent respectively per year. Installed power generation capacity in the country has increased from a meagre 1,400 mw in 1947 to 81,164.41 mw at the end of 1994-95 comprising 20,829.04 mw hydro (25.66 per cent) and 58,110.37 mw thermal including gas, diesl and wind (71.60 per cent) and 2,225.0 mw nuclear (2.74 per cent).

Various measures being taken to improve power generation in the country include commission of new generation capacity, renovation and modernisation of old units, assistance to Electricity Boards in undertaking plant betterment programme, supply of requisite quantity and quality of coal, training of operation and maintenence personnel and strengthening of transmission and distribution system and implementation of short gestation projects, reduction in T & D losses, implementation of demand management and energy conservation measures. The target of power generation during 1995-96 has been 377.15 billion units out of which 297 billion units are programmed for generation by thermal stations 72.3 billion units by hydro stations and 7.85 billion units by the nuclear stations. Thus an increase of about 7.4 per cent over the generation achieved during 1994-95 is envisaged.

The Plant Load Factor (PLF) has shown a steady improvement over the years. It has improved from 53.8 per cent in 1990-91 to 60 per cent in 1994-95. The following table highlights the achievement of the power sector in major areas during 1994-95.

**Energy and power**

Electricity is a concurrent subject at Entry 34 in the List III of Seventh Schedule of the Constitution of India. The responsibility of its development lies both with the Central and state governments. At the Centre, the Ministry of Power is responsible for the administration of the Electricity (Supply) Act, 1948 and the Indian Electricity Act, 1910. The Ministry is also concerned with perspective planning, policy formulation, processing of projects for investment decision, monitoring of the implementation of power projects and training and manpower development.

The Central Electricity Authority (CEA), constituted under the Electricity (Supply) Act, 1948, advises the Ministry of Power on technical and economic matters. The construction and operation of generation and transmission projects in the Central Sector are entrusted to Central sector power corporations, namely, the National Thermal Corporation (NTPC), the National Hydroelectric Power Corporation (NHPC), the North Eastern Electric Power Corporation (NEEPCO) and the

Power Grid Corporation of India Limited (POWERGRID). POWERGRID, which was incorporated on the 23 October 1989, is responsible for all the existing and future transmission projects in the Central sector and also for the formation of the National Power Grid. There are two joint ventures power corporations under the administrative control of the Ministry of Power, namely, Nathpa Jhakri Power Project and projects of the Tehri Hydro Power Complex. The Damodar Valley Corporation (DVC), constituted under the DVC Act, 1948, the Bhakra Beas Management Board (BBMB) constituted under the Punjab Act, 1966, and three autonomous bodies, namely, Central Power Research Institute (CPRI), the National Power Training Institute (NPTI) and the Energy Management Centre (EMC) are also under the administrative control ofthe Ministry. Programmes of rural electrification are within the purview of the Rural Electrification Corporation (REC). The Power Finance Corporation (PFC) provides term-finance to projects in the power sector. There is one subordinate office Badarpur Management Control Cell (BMCC), directly under this Ministry and 16 subordinate offices under the Central Electricity Authority.

Significant progress has been made in expansion of transmission and distribution facilities in the country. Total length of transmission lines of 66 kv and above voltage level increased form 10,000 ckt km in December 1950 to about 2.36 lakh ckt in March 1994. Highest transmission voltage at present is 400 kv and about 30,240 ckt km of 400 kv lines had been constructed upto March 1994. In addition, the first +500 kv HVDC bipole Rihand-Dadri transmission line of about 820 km length is also in operation. An inter-regional link (vindhyachal 2 × 250 mw HVDC back-to-back) connecting western and northern regions is also in operation.

Five regional grid systems, namely, northern, western, southern, eastern and north-eastern covering all the states of the country are already existing. All the regions except north-eastern have fairly well interconnected systems of 220 kv voltage level with progressive overlay of 400 kv transmision systems. The Union Cabinet in 1981 approved in principle the establishment of a Centrally owned and operated National Power Grid. The National Power Grid would eventually comprise strong regional networks with suitable synchronous HVDC links between the regions. Power Grid Corporation of India Limited (*POWERGRID*), created in October 1989, has been vested with the responsibility of developing a National Power Grid. The development of National Power Grid is an evolutionary process and would be achieved over a period of time through development of the regional grid systems and further inter-connections between the regions. National Power Grid will promote integrated operation and transfer of power from one system to another with ultimate objective of ensuring optimum utilisation of available resources in the country.

In order to promote integrated operation of power systems, the country has been demarcated into five regions, namely, north, west, south, east and north-east. Regional electricity boards were set up in 1964 in each of these regions. Northern region covers Haryana, Himachal Pradesh, Jammu and Kashmir, Punjab, Rajasthan, Uttar Pradesh, Chandigarh and Delhi, western region covers Gujarat, Maharashtra, Madhya Pradesh, Goa, Daman and Diu and Dadra and Nagar Haveli; southern region covers Andhra Pradesh, Karnataka, Tamil Nadu, Kerala and Pondicherry; eastern region covers Bihar, Orissa, West Bengal and Sikkim and north-eastern region covers Assam, Manipur, Meghalaya, Nagaland, Tripura, Arunachal Pradesh and Mizoram.

To coordinate operation of the grids of the constituent power systems and to optimise utilisation of the existing generation capacity, regional load despatch centres (RLDCs) have been set up in each region. RLDCs, hitherto functioning under the Central Electricity Authority/regional electricity boards, are being transferred to *Powergrid* in phased manner. In the northern, western and eastern regions, permanent RLDCs equipped with computer based telemetry and the data acquisition system were establilshed around mid 1980s. In the southern region, RLDC equipped with analog telemetry equipment, mimic board, transducers, speech communication, telex and teleprinters facilities is working. In the north-eastern region, an interim regional load despatch centre is operating. Unfied schemes covering the long-term requirements of RLDC and constituents systems in respect of all the five regions are in different stages of formulation. The schemes in respect of southern, northern, and north-eastern regions have got technoeconomic clearance of Central Electricity Authority while the scheme pertaining tothe eastern and western regions are still under finalisation.

Efficient operation of integrated power systems through moderanised computer-based load despatch centres is vitally dependent on efficient data transfer over distance. Thus there is a need for developing a highly reliable communication network. Subsequent to an in-depth analysis of requirements carried out by the Planning Commission, the Central Electricity Authority (CEA)) has developed a Master Telecom Plan for the power sector. Concrete schemes have been framed based on modern communication system. Several such schemes have been techno-economically approved by CEA and most ofthese have also cleared by DOT.

With a number of inter-regional links commissioned

during the Eighth Plan period and subsequent years in form of National Grid and the five regional load despatch centres already in operation, National Electric Power System Information Centre (NEPSIC) has been set up which is equipped with PC-based data acquisition system linking all the RLDCs in the country. The data acquired from RLDC is also available at CEA headquarters for getting an overview of current power system status. Teleconferencing and FAX facilities are also provided. The system is fully functional since June 1993.

State electricity boards have been established in 18 out of 25 states. These are mainly responsible for generation and distribution of electricity in their respective states. Arunachal Pradesh, Goa, Manipur, Mizoram, Nagland, Sikkim and Tripura are yet to establish their electricity boards.

The first major step in this direction had been the setting up of 336 mw Chukha Hydroelectric Project in Bhutan at a cost of Rs. 243.71 crore with Indian technical and financial assistance under an agreement signed in March 1974. The first unit of the project was commissioned in September 1986 and all the four units of 84 mw August 1988. Since then the project has been generating power, the bulk of which has been exported to India. Bhutan has earned the entire cost of the project in about five years time by export of power to India alone besides their internal consumption.

Gratified with the success of Chukha Project the Royal Government of Bhutan are keen on development of their Hydro Resources for the mutual benefit of the two countries. To this end, India and Bhutan have signed an agreement in February 1994 for implementation of Kurichu Hydroelectric Project (3×15 mw) in western Bhutan at a cost of about Rs. 310 crore on a turn-key basis through NHPC within a period of five years. India and Bhutan have agreed to execute Tala HE Project downstream of existing Chukha Project with an installed capacity of 1,020 mw. Discussions have been held between the two countries and modalities for implementation of this mega project are being worked out.

India had constructed a number of mini/micro hydel schemes at Thimpu (360 kw), Gidakom (1000 kw), Wangdi (3000 kw), Gyesta (1500 kw), Khaling (600 kw), Chenarry (750 kw), Lhuntshi (20 kw) during 1960-80. These projects have been identified for rehabilitation in a phased manner by the Government of India. Proposals for taking up impementation of new mini/micro hydro schemes at Ungrichu, Yonglachy, Dongdichu and Chhalori are under consideration.

Energy Conservation has been identified as one of the major thrust areas in the Eighth Plan, as a part of the National Energy Efficiency Programme, with an objective of saving 5,000 mw of installed capacity by the terminal year of Eighth Plan. Apart from the awareness campaign and launching of demonstration projects in agricultural and industrial sectors for promoting energy efficiency technologies, other main activities relate to organising training programmes and studies in the field of energy conservation. A number of internationally supported projects for cooperation on energy conservation in Indian industries and other areas have also been undertaken.

Concerned with the deterioration in the performance of the thermal power stations in the country, Government of India launched a Centrallysponsored programme for renovation and modernisation ( R and M) of thermal power stations to improve their performance. Likewise, a programme for renovation, modernisation and uprating (RM and U) of hydro-electric power stations was formulated by the Central Electricity Authority in 1987. R and M schemes are relevant also in the context of energy conservation and optimum energy usage.

At present, 3,544.58 mw (around 4.4 per cent of India's installed capacity) is in the private sector. The Government of India announced in September 1991 the policy to encourage private enterprises participation in the electricity sector. In pursuance of the policy announcement, the legislation governing the electricity sector was amended in October 1991 and the two part tariff notification was issued on 30 March 1992. The primary objective of the policy was to bring a additionality of resources, increase efficiency in operation and encourge commercial operations in this sector. The response has been encouraging. As on date, interest has been expressed in putting up 196 power projects for a total capacity of 77,720 mw involving an investment of Rs. 2,88,252 crore.

Coal is the main source of energy in the country and it accounts for about 60 per cent of the country's commercial energy requirement. Coal is also an essential input in steel and carbo-chemical industries.

An on 1 January 1995, the coal resources of India (upto a depth of 1,200 metre) have been estimated by the Geological Survey of India at 1,96,891.87 million tonnes.

Coal production which was around 78.71 million tonnes atthe time of nationalisation of the coal industry in 1973-74, rose to a level of 253.80 million tonnes in 1994-95. India is now the third largest coal producing country in the world. The coal production is slated to reach 300 million tonnes by 1996-97. Strategies adopted to achieve higher rate of production are: re-organising existing mines and opening up on new projects, both underground as well as opencast.

Distribution of coal is controlled statutorily under

the Colliery Control Order., 1945. The distribution is to be done by the Coal Controller. However, if for any reason Coal Controller is not able to do so, coal companies have been allowed to distribute coal on the basis of linkages/ sponsorships. Short term linkages for important sectors of economy, like power and cement are decided by Standing Linkage Committee set up under the mInistry of Coal. Linkages to other consumers execpt steel are within the purview of coal companies, which allot coal to actual users as per advice receeived by them from the various sponsoring authorities. New allotments by coal companies to industries are of the order of 5,000 tonnes per month. Off-take of raw coal during 1993-94 and 1994-95 to major sectors of economy is given in table 21.

Under the present delegation of powers, coal projects costing upto Rs. 50 crore are sanctioned by the Board of Directors of the Coal India Limited. The subsidiary companies of Coal India Limited have powers to sanction projects upto Rs. 20 crore. Singareni Collieries Company Limited Board can also sanction coal projects upto Rs. 50 crore. Projects costing more than Rs. 50 crore are sanctioned by the Government. After the nationalisation of the coal industry in 1973 and till December 1994, the number of projects sanctioned (each costing Rs. two crore and above) was 633. A total investment of Rs. 20,718.97 crore has been sanctioned in these projects. Og these, 419 are mining projects and remaining 214 are non-mining projects like washeries, fire control schemes, captive power plants, water supply schemes etc. Out of 633, 340 projects have been completed and 293 are at different stages of implementation. Mining projects on completion will have a capacity of 338.08 million tonnes of coal per annum

Even though history of Indian coal mining dates back more than two centuries, real sprut in coal production took place only after the nationalisation of the coal industry. Coal production in the country is now allmost completely in the public sector companies e.g. Coal India limited (CIL) and Singareni Collieries Company Limited (SCCL) except few captive mines of TISCO, IISCO and DVC. Coal India Limited producing over 90 per cent of the country's total coal production, has seven coal producing subsidiaries, namely, eastern Coalfields Limited (ECL), Bharat Coking Coal Limited (BCCL), Central Coalfields Limited (CCL), Northern Coalfields Limited (NCL), South Eastern Coalfields (SECL), Mahandi Coalfields Limited (MCL) and Western Coalfields Limited (WCL). The eight subsidiary Central Mines Planning and Design Institute Limited (CMPDIL) is the planning and design institute. SCCL is a joint venture of the Centre and Government of Andhra Pradesh. About 72 per cent of the coal production is obtained through opencast mmines which are almost completely mechanised deploying dragllines, shovels, dumpers, drills, dozers, etc. Mechanisation of underground mines has also been taken up in a big way. Most of the equipment used in coal mines ae indigenously available. At present there are 19 coking coal washeries with an annual capacity of 32.56 million tonnes.

Conservation of coal is an integrated part of mine planning and operation. This is ensured by maximum recovery of *in situ* reserves of coal. Since coal deposits in India are mostly in thick seams and occur at shallow depths, special techniques for maximising recovery are being developed.

Difficult geo-mining conditions prevailing in coal bearing areas like steep and irregular coal seam deposits, gassy seams contifuous and multisection seams necessitate the introduction of some suitable technology

for exploitation of such deposits from coal conservation and also safety point in view. Some of the newly introduced methods of mining are: (a) to exploit seams developed in multi-sections and seams with thickness of 6 to 8 m and standing pillars, methods such as blasting gallery and sub-level caving have been adopted in Katras Project, BCCL. Blasting gallery method with sub-pannelings has been planned in Chora Colliery of ECL and GDK-10 and CDK-8 of SCCL Colliery; (b) keeping in view the limitations of conventional underground methods in terms of quantum of output as well as conservation, both Coal India Limited and Singareni Collieries Company Limited have introduced mechanised longwall technology that ensures higher extractability; (c) diversion of rivers, shifting of colonies and townships have been taken up to release sterlised coal underground; (d) adequate measures have been asopted to deal with coalfijeld fires particularly in Jhria Coalfield and latest technology like remote sensing is being applied for fire management; (e) in steep and thick seams of Margheritta Area (Assam), the system of Shield Mining has been introduced. The extraction percentage of coal by traditional system which was 25 per cent to 35 per cent has now improved to nearly 70 per cent or even more in the system of shield mining. The flexible roofing method of mining in the thick seams of North Eastern coalfield has also been applied where the thickness of the seam exceeds 4.5 meter. The system has, however, a limited application ; and (f) since opencast working ensures better conversation, application of opencast working is now followed with much higher cut-off ratios utilising high capacity machineries. Singareni Collieries Company Limited has also made a breakthrough in a small way for extraction of Developed pillars by opencast methods. The company has of late been making efforts to convert existing underground mines into high capacity mechanised Opencast projects at Ramagundam and Kothagudem areas.

The Coal mines Conservation and Development Act, 1974 provides for imposition of excise duty on coal despatches for meeting activities like conservation of coal, development/introduction of new technology in coal mines, safety in Mines and assistance in mining operation. A number of research and development activities in coal sector are carried out under overall guidance and supervision of Standing Scientific and Research Commmittee and its four sub-committees. The applied research is carried out in the fields of production, productivity, safety coal preparation, coal utilisation, environment and ecology.

Special efforts to improve lthe standard of safety in the coal industry have brought down the rate of fatalities per million tonne of output in Coal India Limited to 0.40 and in Singareni Collieries Companies Limited to 2.04 in the year 1994. A Standing Committee on Safety regularly review safety standards in coal mines.

Coal industry employs over seven lakh workers. Since nationalisation of coal mines, welfare of coal miners by way of providing facilities like housing, water supply, medical care, education, etc., is bieng given greater attention.

Lignite reserves in the country have been estimated at around 26,200 million tonnes. Out of the above, 3,300 million tonnes spread over 480 sq km is in the Neyveli Lignite fields in South Acrot Vallalar district and about 2,000 mt has been identified as minerable under the presently adopted mining parameters. Geological reserves of about 1150 mt of lignite have been identified in Jayamkondacholapuram of Trichy district of Tamil Nadu. In Mannargudi and east of Veeranam, geological reserves of around 18,200 mt and 1,340 mt of lignite respectively have been estimated. Smaller deposits exist in Rajasthan, Gujarat and J&K. Lignite reserves at Neyveli are exploited by Neyveli Lignite Corporation (NLC) Ltd. It was incorporated as a private limited company in 1956 wholly owned by Government of India. The Corporation was converted into public company w.e.f. 7 March 1986.

The main constituents of the company are lignite mines, thermal power stations, fertilizer plant and briquetting and carbonisation plant. Mine-I (6.5 million tonnes of Lignite per annum) feeds thermal Power Station-I (600 mw), Briquetting and Carbonisation Plant (2,62,000 tonnes of coke-achievable capacity) and the Process Steam Plant. Mine-II (10.5 million tonnes of lignite per annum) feeds it captive Thermal Power Station-II (7×210 mw). The Fertilizer Plant (achievable capacity. 1,29,200 tonnes of urea per annum) which initially used raw lignite as feed stock changed over to oil gasification in July 1979 on operational and technological consideration. The power generated from Thermal Power Station-I after meeting the NLC's requirements is fed into Tamil Nadu Electricity Board grid which is the sole beneficiary. Power generated from Thermal Power Station-II after meeting the needs of Second Mine is shared by southern states *viz.*, Tamil Nadu, Kerala, Karnataka, Andhra Pradesh and Union Territory of Pondicherry. NLC produced 154.10 lakh tonnes of lignite and generated 10,890.29 million units of power during 1994-95, registered an increase of about 23 per cent and 36 per cent respectively over 1991-92.

Raw lignite sales (12,34,001 tonnes) and power export (8916.36 million units) had registered an increase of about 61 per cent and 40 per cent respectively in 1994-95 over 1991-92. The company has been making profits since 1976-77 and its profit of Rs 171 crore (provisional) for 1994-95 is the highest profit achieved for any year since inception. In 1994-95, the sales turnover has recorded a growth of 33.23 per cent and net profit of 50 per cent over 1993-94.

India is richly endowed with minerals. Under the Constitution, minerals rights and the administration of mining laws are vested in the state governments. The Centre, however, regulates the development of minerals under the Mines and Minerals (Regulation and Development) Act, 1957 and the rules and regulations framed under it. This Statute empowers the Centre to formulate rules for: (i) the grant of prospecting licences and mining leases for schedule minerals, (ii) the conservation and development of minerals., and (iii) the modification of old leases. The Act, came into force on 1 June 1958. Amendments to this Act were made in 1972, 1986, and 1994.

Principal mineral found in the country along with their estimated reserves are given below.

Coal is India's largest mineral resource and presently India is the fifth largest producer of coal in the world. Vast deposits of coal of Gondwana formations occur in West Bengal, Orissa, Bihar, Madhya Pradesh, Andhra Pradesh, Uttar Pradesh and Maharashtra. It also occurs in tertiary formation in Assam, Arunachal Pradesh, Meghalaya and Nagaland. Total known reserves of all types of coals in Gondwana and tertiary coalfields estimated stands at 192 billion tonnes. Out of these, reserves of prime-coking coal have been estimated at 5.3 billion tonnes. Total reserves of lignite stands at 6.5 billion tonnes, located in Tamil Nadu, Gujarat, Rajasthan, Kerala, Pondichery and Jammu and Kashmir.

The total recoverable reserves of bauxite in the

country are placed at 2,525 million tonnes while the total *in situ* reserves are 3,037 million tonnes. The conditional resources of bauxite are about five lakh tonnes. In addition; prospective resources are placed at 90 million tonnes. Orissa, Andhra Pradesh, Madhya Pradesh, Gujarat, Maharashtra and Bihar are the principal states where bauxite deposits are located. Major reserves are concentrated in the East Coast Bauxite deposits of Orissa and Andhra Pradesh.

Total recoverable reserves of chromite are estimated at 8.8 million tonnes. Deposits of economic significance occur in Andhra Pradesh, Bihar, Karnataka, Maharashtra, Manipur, Orissa and Tamil Nadu. However, refractory grade reserves of chromite are very meagre.

The total recoverable reserves of copper ore in the country are 415.86 million tonnes equivalent to 4.14 million tonnes of metal content. The all-India conditional resources of copper are 695.29 million tonnes (1.99 million tonnes of copper metal) and prospective resources are 769.9 million tonnes of copper ore. Major and important copper ore deposits are located in Singhbhum district (Bihar), Balaghat (Madhya Pradesh) and Jhunjhunu and Alwar (Rajasthan). In addition, small copper ore deposits are in Andhra Pradesh, Gujarat, Karnataka, Sikkim, Orissa, Uttar Pradesh and West Bengal.

There are three important gold fields in the country, namely, Kolar Gold Field, Kolar disrict, Hutti Gold Fields in Raichur district (both in Karnataka) and Ramgiri Gold field in Anantpur district (Andhra Pradesh). Total gold metal ore reserves are estimated at 176.9 lakh tonnes.

The total recoverable reserves of iron ore in the country are about 9,606 million tonnes of haematite and 3,143 million tonnes of magnetite. Haematite resources are located in Andhra Prades, Bihar, Goa, Karnataka, Madhya Pradesh, Maharashtra, Orissa and Rajasthan. Magnetite resources are located in Andhra Pradesh, Bihar, Goa, Karnataka and Kerala.

Lead-zinc resources are located in Rajasthan, Gujarat, West Bengal, Andhra Pradesh, Meghalaya, Orissa, Sikkim, Tamil Nadu and Uttar Pradesh. Total recoverable reserves (all grades) of lead and zinc ores are 198.5 million tonnes comprising of metal content of 2,390 thousand tonnes of lead and 9,866 thousand tonnes of zinc metal. The conditonal resources of lead-zinc are 200.29 million tonnes in the country.

The total recoverable reserves of manganese ore are 233.33 million tonnes out of which 41.05 million tonnes are proved , 142.03 million tonnes probable and 50.25 million tonnes of possible category. Main reserves are in Karnataka followed by Orissa, Madhya Pradesh, Maharashtra and Goa. Minor occurences of manganese are in Andhra Pradesh, Bihar, Gujarat, Rajasthan and West Bengal.

The total estimated conditional resource of nickel ore is 294 million tonnes located in Orissa (285 million tonnes) and Bihar (9 million tonnes). Minor occurrence of nickel in Tamil Nadu, Maharashtra and Goa are indicated. The recoverable reserves of tungsten ore have been estimated at 25.89 million tonnes or 77.32 thousand tonnes of $WO_3$ content. The main reserves are at Degana, Rajasthan. It also occurs in Maharashtra, Karnataka, West Bengal and Uttar Pradesh.

The recoverable reserves of barytes are 70.15 million tonnes. The Mangampet deposit occuring in Cuddapah djistrict (Andhra Pradesh) is the single largest deposit in the world containing 67 million tonnes of recoverable reserves. Minor occurences of barytes are located in

Rajasthan, Madhya Pradesh, Maharashtra, Himachal Pradesh, Tamil Nadu, Uttar Pradesh and Bihar.

Diamond deposits occur in three types of geological settings such as kimberlite pipes, conglomerate beds and alluvial gravels. The main diamond bearing areas in India are Panna belt in Madhya Pradesh, Munimadugu-Banganapalle conglomerate in Kurnool district, Wajrakarur kimberlite pipe in Anantpur district and the gravels of Krishna river basin in Andhra Pradesh. Reserves * of about a million carats, there are conditional submarginal of 265 thousand carats.

Dolomite occurrences are widespread in almost all part of the country. The total recoverable reserves of all grades of dolomite are 4,967 million tonnes. Of the total all India recoverable reserves, major share of about 92 per cent reserves is distributed in seven states– Madhya Pradesh, Orissa, Gujarat, Karnataka, West Bengal, Uttar Pradesh and Maharashtra.

Fireclay occurs as a bedded deposit, mostly associated with measures of Gondwana and Tertiary periods. Important deposits are associated with Jharia and Raniganj coalfields in Bihar and West Bengal, Korba coalfields in Madhya Pradesh and Neyveli Lignite field in Tamil Nadu. Notable occurrences of fireclay not associated with coal measures are known in Gujarat, Jabalpur region of Madhya Pradesh and Belpahar-Sundergarh areas of Orissa. The recoverable reserves of fireclay are about 697 million tonnes.

Total recoverable reserves of fluorspar in India are 2.15 million tonnes. Rajasthan and Gujarat are the only producing states in India. Fluorspar occurs in Gujarat, Madhya Pradesh, Maharashtra and Rajasthan.

The recoverable reserves of gypsum are estimated at 239 million tonnes. Out of the above, 70,000 tonnes surgical plaster grade, 39 million tonnes of fertilizer/pottery grade, 38.6 million tonnes of cement/paint grade, four million tonnes of soil reclamation grade and the rest is unclassified. The production of gypsum is confined to Rajasthan, Tamil Nadu, Jammu and Kashmir, Uttar Pradesh, Himachal Pradesh and Gujarat. Rajasthan is the main producer of gypsum followed by Tamil Nadu.

The recoverable reserves of graphite are 3.11 million tonnes. Orissa is the major producers of graphite. Almost the entire reserves under proved category are in Ramanathapuram district, Tamil Nadu. Resources of graphite are in Andhra Pradesh, Orissa, Tamil Nadu, Kerala, Bihar, Gujarat, Rajasthan, Madhya Pradesh and Maharashtra.

The recoverable reserves of ilmenite are 86.75 million tonnes. Ilmenite occurs mainly in beach sand deposits right from Ratnagiri coast in the west to Orissa coast in the east. These minerals are found in Kerala, Tamil Nadu and Orissa.

The all India recoverable reserves of kaolin, including white clay of all categories are about 986 million tonnes. Principal producing states are Bihar, Gujarat, Rajasthan and West Bengal. Kerala, Haryana, Orissa and Madhya Pradesh also produce significant quantities and ball clay is mainly produced in Rajasthan, Andhra Pradesh and Gujarat.

The total recoverable reserves of limestone of all categories and grades are placed at 76,446 million tonnes. The conditional reserves have been estimated at 360 million tonnes. Major producing states are Madhya Pradesh, tamil Nadu, Andhra Pradesh, Gujarat, Bihar, Orissa, Rajasthan and Karnataka.

India is the world's leading producer of sheet mica and accounts for about 60 per cent of global mica trade.

Economic deposits of mica occur in three important belts in Bihar, Andhra Pradesh and Rajasthan.

The total recoverable reserves of magnesite are about 233 million tonnes of which 41 million tonnes are in theproved category. Magnesite is found in Uttar Pradesh, Tamil Nadu and Rajasthan while minor occurrences are in Karnataka, Jammu and Kashmir and Himachal Pradesh.

The total recoverable reserves of kyanite and sillimanite in the country are 2.7 million tonnes respectively. Besides, conditional resources of 175.84 million tonnes of kyanite are also estimated. For sillimanite conditional resources of 5.9 million tonnes and prospective resources of 0.8 million tonnes have been estimated.

Kyanite deposits are located in Andhra Pradesh, Bihar, Karnataka and Maharashtra. Sillimanite resources are in Kerala, Orissa, Madhya Pradesh, tamil Nadu and minor occurrences in Andhra Pradesh, Assam, Bihar, Karnataka, Maharashtra, Meghalaya, Rajasthan and West Bengal.

Deposits of phosphorites are located in Madhya Pradesh, Rajasthan and Uttar Pradesh. Besides, apatite deposits of commercial importance are reported from Bihar, Andhra Pradesh, Rajasthan, West Bengal and Tamil Nadu. Recoverable reserves of rock-phosphate are estimated at 146.95 million tonnes of all grades and of apatite at 13 million tonnes.

Other minerals occuring in significant quantities in India are bentonite (Gujarat, Rajasthan, Bihar, Jammu and Kashmir and Tamil Nadu), corundum (Maharashtra, Madhya Pradesh, Andhra Pradesh * and Gujarat), fullers earth (Rajasthan, Karnataka and Andhra Pradesh), garnet (Tamil Nadu, Rajasthan and Andhra Pradesh Pradesh), pyrites (Bihar and Rajasthan), steatite (Rajasthan, Uttar Pradesh, Andhra Pradesh, Tamil Nadu and Bihar), wollastonite (Rajasthan and Gujarat), zircon (beach sand of Tamil Nadu, Kerala and Orissa) and quartz and silica minerals are wide spread and occur in about all states. Besides, the country has vast resources of building dimension and ornamental stones such as granite, marble and slate. Granite is mainly mined in Tamil Nadu, Karnataka, Andhra Pradesh and Rajasthan, marble in Rajasthan, Uttar Pradesh and Gujarat and slate in Madhya Pradesh, Andhra Pradesh and Haryana.

The petrochemical industry, which forms a part of the chemical industry, is one of the fastest growing sectors in the Indian economy. The annual growth rate of the industry has been around 12-15 per cent compared to about 10 per cent in the chemical industry and 8 per cent of industrial sector as a whole. Petrochemicals, particularly plastics and fibres, make a substantial contribution to the national exchequer directly by way of excise and customs duty and other taxes. The plastic processing industry offers direct employment to over two lakh persons with the potential of over three lakh persons by 2000 AD. Starting from the stage of raw material production to the conversion of finished products, employment gets generated in a cascading manner.

In the initial years, since indigenous capacity was small, the growth was mainly import driven. Consequent to the strong leadership provided by the Indian Petrochemicals Corporation Limited (PCL), a public sector company, and perceiving the greater growth and scope for returns on investments, several private sector companies entered this field. Consumption of all major petrochemicals increased from 7.5 lakh mt in 1979-80 to 29.73 lakh mt in 1990-91 and 34 lakh mt in 1993-94, and is expected to reach the level of over 70 lakh mt by 2000 AD. To meet the growing demand of petrochemicals, Government have sanctioned several mega petrochemical complexes involving a total investment of about Rs. 35,000 crore. This would make India largely self-sufficient in petrochemicals. Petrochemicals have emerged as cost effective energy saving versatile materials serving the needs of the common people.

Exports in petrochemicals have been growing reasonably well. The country has been able to make some exports of polyester staple fibre and LAB. In addition, export of plastic processed goods has increased from Rs. 415 crore in 1992-93 to Rs. 815 crore in 1993-94. The export of man made/synthetic fibres/yarns (including blended spun yarns) was for Rs. 712 crore in 1992-93 and Rs. 514 crore in 1993-94.

There are three public sector organisations in the petrochemical sector under the administrative control of the Department of Chemicals and Petrochemicals. Indian Petrochemicals Corporation Limited (IPCL) is a public sector undertaking incorporated in March 1969. The company has been entrusted with the responsibility of manufacturing and distribution of various petrochemicals like polymers, synthetic organic chemicals, fibres and fibre intermediates. IPCL's mega petrochemicals complex at Vadodara was commissioned in 1993 and the Olefin Complex was commissioned in 1978. The company has set up another Olefin complex in Nagothane in Maharashtra. It has been commissioned and production is stabilising. The third such complex has been approved by the Government in Gandhar in Gujarat. IPCL is a profit making company which earned a net profit of Rs. 562.32 crore during 1994-95.

Petrofils Cooperative Limited (PCL) is a joint venture company of the Government of India and weavers' cooperative societies. It produces polyester filament yarn and nylon filament yarn at its three plants located at Vadodara and Naldhari in Gujarat. The Society has set up spandex plant at Naldhari, which will manufacture spandex yarn for the first time in the country. The spandex yarn having elastic properties is used in swimming suits, underwear garments etc. The company has a turnover of Rs. 322 crore during 1993-94. It has made a net profit of about Rs. 5.40 crore during 1993-94 as against a net loss of Rs. 15.83 crore in 1992-93.

The Central Insititute of Plastics Engineering and Technology (CIPET) is a training institute set up at Madras by the Government as a registered society with the primary objective to develop skilled manpower and provide technical services to the plastic industry. Besides training, the Institute also provides testing, standardisation and quality control, advisory and consultancy services to the plastic industry. To meet the increasing demand of trained personnel in the field of plastics, CIPET has set up nine extension centres at Ahmadabad, Amritsar, Bhopal, Bhubaneswar, Hyderabad, Imphal, Lucknow and Mysore including the headquarter centre at Madras. A service centre and a training centre of CIPET have also been opened at Goa and Patna respectively to cater to the demands of plastic industry in and around these places.

The production of crude oil which reached a peak of 34.09 million tonnes in 1989-90 declined to the level of 26.95 million tonnes in 1992-93. Therefore, to increase the production, a number of short-term and medium-term measures such as early production from satellite fields, use of state-of-the-art technology i.e. horizontal drilling, drainhole drilling etc., were initiated in 1993. As a result of these measures, the decline in crude oil production was arrested in 1993-94 with the production level of 27.02

million tonnes which has further increased to 32.24 million tonnes in 1994-95. The substantial increase in the production in 1994-95 has been due to commissioning of major development schemes such as the additional development of L-II, L-III, Neelam field and South Heera field in the Western Offshore. The crude oil production during 1995-96 is expected to be 37.24 million tonnes. This increase over 1994-95 of around five million tonnes will come mostly from increased production in the Western Offshore fields. The production of crude oil is likely to reach the level of 38.57 million tonnes in 1996-97. Government have also initiated action for increasing indigenous crude oil by offering small and medium sized fields for development through private/joint venture participation. Some small sized fields have been offered for development through private participation.

India is importing a substial part of its oil needs. During 1992-93, the gross import of crude oil and petroleum products was 40.5 million tonnes costing Rs. 17,046 crore in foreign exchange. During 1993-94, the import of crude oil and POL was at 42.9 million tonnes valued at Rs. 17,730 crore. The gross import of crude oil and POl products during 1994-95 was 41.3 million tonnes valued at Rs. 17,838 crore.

# 7

# Conservation of Petroleum Products

High priority is given to the conservation of petroleum products.

**In-house conservation**

*Conservation in upstream sector*

Methods adopted in the upstream sector include reduction of gas flaring, reinjection of gas into the reservoir, installation of waste heat recovery systems, utilization of nonconventional energy sources and monitoring of all conservation efforts by ONGC and OIL.

The flaring of natural gas by ONGC/ OIL has come down from 5.60 MMSCMD on 11% of total production in 1994-95 to 4.24 MMSCMD on 6% of natural gas production in 1997-98.

*Conservation of hydrocarbons in refineries*

The oil refineries are revamping, replacing the low efficiency furnaces and boilers, and installing heat exchangers, economisers and co-generation equipments etc., apart from improved house keeping.

*Lubricants upgradation plan*

There is great potential to conserve through quality upgradation of automotive lubricants. It is planned to produce and sell high grade lubricants of about 2.5 lakhs tonnes per year replacing the erstwhile lower grades in a phased manner.

***Ocean losses***

As a result of various measures taken, ocean losses during transportation has declined over the years.

**End usersof petroleum products and conservation efforts**

Steps being taken are set out below:

*(i) Transport sector*

Adoption of engine design and driving habits conducive to increased fuel efficiency supplemented by training programmes.

*(ii) Industrial sector*

Replacement of old and inefficient heat apparatus and promotion of fuel-efficient practices.

*(iii) Agricultural sector*

Standardization of fuel-efficient irrigation pumpsets and rectification of existing pumpsets.

*(iv) Household sector*

Development of fuel efficient appliances.

**Multimkedia mass awareness campaign**

Mass awareness campaigns have been conducted by the PCRA through the media associating the oil companies.

**Oil conservation forthnight**

Commencing in January 1991, Oil Conservation Week was organised every year thereafter in co-ordination with the concerned Ministries/ Departments of the Union Government, State Government, Public Sector Undertaking Chambers of Commerce etc. throughout the country. The encouraging results prompt extension of Oil Conservation week into the Oil Conservation Fortnight from 1997. During the 9th Oil Conservation Fortnight in January 1999, approximately 1,73,000 activities were organized.

**Petroleum conservatiaon research association**

The Petroleum Conservation, Research Association

(PCRA) was set up in 1976. It sponsors R&D activities for the development of fuelefficient equipment/ devices and organizes multi-media campaigns for creating mass enthusiasms for conservation. As a fall out of PCRA's initiative, a Conservation Cell was established in the Ministry in July, 1989.

PCRA's efforts have contributed to a saving of about Rs. 189 crores in 1997-98.

The highlights of PCRA's activities undertaken during the year are as follows:

*(i) Energy studies*

140 energy audit studies and 289 fuel oil utilization studies were undertaken during 1997-98 - 124 energy audit studies and 238 fuel oil utilization studies have been already completed between April 1998 and December 1998. 306 small-scale industries were helped to achieve fuel oil conservation till during 1997-98 and 1493 follow-up studies were conducted in the industries surveyed by PCRA.

*(ii) Use of energy vans*

Mobile energy vans were provided to all the regions of the PCRA for conducting walk-through energy audits and fuel oil studies in the industrial units.

*(iii) Model depot projects*

During the period April-March, 1998, 155 model depot development studies were completed in various States across the country.

*(iv) Driver training programmes*

266 driver training programmes were conducted during the year.

*(v) Demonstration clinics/workshops/exhibitions*

773 save fuel clinics/ workshops and 27 exhibitions covering widely dispersed target groups of oil users etc. were organized during the year till March 1998.

*(vi) Consumer meets*

PCRA organized 13 consumer meets to bring together energy consumers, equipment manufacturers and energy consultants to solve the energy conservation problems and create awareness.

*(vii) Promotional schemes*

a) 4 Model garages were set up by December, 1998.

b) Testing facility for transition from non-ISI foot valve manufacture to production of energy efficient ISI marked foot valves is being provided.

*(viii) Educational films/TV spots*

Educational films and TV spots on themes of conservation are screened on Doordarshan and All India Radio in all the regional languages.

*(ix) Outdoor publicity media*

PCRA's conservation messages were spread out throughout the country by using various publicity media.

*(x) Press campaign & distribution of printed literature*

PCRA's advertisements are released in small/ medium/ leading publications in every part of the country. The target groups comprised of top executives of industries, farmers, drivers, automobile owners, truck/bus drivers, housewives, school/college students etc.

*(xi) R&D projects*

a) PCRA had taken the following R&D projects on conservation:

b) Development of kerosene pressure stove - increasing thermal efficiency from 55% to 65%.

c) Development of a prototype electric-hybrid car through ARAI, Pune,

d) Development of fuel efficiency monitor for boilers.

e) Development of dash-board mounted specific fuel consumption meter for automobiles through DOE.

f) Development of a kerosene vapour recovery plant through BTRA, Mumbai.

g) Development of modified dispensing equipment for lubricants.

h) Trials are also in progress with 3% methanol-gasoline blend for operation of a Maruti van, CNG for operation of PCRA's staff car development of fuel injection system for passenger cars, development of modified smoke density monitors for these automobiles, development of improved forging furnaces and development of processes for re-refining of used lubricating oils.

Energy, an essential input for economic development, is consumed in a variety of forms in India. Fuelwood, animal waste and agricultural residues are traditional sources of energy that continue to meet the bulk of the energy requirement in the rural areas. These 'non-commercial fuels' are gradually getting replaced by 'commercial fuels' such as coal,l lignite, petroleum products, natural gas and electricity.

The Government has formulated an energy policy with the objectives of ensuring adequate energy supply at a minimum cost, achieving self-sufficiency in energy supplies and protecting environment form adverse impact of utilising energy resources in an unjudicial manner. The development and promotion of non-conventional/alternate/new and renewable sources of energy such as solar, wind and bio-energy, etc., are also getting sustained attention from the Department of Non-

Conventional Energy Sources, created in september 1982. Nuclear energy to * contribute significantly to the overall energy avalalbility in the country.

Electricity is the most convenient and versatile form of energy. Demand for it, therefore, has been growing at the rate faster than other forms of energy. Power industry too has recorded a phenomenal rate of growth both in terms of its volume and technological sophistication over the last few decades. Electricity plays a crucial role in both industrial and agricultural sectors and, therefore, consumption of electricity in the country is an indicator of productivity and growth. In view of this, power development has been given high priority in development programme.

Studies have shown that while the demand for electricity in the entire economy has riisen at the rate of 9.73 per cent during 1986-87, the demand in the residential and agricultural sectors has been increasing at an alarming rate of 14.03 per cent and 14.58 per cent respectively per year. Installed power generation capacity in the country has increased from a meagre 1,400 mw in 1947 to 81,164.41 mw at the end of 1994-95 comprising 20,829.04 mw hydro (25.66 per cent) and 58,110.37 mw thermal including gas, diesl and wind (71.60 per cent) and 2,225.0 mw nuclear (2.74 per cent).

Various measures being taken to improve power generation in the country include commission of new generation capacity, renovation and modernisation of old units, assistance to Electricity Boards in undertaking plant betterment programme, supply of requisite quantity and quality of coal, training of operation and maintenence personnel and strengthening of transmission and distribution system and implementation of short gestation projects, reduction in T & D losses, implementation of demand management and energy conservation measures. The target of power generation during 1995-96 has been 377.15 billion units out of which 297 billion units are programmed for generation by thermal stations 72.3 billion units by hydro stations and 7.85 billion units by the nuclear stations. Thus an increase of about 7.4 per cent over the generation achieved during 1994-95 is envisaged.

The Plant Load Factor (PLF) has shown a steady improvement over the years. It has improved from 53.8 per cent in 1990-91 to 60 per cent in 1994-95. The following table highlights the achievement of the power sector in major areas during 1994-95.

**Energy and power**

Electricity is a concurrent subject at Entry 34 in the List III of Seventh Schedule of the Constitution of India. The responsibility of its development lies both with the Central and state governments. At the Centre, the Ministry of Power is responsible for the administration of the Electricity (Supply) Act, 1948 and the Indian Electricity Act, 1910. The Ministry is also concerned with perspective planning, policy formulation, processing of projects for investment decision, monitoring of the implementation of power projects and training and manpower development.

The Central Electricity Authority (CEA), constituted under the Electricity (Supply) Act, 1948, advises the Ministry of Power on technical and economic matters. The construction and operation of generation and transmission projects in the Central Sector are entrusted to Central sector power corporations, namely, the National Thermal Corporation (NTPC), the National Hydroelectric Power Corporation (NHPC), the North Eastern Electric Power Corporation (NEEPCO) and the Power Grid Corporation of India Limited (POWERGRID).

POWERGRID, which was incorporated on the 23 October 1989, is responsible for all the existing and future transmission projects in the Central sector and also for the formation of the National Power Grid. There are two joint ventures power corporations under the administrative control of the Ministry of Power, namely, Nathpa Jhakri Power Project and projects of the Tehri Hydro Power Complex. The Damodar Valley Corporation (DVC), constituted under the DVC Act, 1948, the Bhakra Beas Management Board (BBMB) constituted under the Punjab Act, 1966, and three autonomous bodies, namely, Central Power Research Institute (CPRI), the National Power Training Institute (NPTI) and the Energy Management Centre (EMC) are also under the administrative control ofthe Ministry. Programmes of rural electrification are within the purview of the Rural Electrification Corporation (REC). The Power Finance Corporation (PFC) provides term-finance to projects in the power sector. There is one subordinate office Badarpur Management Control Cell (BMCC), directly under this Ministry and 16 subordinate offices under the Central Electricity Authority.

Significant progress has been made in expansion of transmission and distribution facilities in the country. Total length of transmission lines of 66 kv and above voltage level increased form 10,000 ckt km in December 1950 to about 2.36 lakh ckt in March 1994. Highest transmission voltage at present is 400 kv and about 30,240 ckt km of 400 kv lines had been constructed upto March 1994. In addition, the first +500 kv HVDC bipole Rihand-Dadri transmission line of about 820 km length is also in operation. An inter-regional link (vindhyachal 2 × 250 mw HVDC back-to-back) connecting western and northern regions is also in operation.

Five regional grid systems, namely, northern,

western, southern, eastern and north-eastern covering all the states of the country are already existing. All the regions except north-eastern have fairly well inter-connected systems of 220 kv voltage level with progressive overlay of 400 kv transmision systems. The Union Cabinet in 1981 approved in principle the establishment of a Centrally owned and operated National Power Grid. The National Power Grid would eventually comprise strong regional networks with suitable synchronous HVDC links between the regions. Power Grid Corporation of India Limited (*POWERGRID*), created in October 1989, has been vested with the responsibility of developing a National Power Grid. The development of National Power Grid is an evolutionary process and would be achieved over a period of time through development of the regional grid systems and further inter-connections between the regions. National Power Grid will promote integrated operation and transfer of power from one system to another with ultimate objective of ensuring optimum utilisation of available resources in the country.

In order to promote integrated operation of power systems, the country has been demarcated into five regions, namely, north, west, south, east and north-east. Regional electricity boards were set up in 1964 in each of these regions. Northern region covers Haryana, Himachal Pradesh, Jammu and Kashmir, Punjab, Rajasthan, Uttar Pradesh, Chandigarh and Delhi, western region covers Gujarat, Maharashtra, Madhya Pradesh, Goa, Daman and Diu and Dadra and Nagar Haveli; southern region covers Andhra Pradesh, Karnataka, Tamil Nadu, Kerala and Pondicherry; eastern region covers Bihar, Orissa, West Bengal and Sikkim and north-eastern region covers Assam, Manipur, Meghalaya, Nagaland, Tripura, Arunachal Pradesh and Mizoram.

To coordinate operation of the grids of the constituent power systems and to optimise utilisation of the existing generation capacity, regional load despatch centres (RLDCs) have been set up in each region. RLDCs, hitherto functioning under the Central Electricity Authority/regional electricity boards, are being transferred to *Powergrid* in phased manner. In the northern, western and eastern regions, permanent RLDCs equipped with computer based telemetry and the data acquisition system were establilshed around mid 1980s. In the southern region, RLDC equipped with analog telemetry equipment, mimic board, transducers, speech communication, telex and teleprinters facilities is working. In the north-eastern region, an interim regional load despatch centre is operating. Unfied schemes covering the long-term requirements of RLDC and constituents systems in respect of all the five regions are in different stages of formulation. The schemes in respect of southern, northern, and north-eastern regions have got technoeconomic clearance of Central Electricity Authority while the scheme pertaining tothe eastern and western regions are still under finalisation.

Efficient operation of integrated power systems through moderanised computer-based load despatch centres is vitally dependent on efficient data transfer over distance. Thus there is a need for developing a highly reliable communication network. Subsequent to an in-depth analysis of requirements carried out by the Planning Commission, the Central Electricity Authority (CEA)) has developed a Master Telecom Plan for the power sector. Concrete schemes have been framed based on modern communication system. Several such schemes have been techno-economically approved by CEA and most ofthese have also cleared by DOT.

With a number of inter-regional links commissioned

during the Eighth Plan period and subsequent years in form of National Grid and the five regional load despatch centres already in operation, National Electric Power System Information Centre (NEPSIC) has been set up which is equipped with PC-based data acquisition system linking all the RLDCs in the country. The data acquired from RLDC is also available at CEA headquarters for getting an overview of current power system status. Teleconferencing and FAX facilities are also provided. The system is fully functional since June 1993.

State electricity boards have been established in 18 out of 25 states. These are mainly responsible for generation and distribution of electricity in their respective states. Arunachal Pradesh, Goa, Manipur, Mizoram, Nagland, Sikkim and Tripura are yet to establish their electricity boards.

The first major step in this direction had been the setting up of 336 mw Chukha Hydroelectric Project in Bhutan at a cost of Rs. 243.71 crore with Indian technical and financial assistance under an agreement signed in March 1974. The first unit of the project was commissioned in September 1986 and all the four units of 84 mw August 1988. Since then the project has been generating power, the bulk of which has been exported to India. Bhutan has earned the entire cost of the project in about five years time by export of power to India alone besides their internal consumption.

Gratified with the success of Chukha Project the Royal Government of Bhutan are keen on development of their Hydro Resources for the mutual benefit of the two countries. To this end, India and Bhutan have signed an agreement in February 1994 for implementation of Kurichu Hydroelectric Project (3×15 mw) in western Bhutan at a cost of about Rs. 310 crore on a turn-key basis through NHPC within a period of five years. India and Bhutan have agreed to execute Tala HE Project downstream of existing Chukha Project with an installed capacity of 1,020 mw. Discussions have been held between the two countries and modalities for implementation of this mega project are being worked out.

India had constructed a number of mini/micro hydel schemes at Thimpu (360 kw), Gidakom (1000 kw), Wangdi (3000 kw), Gyesta (1500 kw), Khaling (600 kw), Chenarry (750 kw), Lhuntshi (20 kw) during 1960-80. These projects have been identified for rehabilitation in a phased manner by the Government of India. Proposals for taking up impementation of new mini/micro hydro schemes at Ungrichu, Yonglachy, Dongdichu and Chhalori are under consideration.

Energy Conservation has been identified as one of the major thrust areas in the Eighth Plan, as a part of the National Energy Efficiency Programme, with an objective of saving 5,000 mw of installed capacity by the terminal year of Eighth Plan. Apart from the awareness campaign and launching of demonstration projects in agricultural and industrial sectors for promoting energy efficiency technologies, other main activities relate to organising training programmes and studies in the field of energy conservation. A number of internationally supported projects for cooperation on energy conservation in Indian industries and other areas have also been undertaken.

Concerned with the deterioration in the performance of the thermal power stations in the country, Government of India launched a Centrallysponsored programme for renovation and modernisation ( R and M) of thermal power stations to improve their performance. Likewise, a programme for renovation, modernisation and uprating (RM and U) of hydro-electric power stations was formulated by the Central Electricity Authority in 1987. R and M schemes are relevant also in the context of energy conservation and optimum energy usage.

At present, 3,544.58 mw (around 4.4 per cent of India's installed capacity) is in the private sector. The Government of India announced in September 1991 the policy to encourage private enterprises participation in the electricity sector. In pursuance of the policy announcement, the legislation governing the electricity sector was amended in October 1991 and the two part tariff notification was issued on 30 March 1992. The primary objective of the policy was to bring a additionality of resources, increase efficiency in operation and encourge commercial operations in this sector. The response has been encouraging. As on date, interest has been expressed in putting up 196 power projects for a total capacity of 77,720 mw involving an investment of Rs. 2,88,252 crore.

Coal is the main source of energy in the country and it accounts for about 60 per cent of the country's commercial energy requirement. Coal is also an essential input in steel and carbo-chemical industries.

An on 1 January 1995, the coal resources of India (upto a depth of 1,200 metre) have been estimated by the Geological Survey of India at 1,96,891.87 million tonnes.

Coal production which was around 78.71 million tonnes atthe time of nationalisation of the coal industry in 1973-74, rose to a level of 253.80 million tonnes in 1994-95. India is now the third largest coal producing country in the world. The coal production is slated to reach 300 million tonnes by 1996-97. Strategies adopted to achieve higher rate of production are: re-organising existing mines and opening up on new projects, both underground as well as opencast.

Distribution of coal is controlled statutorily under

the Colliery Control Order., 1945. The distribution is to be done by the Coal Controller. However, if for any reason Coal Controller is not able to do so, coal companies have been allowed to distribute coal on the basis of linkages/ sponsorships. Short term linkages for important sectors of economy, like power and cement are decided by Standing Linkage Committee set up under the mInistry of Coal. Linkages to other consumers execpt steel are within the purview of coal companies, which allot coal to actual users as per advice receeived by them from the various sponsoring authorities. New allotments by coal companies to industries are of the order of 5,000 tonnes per month. Off-take of raw coal during 1993-94 and 1994-95 to major sectors of economy is given in table 21.

Under the present delegation of powers, coal projects costing upto Rs. 50 crore are sanctioned by the Board of Directors of the Coal India Limited. The subsidiary companies of Coal India Limited have powers to sanction projects upto Rs. 20 crore. Singareni Collieries Company Limited Board can also sanction coal projects upto Rs. 50 crore. Projects costing more than Rs. 50 crore are sanctioned by the Government. After the nationalisation of the coal industry in 1973 and till December 1994, the number of projects sanctioned (each costing Rs. two crore and above) was 633. A total investment of Rs. 20,718.97 crore has been sanctioned in these projects. Og these, 419 are mining projects and remaining 214 are non-mining projects like washeries, fire control schemes, captive power plants, water supply schemes etc. Out of 633, 340 projects have been completed and 293 are at different stages of implementation. Mining projects on completion will have a capacity of 338.08 million tonnes of coal per annum.

Even though history of Indian coal mining dates back more than two centuries, real sprut in coal production took place only after the nationalisation of the coal industry. Coal production in the country is now allmost completely in the public sector companies e.g. Coal India limited (CIL) and Singareni Collieries Company Limited (SCCL) except few captive mines of TISCO, IISCO and DVC. Coal India Limited producing over 90 per cent of the country's total coal production, has seven coal producing subsidiaries, namely, eastern Coalfields Limited (ECL), Bharat Coking Coal Limited (BCCL), Central Coalfields Limited (CCL), Northern Coalfields Limited (NCL), South Eastern Coalfields (SECL), Mahandi Coalfields Limited (MCL) and Western Coalfields Limited (WCL). The eight subsidiary Central Mines Planning and Design Institute Limited (CMPDIL) is the planning and design institute. SCCL is a joint venture of the Centre and Government of Andhra Pradesh. About 72 per cent of the coal production is obtained through opencast mmines which are almost completely mechanised deploying dragllines, shovels, dumpers, drills, dozers, etc. Mechanisation of underground mines has also been taken up in a big way. Most of the equipment used in coal mines ae indigenously available. At present there are 19 coking coal washeries with an annual capacity of 32.56 million tonnes.

Conservation of coal is an integrated part of mine planning and operation. This is ensured by maximum recovery of *in situ* reserves of coal. Since coal deposits in India are mostly in thick seams and occur at shallow depths, special techniques for maximising recovery are being developed.

Difficult geo-mining conditions prevailing in coal bearing areas like steep and irregular coal seam deposits, gassy seams contifuous and multisection seams necessitate the introduction of some suitable technology for exploitation of such deposits from coal conservation and also safety point in view. Some of the newly introduced methods of mining are: (a) to exploit seams developed in multi-sections and seams with thickness of 6 to 8 m and standing pillars, methods such as blasting gallery and sub-level caving have been adopted in Katras Project, BCCL. Blasting gallery method with sub-pannelings has been planned in Chora Colliery of ECL and GDK-10 and CDK-8 of SCCL Colliery; (b) keeping in view the limitations of conventional underground methods in terms of quantum of output as well as conservation, both Coal India Limited and Singareni Collieries Company Limited have introduced mechanised longwall technology that ensures higher extractability; (c) diversion of rivers, shifting of colonies and townships have been taken up to release sterlised coal underground; (d) adequate measures have been asopted to deal with coalfijeld fires particularly in Jhria Coalfield and latest technology like remote sensing is being applied for fire management; (e) in steep and thick seams of Margheritta Area (Assam), the system of Shield Mining has been introduced. The extraction percentage of coal by traditional system which was 25 per cent to 35 per cent has now improved to nearly 70 per cent or even more in the system of shield mining. The flexible roofing method of mining in the thick seams of North Eastern coalfield has also been applied where the thickness of the seam exceeds 4.5 meter. The system has, however, a limited application ; and (f) since opencast working ensures better conversation, application of opencast working is now followed with much higher cut-off ratios utilising high capacity machineries. Singareni Collieries Company Limited has also made a breakthrough in a small way for extraction of Developed pillars by opencast methods. The company has of late been making efforts to convert existing underground mines into high capacity mechanised Opencast projects at Ramagundam and Kothagudem areas.

The Coal mines Conservation and Development Act, 1974 provides for imposition of excise duty on coal despatches for meeting activities like conservation of coal, development/introduction of new technology in coal mines, safety in Mines and assistance in mining operation. A number of research and development activities in coal sector are carried out under overall guidance and supervision of Standing Scientific and Research Commmittee and its four sub-committees. The applied research is carried out in the fields of production, productivity, safety coal preparation, coal utilisation, environment and ecology.

Special efforts to improve lthe standard of safety in the coal industry have brought down the rate of fatalities per million tonne of output in Coal India Limited to 0.40 and in Singareni Collieries Companies Limited to 2.04 in the year 1994. A Standing Committee on Safety regularly review safety standards in coal mines.

Coal industry employs over seven lakh workers. Since nationalisation of coal mines, welfare of coal miners by way of providing facilities like housing, water supply, medical care, education, etc., is bieng given greater attention.

Lignite reserves in the country have been estimated at around 26,200 million tonnes. Out of the above, 3,300 million tonnes spread over 480 sq km is in the Neyveli Lignite fields in South Acrot Vallalar district and about 2,000 mt has been identified as minerable under the presently adopted mining parameters. Geological reserves of about 1150 mt of lignite have been identified in Jayamkondacholapuram of Trichy district of Tamil Nadu. In Mannargudi and east of Veeranam, geological reserves of around 18,200 mt and 1,340 mt of lignite respectively have been estimated. Smaller deposits exist in Rajasthan, Gujarat and J&K. Lignite reserves at Neyveli are exploited by Neyveli Lignite Corporation (NLC) Ltd. It was incorporated as a private limited company in 1956 wholly owned by Government of India. The Corporation was converted into public company w.e.f. 7 March 1986.

The main constituents of the company are lignite mines, thermal power stations, fertilizer plant and briquetting and carbonisation plant. Mine-I (6.5 million tonnes of Lignite per annum) feeds thermal Power Station-I (600 mw), Briquetting and Carbonisation Plant (2,62,000 tonnes of coke-achievable capacity) and the Process Steam Plant. Mine-II (10.5 million tonnes of lignite per annum) feeds it captive Thermal Power Station-II (7×210 mw). The Fertilizer Plant (achievable capacity 1,29,200 tonnes of urea per annum) which initially used raw lignite as feed stock changed over to oil gasification in July 1979 on operational and technological consideration. The power generated from Thermal Power Station-I after meeting the NLC's requirements is fed into Tamil Nadu Electricity Board grid which is the sole beneficiary. Power generated from Thermal Power Station-II after meeting the needs of Second Mine is shared by southern states *viz.*, Tamil Nadu, Kerala, Karnataka, Andhra Pradesh and Union Territory of Pondicherry. NLC produced 154.10 lakh tonnes of lignite and generated 10,890.29 million units of power during 1994-95, registered an increase of about 23 per cent and 36 per cent respectively over 1991-92.

Raw lignite sales (12,34,001 tonnes) and power export (8916.36 million units) had registered an increase of about 61 per cent and 40 per cent respectively in 1994-95 over 1991-92. The company has been making profits since 1976-77 and its profit of Rs 171 crore (provisional) for 1994-95 is the highest profit achieved for any year since inception. In 1994-95, the sales turnover has recorded a growth of 33.23 per cent and net profit of 50 per cent over 1993-94.

India is richly endowed with minerals. Under the Constitution, minerals rights and the administration of mining laws are vested in the state governments. The Centre, however, regulates the development of minerals under the Mines and Minerals (Regulation and Development) Act, 1957 and the rules and regulations framed under it. This Statute empowers the Centre to formulate rules for: (i) the grant of prospecting licences and mining leases for schedule minerals, (ii) the conservation and development of minerals., and (iii) the modification of old leases. The Act, came into force on 1 June 1958. Amendments to this Act were made in 1972, 1986, and 1994.

Principal mineral found in the country along with their estimated reserves are given below.

Coal is India's largest mineral resource and presently India is the fifth largest producer of coal in the world. Vast deposits of coal of Gondwana formations occur in West Bengal, Orissa, Bihar, Madhya Pradesh, Andhra Pradesh, Uttar Pradesh and Maharashtra. It also occurs in tertiary formation in Assam, Arunachal Pradesh, Meghalaya and Nagaland. Total known reserves of all types of coals in Gondwana and tertiary coalfields estimated stands at 192 billion tonnes. Out of these, reserves of prime-coking coal have been estimated at 5.3 billion tonnes. Total reserves of lignite stands at 6.5 billion tonnes, located in Tamil Nadu, Gujarat, Rajasthan, Kerala, Pondichery and Jammu and Kashmir.

The total recoverable reserves of bauxite in the

country are placed at 2,525 million tonnes while the total *in situ* reserves are 3,037 million tonnes. The conditional resources of bauxite are about five lakh tonnes. In addition, prospective resources are placed at 90 million tonnes. Orissa, Andhra Pradesh, Madhya Pradesh, Gujarat, Maharashtra and Bihar are the principal states where bauxite deposits are located. Major reserves are concentrated in the East Coast Bauxite deposits of Orissa and Andhra Pradesh.

Total recoverable reserves of chromite are estimated at 8.8 million tonnes. Deposits of economic significance occur in Andhra Pradesh, Bihar, Karnataka, Maharashtra, Manipur, Orissa and Tamil Nadu. However, refractory grade reserves of chromite are very meagre.

The total recoverable reserves of copper ore in the country are 415.86 million tonnes equivalent to 4.14 million tonnes of metal content. The all-India conditional resources of copper are 695.29 million tonnes (1.99 million tonnes of copper metal) and prospective resources are 769.9 million tonnes of copper ore. Major and important copper ore deposits are located in Singhbhum district (Bihar), Balaghat (Madhya Pradesh) and Jhunjhunu and Alwar (Rajasthan). In addition, small copper ore deposits are in Andhra Pradesh, Gujarat, Karnataka, Sikkim, Orissa, Uttar Pradesh and West Bengal.

There are three important gold fields in the country, namely, Kolar Gold Field, Kolar disrict, Hutti Gold Fields in Raichur district (both in Karnataka) and Ramgiri Gold field in Anantpur district (Andhra Pradesh). Total gold metal ore reserves are estimated at 176.9 lakh tonnes.

The total recoverable reserves of iron ore in the country are about 9,606 million tonnes of haematite and 3,143 million tonnes of magnetite. Haematite resources are located in Andhra Prades, Bihar, Goa, Karnataka, Madhya Pradesh, Maharashtra, Orissa and Rajasthan. Magnetite resources are located in Andhra Pradesh, Bihar, Goa, Karnataka and Kerala.

Lead-zinc resources are located in Rajasthan, Gujarat, West Bengal, Andhra Pradesh, Meghalaya, Orissa, Sikkim, Tamil Nadu and Uttar Pradesh. Total recoverable reserves (all grades) of lead and zinc ores are 198.5 million tonnes comprising of metal content of 2,390 thousand tonnes of lead and 9,866 thousand tonnes of zinc metal. The conditonal resources of lead-zinc are 200.29 million tonnes in the country.

The total recoverable reserves of manganese ore are 233.33 million tonnes out of which 41.05 million tonnes are proved , 142.03 million tonnes probable and 50.25 million tonnes of possible category. Main reserves are in Karnataka followed by Orissa, Madhya Pradesh, Maharashtra and Goa. Minor occurences of manganese are in Andhra Pradesh, Bihar, Gujarat, Rajasthan and West Bengal.

The total estimated conditional resource of nickel ore is 294 million tonnes located in Orissa (285 million tonnes) and Bihar (9 million tonnes). Minor occurrence of nickel in Tamil Nadu, Maharashtra and Goa are indicated. The recoverable reserves of tungsten ore have been estimated at 25.89 million tonnes or 77.32 thousand tonnes of $WO_3$ content. The main reserves are at Degana, Rajasthan. It also occurs in Maharashtra, Karnataka, West Bengal and Uttar Pradesh.

The recoverable reserves of barytes are 70.15 million tonnes. The Mangampet deposit occuring in Cuddapah djistrict (Andhra Pradesh) is the single largest deposit in the world containing 67 million tonnes of recoverable reserves. Minor occurences of barytes are located in

Rajasthan, Madhya Pradesh, Maharashtra, Himachal Pradesh, Tamil Nadu, Uttar Pradesh and Bihar.

Diamond deposits occur in three types of geological settings such as kimberlite pipes, conglomerate beds and alluvial gravels. The main diamond bearing areas in India are Panna belt in Madhya Pradesh, Munimadugu-Banganapalle conglomerate in Kurnool district, Wajrakarur kimberlite pipe in Anantpur district and the gravels of Krishna river basin in Andhra Pradesh. Reserves * of about a million carats, there are conditional submarginal of 265 thousand carats.

Dolomite occurrences are widespread in almost all part of the country. The total recoverable reserves of all grades of dolomite are 4,967 million tonnes. Of the total all India recoverable reserves, major share of about 92 per cent reserves is distributed in seven states– Madhya Pradesh, Orissa, Gujarat, Karnataka, West Bengal, Uttar Pradesh and Maharashtra.

Fireclay occurs as a bedded deposit, mostly associated with measures of Gondwana and Tertiary periods. Important deposits are associated with Jharia and Raniganj coalfields in Bihar and West Bengal, Korba coalfields in Madhya Pradesh and Neyveli Lignite field in Tamil Nadu. Notable occurrences of fireclay not associated with coal measures are known in Gujarat, Jabalpur region of Madhya Pradesh and Belpahar-Sundergarh areas of Orissa. The recoverable reserves of fireclay are about 697 million tonnes.

Total recoverable reserves of fluorspar in India are 2.15 million tonnes. Rajasthan and Gujarat are the only producing states in India. Fluorspar occurs in Gujarat, Madhya Pradesh, Maharashtra and Rajasthan.

The recoverable reserves of gypsum are estimated at 239 million tonnes. Out of the above, 70,000 tonnes surgical plaster grade, 39 million tonnes of fertilizer/ pottery grade, 38.6 million tonnes of cement/paint grade, four million tonnes of soil reclamation grade and the rest is unclassified. The production of gypsum is confined to Rajasthan, Tamil Nadu, Jammu and Kashmir, Uttar Pradesh, Himachal Pradesh and Gujarat. Rajasthan is the main producer of gypsum followed by Tamil Nadu.

The recoverable reserves of graphite are 3.11 million tonnes. Orissa is the major producers of graphite. Almost the entire reserves under proved category are in Ramanathapuram district, Tamil Nadu. Resources of graphite are in Andhra Pradesh, Orissa, Tamil Nadu, Kerala, Bihar, Gujarat, Rajasthan, Madhya Pradesh and Maharashtra.

The recoverable reserves of ilmenite are 86.75 million tonnes. Ilmenite occurs mainly in beach sand deposits right from Ratnagiri coast in the west to Orissa coast in the east. These minerals are found in Kerala, Tamil Nadu and Orissa.

The all India recoverable reserves of kaolin, including white clay of all categories are about 986 million tonnes. Principal producing states are Bihar, Gujarat, Rajasthan and West Bengal. Kerala, Haryana, Orissa and Madhya Pradesh also produce significant quantities and ball clay is mainly produced in Rajasthan, Andhra Pradesh and Gujarat.

The total recoverable reserves of limestone of all categories and grades are placed at 76,446 million tonnes. The conditional reserves have been estimated at 360 million tonnes. Major producing states are Madhya Pradesh, tamil Nadu, Andhra Pradesh, Gujarat, Bihar, Orissa, Rajasthan and Karnataka.

India is the world's leading producer of sheet mica and accounts for about 60 per cent of global mica trade.

Economic deposits of mica occur in three important belts in Bihar, Andhra Pradesh and Rajasthan.

The total recoverable reserves of magnesite are about 233 million tonnes of which 41 million tonnes are in theproved category. Magnesite is found in Uttar Pradesh, Tamil Nadu and Rajasthan while minor occurrences are in Karnataka, Jammu and Kashmir and Himachal Pradesh.

The total recoverable reserves of kyanite and sillimanite in the country are 2.7 million tonnes respectively. Besides, conditional resources of 175.84 million tonnes of kyanite are also estimated. For sillimanite conditional resources of 5.9 million tonnes and prospective resources of 0.8 million tonnes have been estimated.

Kyanite deposits are located in Andhra Pradesh, Bihar, Karnataka and Maharashtra. Sillimanite resources are in Kerala, Orissa, Madhya Pradesh, tamil Nadu and minor occurrences in Andhra Pradesh, Assam, Bihar, Karnataka, Maharashtra, Meghalaya, Rajasthan and West Bengal.

Deposits of phosphorites are located in Madhya Pradesh, Rajasthan and Uttar Pradesh. Besides, apatite deposits of commercial importance are reported from Bihar, Andhra Pradesh, Rajasthan, West Bengal and Tamil Nadu. Recoverable reserves of rock-phosphate are estimated at 146.95 million tonnes of all grades and of apatite at 13 million tonnes.

Other minerals occuring in significant quantities in India are bentonite (Gujarat, Rajasthan, Bihar, Jammu and Kashmir and Tamil Nadu), corundum (Maharashtra, Madhya Pradesh, Andhra Pradesh * and Gujarat), fullers earth (Rajasthan, Karnataka and Andhra Pradesh), garnet (Tamil Nadu, Rajasthan and Andhra Pradesh Pradesh), pyrites (Bihar and Rajasthan), steatite (Rajasthan, Uttar Pradesh, Andhra Pradesh, Tamil Nadu and Bihar), wollastonite (Rajasthan and Gujarat), zircon (beach sand of Tamil Nadu, Kerala and Orissa) and quartz and silica minerals are wide spread and occur in about all states. Besides, the country has vast resources of building dimension and ornamental stones such as granite, marble and slate. Granite is mainly mined in Tamil Nadu, Karnataka, Andhra Pradesh and Rajasthan, marble in Rajasthan, Uttar Pradesh and Gujarat and slate in Madhya Pradesh, Andhra Pradesh and Haryana.

The petrochemical industry, which forms a part of the chemical industry, is one of the fastest growing sectors in the Indian economy. The annual growth rate of the industry has been around 12-15 per cent compared to about 10 per cent in the chemical industry and 8 per cent of industrial sector as a whole. Petrochemicals, particularly plastics and fibres, make a substantial contribution to the national exchequer directly by way of excise and customs duty and other taxes. The plastic processing industry offers direct employment to over two lakh persons with the potential of over three lakh persons by 2000 AD. Starting from the stage of raw material production to the conversion of finished products, employment gets generated in a cascading manner.

In the initial years, since indigenous capacity was small, the growth was mainly import driven. Consequent to the strong leadership provided by the Indian Petrochemicals Corporation Limited (PCL), a public sector company, and perceiving the greater growth and scope for returns on investments, several private sector companies entered this field. Consumption of all major petrochemicals increased from 7.5 lakh mt in 1979-80 to 29.73 lakh mt in 1990-91 and 34 lakh mt in 1993-94, and is expected to reach the level of over 70 lakh mt by 2000 AD. To meet the growing demand of petrochemicals, Government have sanctioned several mega petrochemical complexes involving a total investment of about Rs. 35,000 crore. This would make India largely self-sufficient in petrochemicals. Petrochemicals have emerged as cost effective energy saving versatile materials serving the needs of the common people.

Exports in petrochemicals have been growing reasonably well. The country has been able to make some exports of polyester staple fibre and LAB. In addition, export of plastic processed goods has increased from Rs. 415 crore in 1992-93 to Rs. 815 crore in 1993-94. The export of man made/synthetic fibres/yarns (including blended spun yarns) was for Rs. 712 crore in 1992-93 and Rs. 514 crore in 1993-94.

There are three public sector organisations in the petrochemical sector under the administrative control of the Department of Chemicals and Petrochemicals. Indian Petrochemicals Corporation Limited (IPCL) is a public sector undertaking incorporated in March 1969. The company has been entrusted with the responsibility of manufacturing and distribution of various petrochemicals like polymers, synthetic organic chemicals, fibres and fibre intermediates. IPCL's mega petrochemicals complex at Vadodara was commissioned in 1993 and the Olefin Complex was commissioned in 1978. The company has set up another Olefin complex in Nagothane in Maharashtra. It has been commissioned and production is stabilising. The third such complex has been approved by the Government in Gandhar in Gujarat. IPCL is a profit making company which earned a net profit of Rs. 562.32 crore during 1994-95.

Petrofils Cooperative Limited (PCL) is a joint venture company of the Government of India and weavers' cooperative societies. It produces polyester filament yarn and nylon filament yarn at its three plants located at Vadodara and Naldhari in Gujarat. The Society has set up spandex plant at Naldhari, which will manufacture spandex yarn for the first time in the country. The spandex yarn having elastic properties is used in swimming suits, underwear garments etc. The company has a turnover of Rs. 322 crore during 1993-94. It has made a net profit of about Rs. 5.40 crore during 1993-94 as against a net loss of Rs. 15.83 crore in 1992-93.

The Central Insititute of Plastics Engineering and Technology (CIPET) is a training institute set up at Madras by the Government as a registered society with the primary objective to develop skilled manpower and provide technical services to the plastic industry. Besides training, the Institute also provides testing, standardisation and quality control, advisory and consultancy services to the plastic industry. To meet the increasing demand of trained personnel in the field of plastics, CIPET has set up nine extension centres at Ahmadabad, Amritsar, Bhopal, Bhubaneswar, Hyderabad, Imphal, Lucknow and Mysore including the headquarter centre at Madras. A service centre and a training centre of CIPET have also been opened at Goa and Patna respectively to cater to the demands of plastic industry in and around these places.

The production of crude oil which reached a peak of 34.09 million tonnes in 1989-90 declined to the level of 26.95 million tonnes in 1992-93. Therefore, to increase the production, a number of short-term and medium-term measures such as early production from satellite fields, use of state-of-the-art technology i.e. horizontal drilling, drainhole drilling etc., were initiated in 1993. As a result of these measures, the decline in crude oil production was arrested in 1993-94 with the production level of 27.02

million tonnes which has further increased to 32.24 million tonnes in 1994-95. The substantial increase in the production in 1994-95 has been due to commissioning of major development schemes such as the additional development of L-II, L-III, Neelam field and South Heera field in the Western Offshore. The crude oil production during 1995-96 is expected to be 37.24 million tonnes. This increase over 1994-95 of around five million tonnes will come mostly from increased production in the Western Offshore fields. The production of crude oil is likely to reach the level of 38.57 million tonnes in 1996-97. Government have also initiated action for increasing indigenous crude oil by offering small and medium sized fields for development through private/joint venture participation. Some small sized fields have been offered for development through private participation.

India is importing a substial part of its oil needs. During 1992-93, the gross import of crude oil and petroleum products was 40.5 million tonnes costing Rs. 17,046 crore in foreign exchange. During 1993-94, the import of crude oil and POL was at 42.9 million tonnes valued at Rs. 17,730 crore. The gross import of crude oil and POl products during 1994-95 was 41.3 million tonnes valued at Rs. 17,838 crore.

Research and development activities by Oil and Naturtal Gas Commission (ONGC) and Oil India LImited (OIL) and Gas Authority of India Limited (GAIL) in the field of crude oil and natural gas exploration and production, processing and marketing sectors are carried out at their respective R and D centers. ONGC has established eight institutes, viz., Kishav Dev Malviya Institute of Petroleum Exploration (KDMIPE), Dehra Dun; Institute of Reservoir Studies (IRS), Ahmadabad; Institute of Engineering and Ocean Technology (IEOT), Bombay; Institute of Oil Gas Production Technology

(IOGPT), Bombay; Geophysical Data Processing and Interpretation Centre (GEOPIG), Dehradun; Institute of Petroleum Safety and Environment Management (IPSEM), Goa; Institute of Biotechnology and Geotectonics (INBIGS), Jrhat; and Institute of Drilling Technology (IDT), Dehra Dun.

The main objective of the KDMIPE is to provide back-up services to exploration efforts of ONGC. IRS provides R and D back-up for preparation of development plans of ONGC"s oil and gas fields and application of enhanced oil recovery methods with a view to improve their oil and gas recovery. IDT attends to the development of techniques for drilling difficult wells in high pressure/high temperature regime as well as super deep wells in technically complex areas. IEOT carries out design review for all offshore platforms, deep water production systems. * IOGPT had been set up to provide continuous back-up to situation specific production problems and long term application of appropriate techniques and technologies. GEOPIC is ONGC's premier seismic, gravity, magnetic, logging and geochemical data processing and interpretation center. IPSEM aims at creating awareness for improved safety and environment management and minimize the pollution accidents and loss of life caused by petroleum exploration and production operations. INBIGS, when fully operational, will be able to provide genetic probes for direct detection of hydrocarbons. Additionally, ONGC has set up a joint ONGC-Schlumverger Wireline Research Center at Delhi to meet the long term need of high technology requirement for wireline logging and related fields. OIL has its R&D center at Duliajan, mainly dealing with exploration, oil field chemicals, EOR and production engineering related matters. GAIL is also developing in-house R&D facilities mainly in the area of gas processing storage, distribution and utilisation.

Production of natural gas in 1994-95 was 19.38 BCM as compared to 18.33 BCM in the year 1993-94. The utilisation in 1994-95 was 17.35 BCM as compared to 16.41 BCM in 1993-94. The balance recoverable reserves as on 1 April 1994 were around 700 BCM.

Gas Authority of India Limited (GAIL) was incorporated i 1984 for the transportation, processing and marketing of natural gas and was assigned the priority task of setting up the cross country HBJ pipeline. Presently GAIL is the largest company in India for marketing natural gas. It operates over 3,000 km of pipelines in the country and supplies gas to power plants for the generation of 6,000 mw of power to the fertilizer sector for the production of 10 MTPA of urea and to about 150 industrial units.

GAIL is operating on the plants LPG at Bijaipur (Madhya Pradesh) and Vaghodia (Gujarat). It is putting up two more LPG plants at Lakwa (Assam) and Usar (Maharashtra), a petro-chemical complex at Auraiya (Uttar Pradesh) and proposes to put up a gas processing complex at Gandhar. GAIL has formed a joint venture company with British Gas to implement the Bombay City Gas Distribution Project. It is also upgrading the HBJ pipeline capacity from 18.2 MMSCMD to 33.4 MMSCMD.

The Government of India has been inviting offers from Indian and foreign companies for development of discovered oil fields as well as for exploration of oil and gas in various blocks in India. Against the offer of discovered oil field made in August 1992, contracts for development of five medium sized fields and 12 small sized fields have been signed. The medium sized fields * are MId and South Tapti, Mukta and Panna (Bombay offshore); Ravva (Krishna-Godavari offshore) and Kharsang (Arunachal Pradesh). The small fields are Hazira, Cambay, Bhandut, Matar, Sabarmati, Indora,

Bakrol, Lohar, Dholka, Wavel, Baola and Asjol in Gujarat.

The medium-sized fields would be developed through joint ventures between Oil and Natural Gas Commission (ONGC) Oil India Ltd. (OIL) on the one hand and private companies on the other. These joint ventures could be either incorporated or unincorporated ventures. Where they are incorporated, ONGC/OIL would have a 49 per cent share in the equity of the venture. In unincorporated ventures, ONGC/OIL would take a 40 per cent share in the venture.

The small-sized fields would be developed by commmpanies on their own, with no participation by ONGC/OIL, under production sharing contracts to be signed by the companies with the Government of India. In both cases, companies would also be required to bear their share of statutory levies like royalty, cess, etc. Foreign companies would be levied income-tax at a fixed rate of 50 per cent, while Indian companies would be governed by the relevant provisions of the Income Tax. The Government has the first right of refusal in respect of the contractor's share of oil, with international price being payable. Companies have also been exempted from payment of customs duty on goods imported for use in petroleum operations.

In addition to the above, the Government has signed production sharing contracts for exploration of oil and gas in four blocks under the fourth round of bidding. These blocks are: (i) in Pranhita-Godavari (Gondwana) onshore basin; (ii) Krishna-Godavari offshore basin; (iii) Rajasthan basin and (iv) Cauvery offshore basin.

Government is actively encouraging the acquisition of acreages overseas to enhance the flow of equity oil into the country. As part of this policy, ONGC Videsh Ltd. (OVL) has been aggressively pursuing opportunities overseas to acquire exploration and producing acreages.

OVL entered into a production sharing contract in 1988 with Petro-Vietnam for exploratiion for hydrocarbons in blocks 6,12E and 19 in offshore Vietnam. Subsequently, in 1992. OVL assigned 45 per cent of its interest in the blocks to the alliance of British Petroleum (BP), UK and Statoil, Norway.

The OVL-BP-Statoil consortium carried out further survey and drilling work during the second phase of exploration between May 1992 and November 1994, leading to a discovery of about two trillion cubic feet (TCF) of gas in the Lan Tay and Lan Do structures in block 6. Techno-economic appraisal of the gas discovery with a view to its development is currently in progress. OVL has so far spent about US dollar 30 million on this venture.

OVL signed an agreement with British Gas, UK, in June 1995 for taking a 50 per cent participating interest in the North Zaafarana concession in Egypt. Under this agreement, OVL is scheduled to drill an exploratory well with and expenditure of about US dollar 7 million. It has also signed an agreement with Command Petroleum, Australia in July 1995 for taking a 40 per cent participating interest in the Fejaj permit in Tunisia. Drilling of an exploratory well is currently in progress.

In addition to the above, OVL is also engaged in negotiations with British Gas for taking a participating interest in offshore block in Yemen. It is also actively evaluating exploration and production opportunities in a number of other countries in order to enhance its reserves in overseas acreages so that a significant contribution to the equity oil accruing to the country from overseas ventures can be made.

The total refining capacity in the country as on 1 April 1994 was 53.40 MMTPA spread over 13 refineries.

The actual crude processed was 54.30 MMTPA year 1993-94 representing a capacity utilisation of 101.7 per cent. The cumulative refinery production from April-August 1995 was 24.12 thousand tonnes as against the *pro-rata* installed capacity * While making projections for the Eighth Five Year Plan, it has been estimated that the demand of petroleum products will be around 79 MMTPA in the terminal year of Eighth Plan and around 102 MMTPA by the end of Nineth Plan *i.e.* in the year 2001-20002. To meet the consumption levels, Government approved proposals to set up the following new refineries in addition to implementation/expansion/debottlenecking of existing refineries: (i) Mangalore Refinery (JV)-Three MMTPA; (ii) Numaligarh Refinery-Three MMTPA and (iii) Panipat Refinery-Six MMTPA. With the modernisation of Digboi Refinery, its capacity would be increased from 0.5 to 0.65 MMTPA. Further expansion of Bongaigaon Refinery and Petrochemicals Limited (BRPL) from 1.35 MMTPA to 2.35 MMTPA has already been implemented. Haldia and Vizak refineries plans have been also approved for expansion by one and three MMTPA respectively. Besides, the Government had decided in July 1992 for setting up of three new grass-root refineries during the Eighth/Ninth Plan, each with a capacity of six MMTPA as joint ventures with suitable private parties from India or abroad.

The Government of India has welcomed proposals for private investment including foreign investment in the refining sector following liberalisation of industrial policy. In pursuance of this policy, Letters of Intent have been granted to 11 companies for setting up refineries in the private sector including EOU refineries to the extent ofabout 60 MMTPA. In case all the approved refineries are implemented by the end of century, India will be mot self-sufficient in the refining capacity but also export some products.

Lubrizol India Limited (LIL), a public sector undertaking was incorporated in 1966 in collaboration with the lubrizol Corporation, USA under the Companies Act. The authorised and paid-up share capital of the company is Rs. 19.20 crore. The Government of India holds 60 per cent of the subscribed equity capital of the company and the Lubrizol Corporation, USA 40 per cent thereof. LIL develops, manufactures and markets additive systems for autommotive and industrial lubricants and also develops other speciality chemicals for catering to the needs of the petroleum industry. The company has one manufacturing unit and the second unit for manufacturing of extreme pressure additives at Taloja, district Raigad, was commissioned on 30 March 1995.

The Engineers India Limited (EIL) was established in 1965 in collaboration with the Bechtel Corporation, USA mainly to indigenise engineering and project management capabilities in the petroleum sector. In 1967, the shareholding of Bechtel was taken over the Government of India and since then the company has been a fully-owned public sector undertaking. The authorised and paid up capital of EIL is Rs. two crore as on 31 March 1994. The reserves and surplus of the company have grown to Rs. 197.90 crore as on 31 MArch 1994 and its net worth on that date was Rs. 199.90 crore.

EIL today provides a complete range of project services in the fields of petroleum refining, petrochemicals, oil and gas processing pipelines, ocean engineering, ports and harbours, fertilizer and non-ferrous metallurgy, cement, paper, etc., and has emerged as South Asia's leading design and engineering company. In order to increase its global competitiveness, EIL has adopted a three-pronged strategy, *i.e.* setting up of joit ventures, formation of strategic alliances and stand alone ventures. The company has formed a joint venture company in the name of AMEC Engineers India Limited (AEIL) in 50:50 partnership with M/s AMEC Process and Energy International, in UK.

The EIL has also formed a wholly-owned subsidiary in India under the name Certification Engineers International Limited (CEIL) in order to provide certification, recertification and third party inspection services to the Indian as well as overseas clients. The company is also in process of establishing a wholly-owned subsidiary company in Malaysia under the name EIL, ASIA PACIFIC SDN BHD. It has diverse consultancy assignments in Iran, Algeria, Qatar, Abu Dhabi and Malaysia.

The growing demand for petroleum products has been casting a heavy burden on the economy. Hence a very high priority is being attached to the conservation of petroleum products. A variety of measures taken by the Petroleum Conservation Research Association * (PCRA), a registered society under the Ministry of Petroleum and Natural Gas, to promote conservation of petroleum products cover transport, industrial, agricultural, household and oil sectors which account for the PCRA are creation of mass awareness on the need for the conservation of petroleum prosucts, promotion of measures to curb wasteful practices, and improve the oil use efficiency of equipment, devices and vehicles and research and development for improving oil use efficiency in various end uses. As a result of these efforts it has been possible to achieve quantifiable savings of about Rs. 491 crore during 1994-95 including recurring saving of Rs. 417 crore achieved as a result of efforts made by and through the PCRA.

In addition, new areas or the inadequately covered areas are also being taken up including promotion of inter-seul subsititution. As part of a programme for inter-fuel substitution, CNG was introduced as an alternate fuel in the road transport sector. In all 1,677 petrol driven vehicles have been converted for CNG operation.

Marketing and distribution network of the Indian pteroleum industry is widespread and, by and large, under the control of the public sector oil companies. Apart from over 2,736 km of product pipeline, the industry has a network of about 16,023 MS/HSD retail outlets, 6156-light diesel oil/kerosene dealers and over 4,673 LPG distributors up to April 1995. Fair distribution of products all over the country at stipulated prices is generally ensured.

A major landmark development in the petroleum marketing has been the decanalisation of kerosene, LPG and LSHS and the introduction of parallel marketing of these products to augment their domestic availability. As a result of this liberalisation, the private entrepreneurs can now undertake import of these commodities and sell them at market determined prices. As on 31 July 1995, about 73.5 TMT of LPG and 817.3 TMT of kerosene has been imported. The private sector has also been allowed to invest in the development of infrastructure for petroleum marketing. Private investment has been invited for setting up and operation of depots, tank farms, import facilities, product and crude pipeline and manufacture of railway tank wagons for use by the oil industry. Several products like naptha, hexane, toluene, petroleum coke, carbon black feed stock, lube oil base stock, etc., have been decanalised for better availability of these products.

In order to inform and educate the public about the credentials and credibility of parallel marketers, a system of rating has been introduced in June 1995, by which every parallel marketer is required to obtain a rating certificate from one of the approved rating agencies.

Several joint ventures have been set up in the petroleum sector by both the public and private enterprises. Six joint ventures have been set up by the public sector oil marketing companies with reputed international companies for manufacture and marketing of lubricants, bitumen emulsions, and insfractructure for LPG. Several private sector companies have also entered into joint venture agreements with transnational companies. These are expected to bring in foreign investment as well as help in upgrading the indigenous technologies.

Indian Oil Corporation (IOC) was set up in September 1964, by amalgamating Indian Refineries Limited with Indian Oil Company Limited. The Corporation has three division, namely, (i) Marketing Division with headquarters at Bombay. (ii) Refineries and Pipelines Division with headquarters at Delhi; and (iii) Assam Oil Division with headquarters at Digboi. IOC has a Research and Development Centre at Faridabad in Haryana. The Centre provides technical service to customers and is engaged in development of sophisticated lubrication oils. It is actively working on possibilities of production and utilisation of viable substitute fuels. IOC is also having a wholly-owned subsidiary called Indian Oil Blending Limited (IOBL) which is engaged in blending lubricants.

The market share of the Corporation was 55.76 per cent of the total oil industry's sales in April 1995. The Corporation had in existence 2,295 cooking gas (LPG) distributorships, 6,277 retail outlet (petrol/diesel) dealerships and 3,283 kerosene/light diesel oil dealerships in the country.

Following government's acquisition of two Burmah-Shell companies in January 1976, name of Burmah-Shell Refineries Limited was changed to Bharat Refineries

Limited from 12 February 1976. Being an integrated refining and marketing company, name of the company was changed to Bharat Petroleum Corporation Limited (BPCL) from 1 August 1977.

The company is engaged in processing of crude oil in its refinery at Bombay and storage, distribution and marketing of petroleum products in country. In addition, it is in the process of diversifying into ptero-chemicals using certain refinery streams as feed stock. Market share of BPCL in 1994-95 was 20.01 per cent of total oil industry's sales. As on 1 April 1995, the company had a total of 948 cooking gas (LPG) distributorships, 4,204 petrol/diesel retail outlets and 937 kerosene oil/light diesel oil dealership.

Hindustan Petroleum Corporation Limited (HPCL) was set up on 15 July 1974 by acquiring assets in India of ESSO Eastern Inc. USA and became a wholly government-owned company. On 21 December 1976, Government acquired Caltex Oil Refining (India) and merged it with HPCL. The main activities of HPCL are refining of crude oil, manufacturing lubricating base oil, manufacturing and blending of lubricants, grease and petroleum products and related automative accessories all over the country and marketing of petroleum products including LPG. Market share of HPCL in 1994-95 was 19.54 per cent of total oil industry's sales. As on 1 April 1995, the company had a total of 1307 cooking gas (LPG) distributorships, 4154 retail outlets (petrol/diesel) and 1,580 kerosene/light diesel oil dealerships.

IBP Company Limited has three divisions, namely, oil, chemicals and engineering. Oil division has a country-wide retail network marketing petroleum products which it obtains from other oil companies in the absence of its own refining facility at present. The Company had in existence 1388 retail outlets (petrol/

diesel) dealerships and 356 kerosene/light diesel oil dealership in the country.

As India is one of the lowest cost refiners in the world, experts believe that it might become a net exporter of petroleum products in the coming century and a "swing producer" to stabilise global product markets. Though the first oil well in India was completed late in the last century—drilling for the oil well at Digboi in Assam was begun in September 1889 and completed in November 1890—the search for oil in a big way started only after the country gained Independence. The first well at Digboi was drilled by the Assam Railway and Trading Company. Later the Assam Oil Company (AOC) came into existence, which sold its rights to the Burmah Oil Company.

These were the beginnings of Oil India Limited, which became a fully-owned Government company in the early eighties. Thus at the time of Independence, indigenous production of crude oil was confined to Assam. Since this was hardly enough to meet the country's needs for petroleum products, the Government of India took a conscious decision to develop the country's oil resources, both onshore and offshore.

Creating a Petroleum Division within the Geological Survey of India in October 1955, exclusively for country-wide oil exploration, was the first step. It did not take much time for GSI's Petroleum Division to grow into the Directorate of Oil and Natural Gas, and subsequently into an autonomous Oil & Natural Gas Commisssion through an act of Parliament in October 1959. Now, of course, the Commission is known as Oil & Natural Gas Corporation Limited.

The real fillip to the development of the indigenous petroleum industry was given by the late Keshav Deo

Malaviya, who gave ONGC the necessary push and was also responsible for the creation of Indian Oil Corporation, India's first national refining and marketing corporation.

Later, of course, the refineries and marketing companies owned by Burmah-Shell, Esso and Caltex (not to talk of the small Digboirefinery owned by Burmah Oil Company) were nationalised giving birth to two more national oil companies, i.e. Bharat Petroleum and Hindustan Petroleum. Today there are 14 refineries (including the two mentioned above)—13 in the public sector and one in the joint sector. The Gas Authority of India Limited (GALL) was set up in 1984 for planned utilisation of gas reserves and was given the responsibility to set up the HBJ pipeline.

These are briefly the main operators in the oil and natural gas sector, which is basically a public sector monopoly now. While Oil India's operations, in the initial stages, were confined to the north-eastern region, ONGC's initial successes came in the western region. The first discovery of oil and gas made by ONGC was in 1958 in the Cambay onshore basin in Gujarat. Also in Gujarat, the first giant oilfield was discovered at Ankleshwar in 1960.

In what was termed as "Samudra Manthan" in the early sixties, ONGC decided to step up its offshore exploration activity in earnest. Seismic surveys helped in the discovery of the Aliabet structure at the mouth of the Narmada and later in "Bombay High". A big debate raged in the late sixties whether we should develop "Bombay High" on our own or entrust the job to foreign compaines. The first option was chosen and ONGC acquired its first jack-up type rig "Sagar Samrat" (built for the Commission in Japan) in 1973. "Sagar Samrat" started drilling in "Bombay High" in January 1974 and about a month later oil was discovered at the very first well it drilled in this oilfield, which has met part of the country's crude needs for the past 15 years or so.

This writer was fortunate enough to be among the group of reporters who were on board the "Sagar Samrat" in early 1974 to witness the drilling for the first well. By the time we returned to shore and about to report this first experiment in offshore drilling, news arrived that oil has been found. February 1974 will thus be a landmark in the development of offshore oil production in India.

ONGC has travelled quite far in the 22 years since oil was established in "Bombay High". Crude oil production from offshore areas (which is solely from ONGC) has risen from five million tonnes in 1980-81 to a high of 21.2 million tonnes in 1990-91. It was around 20.2 million tonnes 1994-95. Total crude production both from onshore and offshore areas (i.e. the total output of OIL and ONGC) was around 35.2 million tonnes in 1995-96.

But the country's requirements of petroleum products have grown at a rapid rate, from 30 million tonnes in 1980-81 to almost 75 million tonnes in 1995-96. Current estimates indicate that it would reach a level of about 113 million tonnes by 2001-02.

Looked at from a different perspective. India's domestic oil production vis-a-vis petroleum product consumption indicate that the percentage of slef-sufficiency has declined from 55.6 per cent in 1990-91 to 43.7 per cent in 1995-96 and is estimated to decline further to 23.5 per cent by 2006-7. In other words, the percentage of self-sufficiency in another 10 years (which is not far away) will be half of what it was in 1990-91.

While of course it is true that it is the Centre's responsibility to find adequate funds to develop the oil and gas industry, the above figures only highlight the need to let the oil and gas industry generate more internal resources to finance its future development. It is an open secret that the Government of India's finances are none too rosy and there are too many competing claims on the limited kitty available with the Centre.

All the more reason for immediate reforms in the hydrocarbons sector. Though it is difficult to quantify in monetary terms the benefits of reforms, the R Group has estimated that the net present value of the reforms it has suggested would amount to around Rs. 100,000 crore. And that is a lot of money.

The controversy that is raging at the moment over raising the prices of some of the heavily subsidised petroleum products only serve to highlight the problems that arise in opening up the oil and gas sector in line with the changes that are taking place in other sectors of the economy.

For instance, it is widely admitted (even in official publicity material) that a level playing field should be given to national oil companies "particularly by paying them international market price of oil". This will help them to raise more revenue, but this good intention still remains on paper only.

"If discovered fields are offered in future for improving economic viabiloity, the national oil companies, who have discovered the fields, should be reimbursed the past costs incurred by them", says an official note explaining the short-term measures to be taken for development of the oil sector. This is another contentious issue on which there is more noise than action.

The Government has allowed entry of private sector in a major way into the oil refining sector (proposals, including export-oriented refineries, adding up to 70 million tonnes per annum have been cleared so far). Similarly, parallel marketing in gas has been allowed (though this has yet to pick up) and with the approval in principle for the Southern Gas Grid, several policy decisions with regard to the natural gas sector have also to be taken. For instance, natural gas is underpriced and there is a recommendation that it should be raised.

Development of the natural gas sector (which will, as per present indications, will be largely based on imported gas) means heavy investment in pipelines, port and storage facililties, etc. It takes years to set up these. Here again, to facilitate and encourage investment, a rational pricing policy must be in place, the sooner the better.

Since the country has mastered the art and science of setting up refineries as well as running them, experts believe that india might become a net exporter of petroleum products in the coming century and a "swing producer" to stabilise global product markets. This expectation is based on the fact that India is one of the lowest cost refiners in the world.

But, to quote Dr. Kelkar again, "our present administered prices regime is non-transparent and certainly not efficency compatible. Further, our current tariffs provide negative rate of protection for the refining sector and as such it discourages provate investors to bring in new investments". Hence, what is required is comprehensive reforms of pricing and tariff policy as that alone can promote adequate infusion of capital and efficient use of these resources, he argues.

Now, that prescription applies not only to the refining sector, but to the entire oil and natural gas sector. This is not the place to go into specific details, but a visionary approach is needed similar tot he one shown by many of those who have helped paying the foundation for the oil and gas industry.

The great institutional base built up within the country over the past several decades in exploration, production and refining should be strengthened further, along with the entry of a range of new actors. Major investments are taking place in sectors like automobiles, but these can become infructuous if the main engine of growth (here one means both industrial and agricultural growth) i.e. the oil and gas sector, is not properly taken care of. It is time we put this sector on a faster track.

Both at the central and state level, the Government has initiated and supports many efforts towards capacity-building. The major thrust of development is on the implementation of sectoral programmes, particularly those related to agriculture and allied sectors. Programmes such as the National Rural Employment Programmes (NREP), Rural Landless Employment Guarantee Programme * (IRDP) aim to alleviate rural poverty. Programmes such as Hill Area Development are designed to tackle hostile environmental factors which affect development of certain areas. In the Drought-Prone Areas Programme (DPAP) and Desert Development Programme (DDP), the emphasis is on water and moisture conservation.

India has sovereign rights and jurisdiction in the economic zone extending 200 nautical miles from the coastline. The Government has established a wide-ranging network of legislative and institutional frameworks for protecting and preserving the marine environment.

The programme of the Department of Ocean Development and associated organizations include

Development of Coastal Zones and Islands, Monitoring and modelling of the Marine Environment, Control of Marine Pollution, Wave Power Generation, Ocean Modelling, Sea Level Monitoring and Modelling, and Coastal Mapping.

Marine Satellite Information Secvice centres and a multi-institutional Marine Pollution Coastal Ocean Monitoring and Predictive System have been established.

The National Environmental Awareness Campaign (NEAC), which began in 1986, is a major programme of the Ministry of Environment and forests. The programme seeks to increase environmental awareness through the involvement of governmental and non-governmental organizations. Activities under the NEAC include seminars, workshops, rallies, teacher training, eco-clubs, environmental campus etc.

The Ministry of Environment and Forests set up the Environmental Information System (ENVIS) in 1982 as a decentralized system using a network of databases to ensure integration of national efforts in collecting information related to environment.

ENVIS has ten centres working in diverse areas such as pollution control, coastal ecology, environmentally sound and appropriate technology etc. It has a documentation service and processes queries from national and international useres. A quarterly abstracting journal Paryavaran Abstracts is published after scanning nearly five hundred scientific journals. ENVIS maintians a close liaison with other national information systems like National Information System on Science and Technology (NISSAT) and Biotechnology Information System (BTIS).

The Central Arid Zone Research Institute (CAZRI) was set up at Jodhpur in Rajasthan by the Government of

India to undertake studies on land, soil water and vegetation resources of arid and semi-arid areas. The Institute carries out studies on precipitation, the regional dynamics of the landscape and the impact of climatic conditions and man-animal activities on it in order to determind the optimal natural plant community of major environments, and to optimize the use of water and land. CAZRI is also involved in transfer of technology, publicity and extension work to create awareness about the desertification process, and to achieve public participation in the development programmes of arid and semi-arid regions.

In the area of formal education, the National Policy on Education (1986) stresses the paramount need to create consciousness about the environment. This must permeate all ages and sections of the society, beginning with the child. The Policy gives unqualified priority to universalization of elementary eduction and substantial improvement in the quality of education. Detailed school mapping exercises have been planned under a master plan for universal provision of facilities for environment education. The National Council of Educational Research and Training (NCERT) has been assigned the responsibility of developing model syllabi and instructional packages in ten core cureicular ares, of which protection of environment is one.

The Ministry of Human Resource Development (MHRD) has taken a major initiative in the field of environment education through the launching of the Environment Orientation to School Education scheme. Under this scheme special cells have been created in the state departments of education. Support is also extended to NGOs to facilitate the development of locale-specific programmes and materials.

The Ministry of Environment and Forests supports

two centres of excellence in the area of environmental educationl. These are the Centre for Environment Education, Ahmedabad, and the CPR Environmental Education Centre, Madras. The Centre for Environment Education, Ahmedabad, is involved in developing innovative programmes and materials to increase awareness about the environment.

The National Museum of Natural History (NMNH), New Delhi, is a unique facility which provides people an opportunity to acquire a direct understanding of the world of nature, the inter relationships among plants, animals, and the environment, and the need to develop a new approach and ethic towards the natural environment. NMNH also has centres at Mysore, Bhubaneshwar and Bhopal.

The Government of India supports research projects for the study of ecosystems and the causes of their degradation. In this regard, two committees—the Environmental Research Committee (ERC) and Man and the Biosphere (MAB) Research Committee function as advisory bodies under the Ministry of Environment and Forests. The research is followed up by formulation of action plans for optimal utilistion of resources leading to sustainable development.

Man and the Biosphere programme is an inter-disciplinary programme of research and training which emphasized and ecological approach to the study of inter-relationships between humans and their environment. The programme aims to provide scientific basis to solve practical problems of resource management through understanding the environmental problems in the ecosystem context.

The Environmental Research Committee addresses problems of chemical, engineering and technological aspects of environmental management, and promotes research in all subjexts concerned with the human environment that are not covered by the MAB programme. ERCs thrust areas include environmental aspects of rural and urban settlemens, resource management, environmental degradation, planning, training and education. It promotes integrated action-oriented programmes which deal not only with research but also its demonstration and extension. Such action-oriented research has been taken up in the Himalayan region, and in the Western and Eastern Ghats, besides multinational project of integrated studies on the Kaveri river.

The Ministry of Environment and Forests has so far supported about 500 environmental research projects in different parts of the country. Of these, about 300 had been completed by March 1990. The findings of the research projects are published in a departmental publication and also in scientific journals and the popular press. Some of the findings have direct applicability while others contribute to the data base for environmental planning and management.

Various other research organizations set up by the Government and other agencies are concerned with different aspects of evnironment. The physical Research Laboratory (PRL) Ahmedabad, is a premier national centre for research in space and allied sciences; the Indian Institute of Remote Sensing (IIRS), Hyderabad, imparts training in remote sensing techniques and promotes research in areas like thematic mapping of land.

The functions of the Council of Scientific and Industrial Research (CSIR) include institutional financing, awarding fellowships, collecting and disseminating information on research and industrial matters. It has a chain of 39 laboratories and about 80 field centres. From aeronautical products to oceanography, and from drugs to salt and marine chemicals research, CSIR is involved in helping the country enter frontier areas of research.

Its centres include the Central Drug Research Institute, Lucknow; National Environmental Engineering Research Institute, Nagpur; Indian National Scientific Documentation Centre, New Delhi; National Chemical laboratory, Pune; Central Institute of Medicinal and Aromatic Plants, Lucknow; Industrial Toxicology Research Centre, Lucknow; Indian Institute of Chemical Technology, Hyderabad; and Central Food Technology Research Institute, Mysore.

Council for Advencement of People's Action and Rural Technology (CAPART), set up in 1986 is the central agency for funding rural development projects of voluntary agencies. It assists voluntary efforts which aim to implement locale-specific rural development projects. Funding for projects coming under several government programmes like the Drought Prone Area programme, Integrated Rural Development Programme etc., are disbursed through CAPART.

CAPART gives financial assistance to registered voluntary organization. Up to 80 per cent of the project expenditure is made available and the remaining has to be raised by the organization for other sources.

The Department of Science and Technology, Government of India, is involved in research and development related to several environmental issues throuhg its institutions.

The Indian Institute of Tropical Meteorology, Pune, is involved in studies of atmospheric ozone, effect of aerosols on climate change, effect of stratospheric changes and anthropogenic activities on climate change, carbon dioxide studies etc.

The Birbal Sahni Institute of Paleobotany, Lucknow, is engaged in paleobotanical research which aims to build up an evlutionary sequence charting the history of modern vegetation. It is also involved in investigating past climates.

The Wadia Institute of Himalayan Geology, Dehra Dun, has been studying various aspects of the chemistry of Himalayan glaciers. It has also conducted studies on the impact of growing human population on the Himalayan ecology.

The Indian institute of Astrophysics, Bangalore, studies solar activity while the Indian Institute of Geomagnetism, Bombay, has a programme for the study of atmospheric and solar terrestrial weather relationships.

The Survey of India, Dehra Dun, is responsible, among other things, for tide gauge observations along the Indian coastline and for the study of anticipated problems of sea-level rise and impact on coastal environment.

The Centre for Atmospheric Studies at the Indian Institute of Technology, New Delhi, studies the effect of aerosols on climate change, air pollution over India, and other related issues.

The Department of Science and Technology is also actively involved in the national efforts of the International Geosphere-Biosphere programme.

The practice of scientific forestry in India dates back to over 120 years. Systamatic research and trainign in foresting commenced nearly 70 years ago. Research and forestry education now come under the purview of the Indian Council of Forestry Research and Education, which conducts its programmes through six regional institutions and a number of universitites and other organizations. Its six regional institutions, including the Forest Research Institute at Dehra Dun which is a premier institution in forestry, carry out extensive field and laboratory research. The Indian Institute of Forest Management (IIFM) Bhopal, was established in 1982 to meet the growing need for managerial expertise in forestry and allied sectors. The institute also runs management development programmes for in—service managers of forest departments, forest development corporations, forest based industries, financial institutions and voluntary organizations. In addition, the Institute is involved in applied research and provides consultancy service.

Forest management in the field is planned and implemented by the Indian Forest Service (IFS). Two year postgraduate training in forestry is imparted to IFS officers at the Indira Gandhi National Forest Academy, Dehra Dun. There are also three regional State Forest Service colleges and numerous rangers' colleges for training middle level and field professionals.

NGOs in India have played a vital role in raising awareness about the issues related to environment and development, and in mobilizing people to take action. They have employed a variety of techniques and media. The Kerala Sastra Sahitya Parishat, which was the catelytic agency involved in mobilizing public opinion agaisnt the Silent Valley hydroelectric project, uses traditional and folk media to communicate its messages. The Centre for Science and Environment (CSE), New Delhi, has brought out three widely circulated volumes on the state of India's environment, in addition to several other publication. CSE has also played a key role in bringing in the South perspective in International discussions of environment and development issues.

Eklavya, Bhopal, develops innovative and relevant school programmes and material. The Assam Science Society which has a membership of professional and students, attempts to enhance science education.

The Narmada Bachao Andolan has brought together scattered voices of protest against the damming of the river Narmada and has raised awarness not only in the affected area and in the rest of India, but alos among the international community. The Vivekanand Kendra, Tamil Nadu, trains hundreds of workers in the fields of health, education and development.

A major focus of its activities is in Arunachal Pradesh where it runs 14 residential schools for tribal children. The People's Commission on Environment and Development, New Delhi, is a forum creatd to bring together and articulate citizen's concerns to put before the UNCED. Kalpavriksh, New Delhi, organizes awareness programmes and carries out campaigns on specific issues by lobbying, holding demonstrations and fighting legal cases.

The Ministry of Environment and Forests has instituted a number of awards to recognize outstanding contributions of individuals and organizations in various environment related endeavours.

National Awards for Prevention and Control of Pollution have been instituted to recognize the achievements of industries for their contribution in the prevention and control of pollution.

Indira Priyadarshini Vrikshmitra Awards are given to individuals and organizations for outstanding work in the field of afforestation and wastelands development.

Indira Gandhi Paryavaran Puraskar is awarded to either an individual or organization for contribution in the field of environment.

Pitamber Pant National Fellowship recognizes excellence in research in any branch of environmental science.

The Centre for Mining Environment at Dhanbad (Bihar) was establised in 1987 by the Ministry of environment and Forests to generate scientific data for sustainable mining in the country. The Centre conducts postgraduate and doctoral level courses, as well as training programmes for in service professionals. Research areas include land use management, noise and vibration problems in mining areas, air pollution in fire areas and its effects on health.

Remote sensing for survey of resources is carried out by India's earth observation satellite system, the IRS series of satellites. Projections of crop yields, land-use mapping, monitorin of forest cover and biomass, identification of agro-climatic zones are today possible, and provide a basis for micro-level planning. Drought monitoring on a real time basis is also becoming possible, as is the use of remote sensing for mitigating damage due to floods. Detailed remote sensing surveys have also helped to considerably narrow down areas for groundwater exploration. Satellite based glacier inventory of the Himalayan states has been found promising for planning and operating mini and micro hydroelectric stations.

Fishers prospect charts, derived from satellite monitoring of sea surface temperature anamolies, are in regular use. Remote sensing has also been used extensively for forest mapping, in India. It is through this that a correct picture of the extent of forest cover and the relative changes in it have been obtained.

The National Natural Resource Management System of the Ministry of Environment and Forests involves utilization of remote sensing technology for accurate inventory of resources such as land, water, forests, minerals, ocean, etc., and to utilize this information for monitoring changes in ecological systems.

The objective of all development is to add to the economic well-being of the people so that their standard of living can be improved. Development projects are, therefore, taken up to convert the natural resources into goods and services. It is imperative to incorporate environmental aspects into the development projects right at the inception stage to prevent the erosion of the resouces base itself. Impact assessment is a handy tool to assess the environmental compatibility of the projects in terms of their location, suitability of technology, efficiency in resource utilisation and recycling etc. Impact assessment was introduced in 1978 and now covers almost all major projects.

At present environmental impact assessment is being done for the following types of project: (a) (i) river valley; (ii) thermal power; (iii) mining; (iv) industries; (v) atomic power; (vi) rail, road, highways, bridges; (vii) ports and harbours; (viii) airport; (iv) new towns and (x) communication projects, (b) projects which require approval of the Public Investment Board/Planning Commission/Central Electricity Authority; (c) projects referred to the Ministry of Environment and Forests by other ministries; (d) projects which are sensitive and located in environmentally degraded areas; (e) public sector undertakings of the Centre where the project cost is more than Rs. 50 crore. A notification has been issued in January 1994 which makes Environmental Impact Assessement statutory for 29 categories of developmental projects under various sectors such as industrial, mining, irrigation, power, transport, tourism, communication, etc. The notification contains details aimed at rationalising and standarding the procedure for environmental clearance. Extensive delegations to the stae governments are also provided in this notification. An amendment to this notification stipulates inter alia that all applications complete in every material aspect have to be examined and decision conveyed to the applicants within 30 days in the case of site clearances and 120 days in the case of environmental clearnce of projects. Once an application has been submitted by project authority the preliminary scrutiny of the project is done by the respective technical divisions and the overall appraisal of the projects is undertaken by specially constituted environmental appraisal committees of experts. In addition, special groups/committees and task forces are constituted as and when needed for expert inputs on major projects. After a detailed scrutiny and assessment, the appraisal committee makes its recommendation for approval or rejection of the projects. Depending on the nature of the project, certain safeguards are recommended. For monitoring and timely implementation of safeguards suggested, six regional centres have been set up by the Ministry at Shillong, Bhubaneswar, Chandigarh, Bangalore, Lucknow and Bhopal.

Under the Forests (Conservation) Act, 1980 diversion of forest land for non-forest purpose requires prior approval from the Central Government. While proposals involving forest land less than 20 hectare can be decided by the state forest departments, proposals involving more than that are appriased by the Advisory Committee of the Ministry, constituted under the Forests (Conservation) Act, 1980 as amended in 1988.

When a project requires both environemental and forest clearance, the proposals are simultaneously processed under the Single Window Celearance Scheme. All cases with complete environmental data and action plans are decided within three months. In the case of diversion of forest land, the decision is taken within six months.

Major environmental impacts of river vally projects which need consideration are: (i) degradation of catchment areas; (ii) command area development; (iii) rehabilitation of those affected; (iv) incresed incidence of water-borne diseases; (v) reservoir induced seismicity; and (vi) deforestation and loss of flora and fauna including gene-pool reserves.

Major environmental impacts of mining operations are: (i) degradation of land; (ii) pollution of surface and ground water resources; (iii) pollution of air; (iv) deforestation including loss of flora and fauna; (v) rehabilitation of affected populationincluding tribals; and (vi) impact on historical monuments and religious places. A major component of the mining operations in India is the opencast mining which severely affects land use pattern. Mining operations have serious adverse impact on the growth of vegetation and general landscape. Minerals extracted interact with surface and ground water thus polluting the water resources. Loss of top-soil due to deforestation also depletes ground water resources and results in drying up of perennial sources like springs and streams especially in hill areas.

Major environmental impacts of thermal power projects include; (a) air pollution; (b) water pollution; (c) deforestation; (d) rehabilitation; and (e) land degradation. Flue gases emerging from stacks containing sulphur dioxide, oxides of nitrogen, carbon monoxide, etc., are detrimental to human beings and vegetation. Water pollution from thermal stations can due to release of slurry which is a mixture of flyash and water. Thermal pollution is due to release of cooling water which can affect acquatic life. Solution to disposal of ash problem is in its recycling by converting it into building blocks and its use in other construction works. Another step which helps in abating pollution cuased by ash is stabilisation of ash dumps through suitable vegetation.

Major environmenal impacts of industrial projects include (i) are pollution; (ii) water pollution; and (iii) disposal and utilisation of solid waste. Impacts of projects in specific areas are examined in great detail and suitable control measures suggested. Linkages of project requirements to utilisation of resources in an optimal way is an essential pre-requisite. Concept of recycling, reuse and adoption of clean technologies is increasingly becoming predominant.

Projects considered under the transport sector include laying of railway lines, roads and bridge construction, airport construction and establishing of ports and harbours. The environmental parameters affected by the transport projects have been classified into (i) natural physical resources; (ii) natural ecological resources; (iii) human/economic development resources; and (iv) quality of life values including aesthetic and cultural values. Adverse impacts on above environmental parameters are to be identified and mitigation measures provided for to offset such impacts.

Under the Environment (Protection) Act, 1986, a notification on Coastal Zone Regulation has been issued declaring coastal stretches of seas, bays, estuaries, creaks, rivers and backwater within 500 meter of High Tide line as Coastal Regulation Zones. Setting up of new industries or expansion of existing industies except those directly related to waterfront, manufacturing, handling, storage or disposal of hazardous substances and setting up and expansion of units/mechanisms for disposal of wastes and effluents etc., are prohibited in these Costal Regulation Zone. All the seven coastal states are required

- to prepare coastal management plans which would provide protection to ecologically fragile coastal areas rich in biological diversity and provide for land use zoning. The Coastal Regulation Zone notification, 1991, has been amended.

In nuclear power plants, safety from radiation during the operation of the plants and after, and disposal of nuclear wastes are of prime concern. Major environmental impacts of nuclear power projects which need consideration are; (i) radio-active contamination of air, water and soil; (ii) thermal pollution due to discharge of cooling water; (iii) deforestation and loss of flora and fauna; (iv) rehabilitation; and (v) radio-active waste disposal. Exposure to radio-active radiations in excess of the prescribed limits are detrimental to human beings, aquatic life, flora and fauna. The long half life periods for radio-active decay necessitate sealing of the reactor vessel and components for a dormant period of about 30 years after decommissioning of the plant.

Afforestation of wastelands through proper financial assitance by various agencies would provide income and employment opportunities to the poor and improve the quality of the environment. The government can play a facilitating role by removing obstacles and simplifying procedures. The lack of ground-level data has affected the afforestation programme. The afforestation of wastelands has now emerged as an important feature in the present socio-economic and political scenario in India, which aims at solving the problems of scarcity of timber, firewood, fodder and other forest produce as well as reclamation of wastelands and degraded forests. India has vast tracts of wastelands, and these lands are mostly owned by government and village Panchayats and are highly degraded. Tree plantation is the socially optimum and ecologically-sound use of such lands. It may not be economically desirable for a farmer to plant trees on good lands which have a very high opportunity cost in terms of value of agricultural production forgone. However, tree planting may be profitable for a farmer in region prone to recurring drought and having unproductive soil which is not fit for growing agricultural crops.

Although the practice of planting trees is as old as cultivation of other crops, the need for government intervation to promote afforestation was articulated by the National Commission on Agriculture (NCA) in 1976. The government of India accepted the NCA's recommendation and subsequently various afforestation programmes like farm forestry, rehabilitation/ reforestation of degraded lands, formation of community woodlots and strip plantation were started in some States in the late seventies. Recent evidences from various parts of the country indicate that the success of afforestation programmes has been remarkable. In India, there is still a vast scope for implementing afforestation programmes in regions which are not yet brought within the fold of tree plantation schemes and in which there is acute shortage of firewood, timber and other forest produce.

In conjunction with technical guidance and financing, availability of wastelands for afforestation is the other crucial component of the wastelands development and afforestation programmes determing their success. There are many constraints which are hampering the implementation of afforestation programmes in various parts of the country. The non-availability of wastelands for afforestation programmes is one of them. In the absence of a comprehensive survey of land use, several estimates have been made about the extent of wastelands in India. One of the estimates of wastelands indicate that about 175 million hectares of (m ha) land fall in this category (Sigh et al, 1981). The other estimate by the Society for the Promotion of Wastelands Development (SPWD) puts it at 129 m ha-93 m ha in non-forest area and 36 m ha in forest area (SPWD, 1984). The National Wastelands Development Board (NWDB, 1989) estimates wastelands to the extent of 120 m ha with 40 m ha in forest lands and 80 m a in agricultural lands. According to Singh (1994), more than half of the geographical area of India consists of degraded lands. The estimates for wastelands range between 38.4 m ha (11.7% of total geographical area of the country, Directorate of Economics & Statistics, GOI, New Delhi 1978-79) to 175 m ha (53.2% of total geographical area of the country, Ministry of Agriculture & Co-operation, New Delhi, 1982) (Gautam and Narayan, 1988:96). However, Bentley (1984) has estimated that 200 m ha of land in India are partially degraded in terms of short-term productivity. According to Khan (1987), the wastelands which may ultimately be available for development would not be more than 80 m ha, bulk of which is degraded forests and marginal agriculatural lands. There are many other estimates of wastelands in India.

The information needed for assessing the potential of non-forest and cultivated lands, like ownership, extent and type of degradation, and present and future uses, has never been collected on a systematic basis for the entire country (Romm, 1981). Recently, some initiatives have been taken to improve the availability of grass roots level data for this purpose. The Government of India has already implemented a National Wastelands Identification Project to identify the extent and type of wastelands in 146 districts in 19 States.

One of the most serious problems threatening the country today is its population growth. Although the foodgrain production in the last few years has kept pace with the population increase, the daunting task of feeding each and everyone in the next century is the biggest challenge before us. In our attempts to meet such increasing demands, the improper and over—use of chemical inputs had deteriorated the agro—ecosystems to a considerable extent. Moreover, the pressure due to growing human and cattle population on the land has added to the deterioration of land status of the country. The increasing deterioration of land due to soil—erosion, injudicious use of chemical fertilizers, water logging, salinity/alkalinity, shifting cultivation, etc. necessitates a more scientific approach towards the utilisation of these lands, often termed as degraded or waste—lands. The growing awareness world over on the environment conservation and the emphasis on the concept of 'sustainability' has focussed on the area of 'wasteland utilization' as an importaht component of 'sustainable development.'

There are various aerial estimates of wastelands in the country varying from one—third to one half of the country's total area. The primary reason of the variation in such estimates could be ascribed to the fact that until recently, wastelands had neither been systematically defined nor identified. The first comprehensive attempt to map out such areas and categories them, was done by the National Commission on Agriculture (1976), which estimated different types of wastelands and suggested guidelines for reclaiming and developing such land. The Commission had estimated the extent of wastelands in the country to be 175 million hectares which is more than half the total geographical area in he country. However, this estimate was not based on scientific data. As per an estimate by the Society for Promotion of Wastelands Development (1993), the area under wastelands is around 129 million hectares or about one—third of country's total geographical area.

According to the statistics presented, the state with the greatest expanse of wastelands in the country is Madhya Pradesh with 20.14 million ha very closely followed by Rajasthan with 19.93 million ha. The states with over 10 million ha of wastelands each are Andhra Pradesh and Maharashtra. Gujarat, Karnataka and Uttar Pradesh have each approximately 9 million ha of wastelands.

To a layman, wasteland is a piece of land which is lying uninhabited or uncultivated. These lands are also commonly perceived to produce much less than their potential. Despleted of the green cover and productivity, such lands are often in a critical condition.

Boradly, wastelands may be defined as land where the production of biomass is less than its opotimum productivity. Wasteland also refers to lands which are economically unproductive, ecologically unstable and subject to environmental deterioration.

According to the Technical Task Group, constituted by the Planning Commisison and NWDB (National Wastelands Development Board), wasteland is defined as that land which is degraded and is presently lying unutilised except as current fallows due to different constraints.

Wastelands have been classified by NWDB into culturable and unculturable wastelands.

*Culturable Wastelands:* Land which is capable of or has the potential for the development of vegetative cover and is not being used due to different constraints of varying degree is termed as culturable wasteland. The culturable wastelands comprise the following categories:

— Gullied and/or ravinous land;

— Undulating upland with or without scrub;

— Surface–waterlogged lands and marsh;

— Salt–affected land;

— Shifting—cultivation area;

— Degraded forest—lands;

— Degraded pastures/grazing—lands;

— Degraded non forest—plantation land;

— Strip—land;

— Sands; and

— Mining/industrial wastelands.

*Unculturable Wastelands:* Lands, which can not be developed for vegetative cover, are defined as unculturable wastelands. The unculturable wastelands comprise the following categories:

— Baren rocky/Stony wastes/Sheet–rock area;

— Steep–sloping area; and

— Snow–covered and/or glacial area.

Besides the above categories of wastelands, the following could also be included:

— Over cultivated soils leading to depletion of micro–nutrients;

— Acidic soils; and

— Land overgrown with aggressive weeds.

The major causes of land being rendered waste include—deforestation, overgrazing, faulty water management practices, extensive mining activities, etc. Deforestation and overgrazing distinctly hastens the process of soil erosion and land degradation. Faulty water managemnt practices lead to problems such as water logging, soil salinity/alkalinity, etc. Deforestation has often been described as the most primary reason of land degradation and the factors in deforestation are—conversion of forest land into agricultural land, the urban and industrial demand for forest products, indiscriminate quarrying for mineral resources, etc. Besides the above mentioned casuses, the environmental factors like slope, intensity of rainfall and the pedogenic characteristics of a particular area interact to increase the formation of wastelands.

Our forest cover has dwindled notwithstanding three successive National Forest Policies. A scientific land use policy alone can ensure sustained production, ecological balance and environmental benefits. It is time that the Forest Policy is reviewed and a new strategy adopted keeping in view that conservation includes preservation, maintenance, sustainable utilization, restoration and enrichment of the environment.

Man depends on natural resources from his forest environment for all his basic needs. No doubt, the majority in the industrialized countries is no longer dependent on the natural living resources but the bulk of the rural and a section of the urban population in India and the rest of the developing world continue this dependence, especially for their fuel, fodder and timber needs. The forest serves many valuable functions as has been reflected in the national forest policies. Moreover, forest plays an active role as a storehouse of living organisms of potential use and as a regulator of rainfall, soil and water regime, source of many basic needs of the weaker sections of the rural population. The relationship between land, climate and forest is such that if the soil is allowed to deteriorate or lost, degradation of both land and vegetation becomes inevitable. Unfortunately, in the developing countries like India, biotic pressures are intense.

The situation is worsening in spite of the lofty aims propagated by the three successive national forest policies. In India, although the first policy is nearly a century old, the present forest cover is worse than when it was originally proposed. The failure of the national forest policies is perhaps due to their focus on government forests rather than to the land and soil in general. There has been a lack, of scientific land use policy having legal backing and public support. For these reasons, the definition of 'forest' has come to imply land area constituted as reserve forests and not general tree cover.

Biotic Pressure: The tremendous increase in human population, the resultant poverty nd the heavy dependence on agriculture have resulted in the use of wood as the main fuel. India's ecology is today no better with the deficit of firewood at 145 million $m^3$ and 43 million ha of land brought under the plough between 1951 and 1976 for the extension of agriculture. The loss of forest area for various purposes during 1951-76 was substantial.

The situation has still remained the same and the condition has not changed as is evident from the cases of some of the States. The problem has worsened due to excessive grazing coupled with forest fire. About 52 per cent of India's forests are incapable of regenration largely due to the combined effects of biotic pressures.

In a developing country like India, forests have suffered badly because of the failure in land management practices. To what extent can we put the blame on forest policies? Are the policies wrong or inconsistent or is it that the policies have remained merely ceremonial documents devoid of the will to implement or people's support? An analysis of the forest policies of India would reveal that the main cause of failure has been, perhaps, viewing forests in isolation rather than taking into consideration the country's soil as a whole. It is after all the soil which supports all kinds of plant life in the biosphere.

Forests are a renewable source and contribute substantially to economic development. They play major role in enhancing the quality of environment. The country has an area of 752.3 lakh hectare notified as forests, of which 406.1 lakh hectare is classified as reserved and 215.1 lakh hectare as protected. Unclassified forest area is spread over 131.1 lakh hectare. About 19.47 per cent of the total geographical area of the country is under actual forest cover.

India is one of the few countries which ahs a forest policy since 1894. It was revised in 1952 and again in 1988. Main plank of the revised forest policy of 1988 is protection, conservation and development of forests. Its aims are: (i) maintenance of environmental stability through preservation and restoration of ecological balance; (ii) conservation of natural heritage; (iii) check on soil erosion and denudation in catchment area of rivers, lakes and reservoirs; (iv) check on extension of sand dunes in desert areas of Rajasthan and along coastal tracts; (v) substantial increase in forest/tree cover through massive afforestation and social forestry programmes; (vi) steps to meet requirements of fuel wood, fodder, minor forest produce and soil timber of rural and tribal populations; (vii) increase in productivity of forest to meet the national needs; (viii) encouragement of efficient utilisation of forest produce and optimum substitution of wood, and (ix) steps to create massive people's movement with involvement of women to achieve the objectives and minimise pressure on existing forests.

The entire gamut of forest activities are being given

a new orientation in the light of the National Forest Policy of 1988. Some of the important areas for immediate and effective protection of forests include afforestation and development of wastelands, reforestation and replantation in existing forests, settlement, restriction on grazing, encouragement for wood substitutes and supply of other kinds of fuel, elimation of forest contractors, discouragement of monoculture practice etc.

Increasing destruction and degradation of forests and treelands especially in the Himalayas and other hilly areas, is contributing to heavy erosion of top soil, erratic rainfall and recurring floods. It is also causing acute shortage of firewood and loos of productivity due to eroded and degraded lands. The Forest (Conservation) Act, 1980 enacted to check indiscriminate deforestation/ diversion of forest lands for non-forestry purpose was amended in 1988 to make it more stringent by prescribing punishment for violations.

Another area of concern has been degradation of forests due to biotic pressure. Guidelines have been framed for preparation of working plans and felling in forests. Some of the salient features are: (i) working plans shoudl be up-to-date and stress conservation; (ii) preliminary working plan should have multi-disciplinary approach; (iii) tribal rights and concessions should be highlighted and with control mechanisms; (iv) grazing should be studied in detail and specific prescriptions should cover fodder propagation; (v) shifting cultivation and encroachments need to be controlled; (vi) clear-felling with artificial regeneration should be avoided as far as possible and clear felling blocks should not exceed 10 hectare in hills and 25 hectare area in plains, and (vii) banning all felling above 1,000 metre altitude for a few years should be considered to allow these areas to recover. Critical areas in hills and catchment areas prone to landslides, erosion etc., should be totally protected and quickly afforested.

Guidelines have been issued in June 1990 to state governments for involving village communities and voluntary agencies for regeneration of degraded forest lands on usufruct shraing basis. As a follow up of these guidelines, 14 states have issued appropriate orders. These states are: West Bengal, Orissa, Bihar, Madhya Pradesh, Rajasthan, Gujarat, Maharashtra, Tripura, Himachal Pradesh, Haryana, Jammu and Kashmir, Andhra Pradesh, Karnataka and Tamil Nadu. Other states are being persuaded to issued such orders.

Firewood occupies a predominant place as an energy source in rural areas. As against the estimated requirement of about 15.7 crore tonnes of fuelwood per annum, recorded production is only 5.8 crore tonnes. Due to scarcity of firewood, considerable quantities of cowdung and agricultural residues are burnt as fuel leading to air pollution. It is expected that programmes of renewable energy sources and augmenting fuel growth in wastelands will help in closing the gap.

Fire is one of the major factors responsible for destruction of forests in the country. In India, most of the fires are man-made and are generally deliberate and on rare occasions accidental. The causes of deliberate fire incidences are grazing, mahua seed and flower collections, tendu leaf collection, poaching and shifting cultivation, etc. In order to reduce the incidents of fire in India, the following steps have been undertaken by the forest department: (i) development of firelines and (ii) establishment of watch towers besides employing fire watchers during fire seasons. In order to develop the techniques for detection, prevention and suppression of fire in the country, a UNDP assisted Modern Forests Fire

Control Project was initiated in 1984 in Chandrapur, Maharashtra and Haldwani/Nainital, U.P. Techniques like development of better communication network and effective use of hand tools and other equipments developed under the projects have proved successful in reducing the fire damage. In addition, fire danger rating system, wireless network, fire reporting system and hand tools etc., were designed. This scheme is being continued in 11 states of the country.

The National Wildlife Action Plan adopted in 1983 provides the framework of strategy as well as programme for conservation of wildlife. At present the protected area network comprises 80 national parks and 441 sanctuaries covering 4.5 per cent of the total geographical area of the country. The Wildlife (Protection) Act, 1972 adopted by all states except Jammu and Kashmir (which has its own Act), governs wildlife conservation and protection of endangered species. The Act prohibits trade in rare and endangered species. India is also a signatory to the Convention on International Trade in Endangered Species of Wild Flora and Fauna. Under this, export or import of endangered species and their products is subject to strict control. Commercial exploitation of such species is prohibited.

The Centre provides finanacial and technical assistance to states for: (i) development and improved management of national parks (ii) protection of wildlife and control of poaching and illegal trade in wildlife products; (iii) eco-development in areas around national parks and sanctuaries; (iv) conservation of elephant and its habitat; and (v) conservation of rhinos in Assam. The Wildlife (Protection) Act, 1972 has been amended to make the provisions more effective.

Endangered species of plants and animals have been brought under the purview of the Act. A Central Zoo

Authority has been set up to look after the management of zoological parks in the country. The Authority has since notified rules for recognition of zoos which stipulates the standards for upkeep, maintenance and veterinary care of animals. It coordinates the activities of over 200 existing zoos and also supervises the exchange of animals on a scientific basis. Project Tiger, one of the premeir conservation efforts of the country has completed 20 years in April 1993. Under this scheme 21 Tiger Reserves have been set up all over the country. A Global Tiger Forum has been set up for Tiger Range countries and an interim secretariat has been set up at New Delhi. A Tiger Crisis Cell has been set up to obtain all the information essential for conservation of the tiger.

The Animal Welfare Board of India, established in 1962 under the provisions of the Prevention of Cruelty to Animals Act, 1960 is an autonomous organisation of the Ministry of Environment and Forests working for the cause of animal welfare in the country. A series of camps for training the members of SPCAs and Animal Welfare Organisations are being held all over the country, in collaboration with the Royal Society for Prevention of Cruelty to Animals, London. The Board also celebrates Animal Welfare Fortnight from 14 January every year.

At the time of India's Independence, our priority was the provision of the basic human needs of food, fuel, shelter, health, employment, etc., to our vast population. As such the focus of our Five Year Plans was on agriculture, health, family welfare etc. In the Fourth Five Year Plan, problems related to environment received direct attention and a Committee was set up in 1972 to look into these problems and suggest a solution in consulation with experts and concerned minstries/ departments of the government. Another Committee was set up in January 1980, for reviewing the existing legislative measures and administrative machinery for ensuring environmental protection and for recommending ways to strengthen them. On the recommendation of this high-powered Committee, the Department of Environment was set up in 1980. Consequently in 1985, it was upgraded to a full-fledged Ministry of Environment and Forests to serve as the focal point in the administrative structure for the planning, promotion and coordination of environmental and forestry programmes.

Environmental problem in India can be classified into two broad categories: (a) those arising as negative effects of the very process of development and (b) those arising from conditions of poverty and under-development. The first category has to do with the impact of efforts to achieve rapid economic growth and development. Poorly planned developmental projects are usually environmentally destructive. The second category has to do with the impact on the health and integrity of our natural resources such as land, soil, water, forests, wildlife, space, etc., as a result of proverty.

There are about 30 major enactments related to protection of environment now being administered by the Central and state governments. Prominent among these are: Wildlife (Protection) Act, 1972; The Forest (Conservation) Act, 1980; The Water (Prevention and Control of Pollution) Act, 1974; The Air (Prevention and Control of Pollution) Act, 1981; The Water (Prevention and Control of Pollution) Cess Act, 1977; The Environment (Protection) Act, 1986; The Public Liability Insurance Act; 1991; The Motor Vehicle Act, 1938 as amended in 1988; The Factories Act and the Insecticides Act. These are implemented through several organisations like Central and state pollution control boards, chief inspectors of factories and insecticides inspectors of agriculture departments, etc.

The Environment (Protection) Act, 1986, brought into force from 19 November 1986 is a landmark legislation as it is an umbrella Act for the protection of environment and aims at plugging the loopholes in the other related Acts. The salient features of this Act are as follows: (a) conferring powers on the Central Government to; (i) take all necessary measures for protecting quality of environment; (ii) coordinate activities of states, officers and other authorities under the Act or under any other law related to the objects of this Act; (iii) Plan and execute a nationwide programme for prevention, control and abatement of environmental pollution; (iv) lay down standards for discharge of environmental pollutant; (v) empower any person to enter, inspect, take samples and test; (vi) establish or recognise environmental laboratories; (vii) appoint or recognise analysts; (viii) lay down standards for quality of environment; (ix) restrict areas in which industries, operations or process may not be carried out or shall be carried out subject to certain safeguards; (x) lay down safeguards for prevention of accidents and take remedial measures in case of such accidents; (xi) lay down procedures and safeguards for handling hazardous substances; (xii) constitute an authority or authorities for exercising powers; (xiii) issue directions to any person, officer or authority including the power direct closure, prohibition or regulation of any industry, operation or process or stoppage or regulations of supply of electricity, water or any other services; (xiv) require any person, officer, state government or authority to furnish any prescribed information; and (xv) delegate powers to any of a state or authority; (b) it confers powers on persons to complain to courts regarding any violation of the provisions of the Act, after a notice of 60 days to prescribed authorities; (c) the Act makes it obligatory for the person incharge of a place to inform the prescribed authorities regarding any accidental discharge or apprehended discharge of any pollutant in excess of prescribed standards. Authorities on receipt of such information or otherwise shall take remedial measures are recoverable with inerest from the pollute; (d) it prescribes penalties for violation of the provisions of the Act. No distinction is shown between government of the Act. These include issue of rules, notification of standards, action regarding environmental laboratories, strengthening of state departments of environment and pollution control boards, delegation of powers, identification of agencies for carrying out various activities for hazardous chemical management and setting up of environemtn protection councils in the states. The Water (Prevention and Control of Pollution) Act, 1974 and the Air (Prevention and Control of Pollution) Act, 1981, have been made more stringent. Steps have been taken to: (i) prevent pollution at source; (ii) encourage, develop and apply the best available practicable and technical solutions; (iii) ensure that the polluter pays for the pollution and control arrangements; (iv) focus protection on heavily polluted areas and river stretches; and (v) involve the public in decision-making.

The rapid increase in industrialisation and urbanisation has exerted extra pressure on the infrastructural facilities of human settlements manifesting in environment problems like increased incidence of air, water and noise pollution.

The ambient aire quality major towns and cities in the country is being monitored under the National Ambient Air Quality Monitoring (NAAQM) programme. The monitoring results indicate that Sulphur Dioxide and Nitrogen dioxide levels are mostly within the permissible limits whereas Suspended Particulate Matter (SPM) values are higher than the prescribed limits at some places due to vehicular and air pollution, burning of fossil fuel and natural dusty conditions.

The pollution caused by vehicles contributes significantly towards air pollution. The problem of suspended particulate matter is more acute during the summer due to local dusty conditions. During the winter months, lower ambient temperatures, lower mixing depth temperature inversion, higher traffic density, higher consumption of domestic fuels, aggravate the pollution problems.

The data on ambient water quality of rivers indicates that levels of coliform count and Biological Oxygen Demand (BOD) are generally high resulting in deterioration of water quality. This is primarily due to inadequate sanitation facilities and discharge of waste water into the surface water bodies without proper treatment.

Urban noise levels in major cities also indicate and incresing trend due to rise in human population, automobiles and industrial activities. Specific studies reveal that noise levels in industrial areas are generally within the prescribed limits but exceed the standards in respect of commercial, residential and silence zones during certain hours. The problem is more conspicuous near the traffic intersections and commercial centres.

The on-going initiatives of Government to improve environment include preventive as well as promotive measures. Fiscal incentives are provided by the Government to encourage the installation of appropriate pollution abatement equipment in the form of custom waive off and soft loans. While the industries are encouraged and the fiscal incentives are provided for installing equipment for control of pollution, punitive measures including legal action is taken against the defaulting units.

To achieve the goal pollution abatement, emission and effluent standards for air, water and noise have been notified. Regular monitoring is carried out and the enforcement efforts have been intensified. At present, a majority of identified units have already installed the requisite pollution control equipment. According to the data collected by the Central Pollution Control Board (CPCB) on September 30, 1996, out of 1,551 units belonging to 17 categories of highly polluting industries, 1,259 units had facilities to comply with the environmental standards, 112 were closed and 180 were not having adequate facilities. Show cause notices under Section 5 of the Environment (Protection) Act 1986 have been issued to all the defaulting units.

Apart from notifications of effluent and emission standards for the major categories of polluting industries, national ambient air quality standards including ambient noise standards have been notified. Industries have been directed to instal necessary pollution control equipment within a stipulated time frame. More stringent norms for vehicular emissions have been notified under the Central Motor Vehicles Rules which have come into effect from April, 1996. Supply of unleaded petrol in four metropolitan cities of Mumbai, Calcutta, Delhi and Chennal has been introduced with effect from April 1, 1995 for use in four wheel vehicles fitted with catalytic converters. The use of unleaded petrol will be gradually expanded to other cities in the country.

Twenty-four critically polluted areas in the country have been identified and action plans have been drawn up to improve the quality of environment in these areas. Adoption of clean technologies of production and formation of Waste Minimisation Circles is being encouraged to minimise environmental pollution. Under the World Bank aided Industrial Pollution Control Project, technical and financial assistance is provided for setting up Common Effluent Treatment Plants (CETPs) in clusters of small scale industrial units. An "Eco-Mark" scheme has been launched to certify various products of the industries which fulfil the prescribed pollution control standards to achieve the objective of environment-friendly production, packaging and waste disposal. To increase public awareness and participation, several public awareness campaigns on effects of pollution and measures to control it have been launched.

The Polity Statement for Abatement of Pollution indicates adoption of best available clean and practicable technologies, rather than end-of-the-pipe treatment, as the key elements for pollution prevention. As a part of this thrust, the Ministry of Environment & Forests has set up a Clean Technologies Division for identifying cleaner technologies that can be introduced in different development sectors. Techniques like coal beneficiation are being promoted. The programme envisages setting up a National Clearing House for cleaner technologies as the overall co-ordinating agency and sectoral centres in different areas of development to focus on their activities. Another initiative taken to motivate environmentally oriented technologies and practices is mandatory submission of Annual Environmental Statements which would be subsequently evolved into environmental audit.

Prior environmental clearance of development projects based on impact assessment is being increasingly emphasised. Such clearance has been made mandatory for 29 specified categories of development projects through a statutory notification issued in January, 1994. This has been done with a view to mitigating the adverse environmental effects of these projects and in integrating the environmental concerns into development. This mechanism is also of help in catalysing the process of inducing cleaner environment-friendly technologies into the developmental process.

The success of the Ganga Action Plan has encouraged its replication for water pollution abatement in tributaries of the Ganga (Yamuna, Gomati and Damodar) under Ganga Action Plan Phase-II. A wider scheme called the National River conservation Plan covering pollution abatement works for grossly polluted stretches in 18 major rivers in 10 States of the country has also been initiated. Further, a programme for conservation of selected lakes has also been formulated by the Ministry.

The National Environmental Tribunal Act, providing relief, compensation and restitution to victims of accidents while handling hazardous substances, and for environmental damages, came into force from 17 June, 1995. The Act provides (i) strict liabilitiy for damages arising out of any accident occurring while handling any hazardous substances and (ii) Establishment of National Environmental Tribunal for effective and expenditious disposals of cases arising from such accidents with a view to give relief and compensation for damage to persons, property and the environment and (iii) matters connected therewith or incidental thereto.

The National Environment Appellate Authority (NEAA) has been set up by the Government in January 1997. Public hearings have now been built into the environment impact assessment. The machinary for hearing appeals against environment pollution impact assessment is also being set up. The measures are to ensure greater transparency and faster decision-making in matters concerning the environmental impact of industrial projects.

As per the Policy Statement of Abatement of Pollution announced in February 1992, the key elements for pollution prevention are adoption of the best available clean and praticable technologies rather than end of the pipe treatment. The focus is on source reduction and substitution of chemicals, with safe alternatives. The thrust has, therefore, been made for considering process changes which involve significant improvements in energy and water conservation. To follow up on the various issues covered in the Policy Statement for Abatement of Pollution, the National Conservation Strategy and the Forest Policy Statement, several new programmes and studies have been initiated and commissioned. An Environment Action Programme has been formulated covering a wide ambit of subjects such as clean and low-waste technologies, improvement of water quality, institutional and human resources development, forestry and natural resources accouning.

To integrate natural resource accounting into the national accounting process, collection and analysis of environmental data has been initiated. It is proposed to produce a computerised map of the critically polluted areas through digitisation, on a format based on Geographic Information System. Base thematic maps on 1.6 M scale have been prepared for the country on the following themes: (i) major river basins and drainage network; (ii) administrative divisions; (iii) designated best use classification of streams; (iv) location of water and air pollution monitoring stations; (v) location of critically polluted areas; and (vi) major cities of India (above one lakh population).

The gazette notification on environmental audit issued in 1992 has been amended and now applies to all units seeking environmental clearance, and such units are required to submit environmental statements for the period ending 31 March on or before 30 September every year beginning from 1993 To facilitate industries in preparing environmental statements, model environmental statement reports for six categories of industries have been prepared. A booklet titled "Environmental Statement as part of environmental audit" has also been prepared by the Ministry. A software package 'Paryavaran' along with a user manual, has been prepared for analysis of information submitted in these environmental statements and is being distributed to all the SPCBs.

An 'Eco-Mark' label has been introduced to label consumer products that are environment friendly. Sixteen products have been identified for labelling and standards for toilet soaps and detergents, paper, paints, architectural paints and laundry soaps have been notified for awarding this label. The procedure for granting consent to small scale industries has been simplified. A new format for the consent application and for authorisation required under the Environment (Protection) Act, 1986 has been developed and notified. Under the scheme "Adoption of clean technology in the small scale industries and to extend necessary technical support", training and awareness programmes for personnel in small Industry Development Organisation and entrepreneurs are being organised. A manual "From Waste to Profits" giving guidelines for waste minimisation has been prepared.

The Central Pollution Control Board (CPCB) is the national apex body for assessment, monitoring and control of water and air pollution. The executive responsibilities for enforcement of the Acts for Prevention and Control of Pollution of Water (1974) and Air (1981) and also of the Water (Cess) Act, 1977 are carried out through are Board. Twenty three states and union territories have already adopted the Act and respective state pollution control boards have been constituted. These states are Andhra Pradesh, Assam, Bihar, Goa, Gujarat, Haryana, Himachal Pradesh, Jammu and Kashmir, Karnataka, Kerala, Madhya Pradesh, Maharashtra, Meghalaya, Mizoram, Orissa, Punjab, Rajasthan, Sikkim, Tamil Nadu, Tripura, Uttar Pradesh, West Bengal, Delhi and Pondicherry. Arunachal Pradesh has adopted the Act, but is yet to constitute the board. Enactment of the Enviornment (Protection) Act, 1986 has further extended the scope of the activities of the Board. Under the Environment (Protection) Act, 1986, effluent and emission standards in respect of 61 categories of industries have been notified. So far, 84 laboratories have been recognised as environmental laboratories. Minimum National Standards (MINAS) for effluents and emissions from specific industries have been formulated and control measures are being implemented in a phased manner. A notification consolidating all the environmental standards including general effluent, emission and noise standards has been issued. It also includes standards for waste water generation in respect of 11 categories of industries. Further mass emission norms which would come into effect from 1 April 1996 have also been issued for petrol and diesel driven vehicles under the Central Motor Vehicles Rules of the Ministry of Surface Transport. Unleaded petrol of Delhi, Bombay, Madras and Calcutta from 1 April 1995. Petrol with a maximum lead content of 0.15 g/l has been introduced at all the retail outlets of these four metro cities since June 1994.

Seventeen categories of heavily polluting industries have been identified namely, cement, thermal powre plants, distilleries, sugar, fertilizer, integrated iron and steel, oil refineries, pulp and paper, petrochemicals, pesticides, tanneries, basic drugs and pharmaceuticals, dye and dye intermediates, caustic soda, zinc smelter, copper smelter and aluminium smelter. Action is taken against the defaulting units in these categories on priority. On the basis of the designated best use of criteria CPCB has identified 13 grossly polluted stretches of Sabarmati, Subernarekha, Godavari, Krishna, Indus (tributaries), Sutlej, Ganga (tributaries), Yamuna, Hindon, Chambal, Damodar, Gomati, and Kali rivers to formulate short-term result oriented programmes. The CPCB, in consultation with SPCBs has identified 22 critically polluted areas in the country which need special attention for control of pollution. These are Vapi (Gujarat), Singrauli (U.P.), Korba, Ratlam, Nagoda (Madhya Pradesh), Digboi (Assam), Talcher (Orissa), Bhadravati (Karnataka), Howrah (West Bengal), Dhanbad (Bihar), Pali and * Pataucheru (Andhra Pradesh), Chembur (Maharashtra), Najafgarh (Delhi), Govindhgarh (Punjab), Udyog Mandal (Kerala) and Parwanoo and Kala Amb (HP). The progress in abatement of pollution in these areas is being reviewed. A Bill has been introduced in the Parliament for establishing a National Environment Tribunal.

There are a host of human interventions including development activities which have resulted in considerable environmental degration. Major human interventions in forests are deforestation, commercial logging, setting up protected area, partial closure of forests, etc which are described below:

— There is increasing deforestation due to commercial exploitation, building of dams, mining and construction activities. Of the world's estimated 8.4 billion hectares of forests in 1990, tropical forests covered 1.76 billion ha. During 1981-90, tropical forests were lost at the rate of 0.8 per cent (15.4 million ha) a year, as per estimates of the World Resources Institute. The net annual deforestation during 1981-90 exceeded two per cent in 10 tropical countries of Asia and Africa.

— Commercial logging for industrial activities is increasing rapidly. Eighty-four per cent of such logging took place in closed tropical broadleaf forests in primary (undisturbed forests) during the 1980s. Logging activity is a causal factor for forest degradation and is reflected in rough wood production which increased by 19 per cent between 1979-81 to 1989-91. Globally, almost 50 per cent of such rough wood is used for industrial purposes, the rest for heating and cooking.

— Setting up of protected areas for conservation purposes has led to complications and conflict-situation with indigenous communities and also denial of many of their rights and privileges.

— Closure of parts of forests for setting up of industries or agro-based activities for private, semi-private lands, construction of railways, roads and new settlements has led to shrinkage of forest cover and increased hardship for local communities in their day-to-day existence.

— Interventions for adhering to international agreements have also alienated many local communities and some of their practices, eg, tribal hunting of wild animals which goes against biodiversity agreements.

— Policies of economic liberalization, privatization and globalization have both, directly and indirectly, led to reduction of forest cover and cuts in subsidies and grants affecting food subsidies and other welfare schemes involving poor and marginalized communities.

The environmental research programme aims to develop strategies for sustainable resource management and create facilities and trained manpower to conduct research in priority areas. Research projects are supported under three main schemes: (a) Man and Biosphere Programme; (b) Environment Research Programme; and (c) Action-oriented research programme for Eastern and Western Ghats. A number of small, specific research projects are also beng supported. Expert committees and expert working groups make recommendations for undertaking research in priority areas, scrutinise proposals, evaluate progress and recommend suitable mechanisms for implementation of the research projects. Priority areas of research are identified in five fundamental elements viz., land, water, air, space and energy. To strengthen the environmental research and training base, the following Centres of Excellence have been set up: Ecological Research and Training Centre, Bangalore: Centre for Mining Environment, Dhanbad: Centre for Environmental Education, Ahmadabad: CPR Environment Education Centre, Madras and the Salim Ali Centre for Orinthology and Natural History, Coimbatore.

This Institute, established in 1988, is an autonomous organisation of the Ministry of Environment and Forests for developing strategies, technologies and knowledge base for ecologically sound developoment of the Himalayan region. Besides undertaking action-oriented research projects the Institute has also installed three weather monitoring stations for collecting and analysing climatic data for the Himalayan region. Units of the Institute are also located at UP, Sikkim, Nagaland and Himachal Pradesh.

Forestry research is the primary responsibility of the Indian Council of Forestry Research and Education. It has the following forestry research institutes and centres under it: (i) Forest Research Institute, Dehra Dun; (ii) Institute of Arid Zone Forestry Research, Jodhpur; (iii) Institute of Rain and Moist Deciduous Forests, Jorhat; (iv)

Institute of Wood Science and Technology, Bangalore; (v) Tropical Forestry Research Institute, Jabalpur; (vi) Institute of Forest Genetics and Tree Breeding, Coimbatore; (vii) Temperate Forest Research Centre, Shimla (viii) Centre for Forest productivity, Ranchi and (ix) Centre for Social Forestry and Environment, Allahabad. In addition, the Indian Plywood Industries Research and Training Institute, Bangalore, has been transferred to the Ministry of Environment and Forests from the Ministry of Industry. Besides forestry research in wood panel products, this Institute imparts training to workers in optimum utilisation of timber.

Research programmes in wildlife are carried out by the Wildlife Institute of India, Dehra Dun and the Salim Ali Centre for Orinthology and Natural History, Coimbatore. Several projects on habitat evolution, elephant movement, ecology of gharial and turtles, status of endangered species behavioural ecology, bio-diversity, resource study, conservation, ecology and management of specific animals etc., are being carried out by both these institutes.

Priority is accorded by the Ministry of Environment and Forests to promote evironmental education, create environmental awareness among various age groups and to disseminate information through Environmental Information System (ENVIS) network to all concerned. Special emphasis is given to non-formal environmental education through seminars/symposia/workshops, training programmes, eco-camps, audio-visual shows etc. The Ministry has been organising a National Environment Awareness Campaign (NEAC) since July 1986. As a part of this Capaign, 19 Novmber to 18 December every year is observed as the National Environment Month. Students/youth, techers, women, tribals, administrators, professionals, legislators, industrial workers, Armed Forces and the general public are covered under this Campaign. During 1994-95 about 2,200 organisations have been granted financial assistance by the Ministry to organise various activities for creating environmental awareness. The Ministry also provides financial support for setting up eco-clubs at schools and for production on films on environment.

A new scheme "Paryavaran Vahini" has been launched during 1992-93 to create environmental awareness and to ensure active public participations by involving the local people in activities relating to environmental protection. Parayavaran Vahinis are proposed to be constituted in 183 selected districts all over the country which have high incidence of pollution and density of tribal and forest population. The Vahinis also play a watch dog role by reporting instances of environmental pollution, deforestation, poaching, etc. They function under the charge of District Collectors with active cooperation of the state/union territory governments. this scheme is entirely financed by the Ministry of Environment and Forests.

The National Museum of Natural History (NMNH) set up in New Delhi in 1978, is concerned with the promotion of non-formal education in the area of environment and conservation. Besides permanent exhibit galleries on various aspects of environment, the museum also conducts temporary exhibitions and a large number of educational programmes and activities for school children, college youth and the general public. A Regional Museum of Natural History has been established at Mysore and two more and planned at Bhopal and Bhubaneswar.

The Indian Council for Forestry Research and Education is the focal point for forestry education and extension developmnet in the country. Indira Gandhi

National Forest Academy, Dehra Dun imparts in-service professional training to Indian Forest Service (IFS) professionals. State forest service colleges provide training to the officers of the State Forest Service (SFS). The Indian Plywood Industries Research and Training Institute, Bangalore organises short-term courses in the area of wood science.

The Indian Institute of Forest Management, Bhopal, also provides training in forest management and allied subjects to persons from the Indian Forest Service, forest development corporations and forest related industries to develop forestry management skills. The Wildlife Institute of India, Dehra Dun conducts various programmes to provide in-service training in wildlife management for forest officers, wildlife ecologists and other professionals.

Environmental Information System (ENVIS) has been set up by the Ministry in 1982 as a decentralised information system network for collection, storage, retrieval and dissemination of environmental information to decision makers, policy planners, scientists, engineers, environmentalists, research workers and the general public all over the country. Besides the Focal Point in the Ministry, the ENVIS network presently consists of 20 subject oriented centres known as ENVIS centres, set up in various institutions/organisations of the country on priority areas of environment such as environmentally sound and appropriate technology, bio-degradation of wastes, desertification, estuary, mangroves, corals and lagoons, media and environment, environmental education, solid wastes disposal, animal ecology, Himalayan ecology, etc. The Focal Point brings out a quarterly abstracting journal "Paryavaran Abstracts" containing information about environmental research in the Indian context.

ENVIS has been designated as National Focal Point (NFP) and Regional Service Centre (RSC) for South Asia sub-regional countries by INFORTERRA (an international referral system for sources of information on environment) of United Nations Environment Programme (UNEP). As NEP, ENVIS updated more than 250 Indian Potential Sources in the International Directory of UNEP for providing information in the field of environment and its related areas.

The Ministry functions as a nodal agency for United Nations Environment Programme (UNEP), South Asia Cooperation Environment Programme (SACEP) and International Centre for Integrated Mountain and Development (ICIMOD) and various international agencies, regional bodies and multilateral institutions. In coordinates all bilateral cooperation in the field of invironment. India has such cooperation programmes with the Netherlands, Norway, Sweden, Denmark, Great Britain, USA, the Russian Federation, Canada, Japan and FRG in addition to forestry programmes with external assistance.

India is signatory to the following important international treaties/agreements in the field of environment: (i) International Convention for the regulation of Whaling; (ii) International Plant Protection Convention; (iii) The Antarctic Treaty; (iv) Conventon on Wetlands of internatonal importance especially as waterfowl habitat; (v) International Convention on international trade in endangered species of wild flora and fauna; (vi) Protocol of 1978 relating to the international convention for the prevention of pollution from ships, 1973; (vii) Vienna Convention for the protection of the ozone layer; (viii) Convention on Migratory Species; (ix) Basel Convention on trans-boundary movement of hazardous substances; (x)

Framework Convention on climatic change; (xi) convention on conservation of bio-diversity; (xii) Montreal Protocol on the substances that deplete the ozone layer and (xiii) International Convention for Combating Desertification.

Instituted in 1987, the Indira Gandhi Prayavaran Puraskar, consisting of a cash component of rupees one lakh, a silver trophy and a citation, is awarded every year to an organisation and to an individual for significant contributions in the field of environment.

The Indira Priyadarshini Vrikshamitra Awards have been constituted by the Ministry of Environment and Forests in 1986 to recognise outstanding contributions of individuals and organisations in the field of afforestation and wastelands development. Ten awards are given every year to individuals, educational institutes, Panchayats, voluntary agencies and government agencies. Each award carries a medallion, a citation and a cash component of Rs. 50,000.

The Maha Vriksha Puraskar, instituted by the NAEB during 1993-94 will be given every year to individuals/ organisations for trees of notified species having the largest girth and height and in good health and vigour. These awards would consist of a cash prize of Rs. 25,000, a plaque and a citation.

Since 1991, national awards are being presented every year to eligible industries in recognition of their contributions to the prevention and control of evnvironmental pollution.

Human activities have pushed our planet to the brink of disaster necessitating a comprehensive global action to retrieve the situation. While exploring newer forms of renewable sources of energy to address the environmental malady, our planners and administrators need to address the most urgent task of improving energy efficiency. The rural areas should depend on minihydel projects and bioenergy as far as possible. A serious and lasting government commitment to the development and use of energy efficient and renewable technologies is the need of the hour. Like it or not, we find ourselves in a world where we are responsible for each other's well-being. In the last few years of this millennium, difficult questions of social equality, national sovereignty, and individual rights and responsibilities are emerging. A person may be able to afford a large, energy-consumptive automobile, but can the planet afford it? Indeed, the larger question boils down as to how many carbon-emitting automobilies can the planet tolerate without the habitability of the earth being disturbed. At a more mundane level, a couple may desire and be able to support several children, but can the planet afford several children per family? Does our generation have the right to extinguish plant and animal species that have evolved over millions of years? Do we not have the obligation to preserve our biological heritage for our future generations?

An affirmative answer to these questions depends on restoring and prserving the conditions that make the earth habitable, a place capable of supporting a diversity of life and modern civilization. Human activities have pushed the planet to the brink of disaster.

A comprehensive global action plan to remedy the situation should include: developing energy strategies that have climate protection as their cornerstone; expanding the earth's forest cover so as to prevent global warming; doubling the per capita grain production and lastly, breaking the momentum of population growth.

While these are the macro-level targets for making this globe a sustainable one in the forthcoming century, at the micro-level it amounts to a severe test on the capacity of world leaders as well as the local ones in their efforts in ecological economic betterment of the populations under their jurisdiction.

It is no wonder that the modes of energy production that are in vogue around the world are primarily responsible for the change in the earth's climate. The huge quantities of oil, coal and natural gas that fuel the global economy account for most of the carbon dioxide emissions responsible for global warming through the greenhouse effect. Producing less carbon dioxide requires using less fuel from among the traditional category. This in turn means exploring other non-conventional energy sources, enough to substitute the fossil sources.

Even though India is one of the few Third World countries which has constitutionalized protection and improvement of environment, the various enactment suffer from several lacunae including the non-recognition of the crucial role that PRIs can play in the endeavour. The involvement of PRIs as the watch-dog of environmental protection at the grass roots level needs to be duty recognized. The Constitution (73rd Amendment) Act 1992 now provides these institutions an opportunity to play their legitimate role. Environment protection represents one of the more recent and yet one of the more profound aspects new public affairs dimension in public administration.

Environmental issues have aroused too much intellectual and academic interest both in developing and underdeveloped nations. They include envioronmental degradation, deforestation and desertification, atmospheric pollution and imbalances as well as disertifications in ecology resulting from the way natural resources—land, water, forests, minerals, etc are harnessed for fulfilment of human needs. The UN

Conference on Human Environment in 1972 proclaimed that the defence and improvement of human environment both natural and man-made had become an imperative good for mankind, to be pursued together with fundamental goals of peace and worldwide economic and social development.

The achievement of these goals was the responsibility of citizens, communities, enterprises and institutions at every level. Later on, the World Conservation Strategy (1980) and the Brundthland Report also noted the irreversible destruction of ecosystems of the poor countries and the implicit threat to the world security and the consequent political instability and social problems. The problem of environmental crises of the developing countries is different from that of the developed countries. The establishment of viable community-based institutions for environment protection was suggested with full legal, administrative and technical support. These institutions should be empowered to plan, to work out the modality and to implement the various measures for environment protection and conservation. The Panchayati Raj as an institution of local rural government is the excellent model for it in rural India.

Among the developing countries, india is also facing environmental problems and crises. The enormous increase in population is the most potent cause for acceleration of the overutilization of productive resources and downgrading the quality of environment.

India has a domesticated animal population of nearly 500 million. Considering that only 3.5 per cent of the land area are under grass, the population is supported by the forest and agriculture residues which are thereby diverted from agricultural land. Out of the total cultivable land, 175 million ha are degraded needing special treatment to restore productivity. Of the 75 million ha designated as forest land, only 35 million ha are close forest. Despite all efforts, India has continued to lose forest cover. The deforestation causes loss in bivodiversity. Over 1,500 species of plants and animals are on the endangered list. Levels of air and water pollution are much beyond acceptable limits. These challenges disturb the environment equilibrium and the life of mankind.

The basic aim of our National Forest Policy must be to ensure environmental stability and maintenance of ecological balance including atmospheric which are vital for the sustenance of all forms of life—human, animal and plant. Rural India has different kinds of environmental crises compared to other countries. The rapid growth of rural population has placed inexorable burden on farm as well as on other land resources, on forests, on water resources and worsened the quality of life of the rural poor in respect of housing, health, ecological surroundings and other essentials.

The Un Declaration on Human Environment in 1972 signalled India to initiate positive steps in the direction towards environment improvement. The Constitution of India has conceptualized its thinking on environment in the form of the Directive Principles of State Policy in favour of protection and improvement of environment, and safeguarding of forests and wildlife (Article 48A), a fundamental duty to protect and improve the natural environment including forests, lakes, rivers and wildlife and to have compassion for living creatures [Article 51A(g)], and a subject in the Consurrent List in its Seventh Schedule (Item 17A and 17B). Both the Directive principles and Fundamental Duty are non-justiciable, but these provide the necessary constitutional sanction if the State intends to adopt a law in the matter.

The other component of the infrastructure for environment improvement and protection is provided by the existing legislation. There are 30 major enactments such as Water Cess Act, Forest Act, Forest Conservation Act, Wildlife Protection Act, Environment Protection Act, of Union and State Governments.

Administrative actions—regulatory, negotiational and persuasive—under these enactments are mainly taken by the Central and State administrative organizations—the Central Ministry of Environment and Forests, the Central Pollution Control Board and the State Departments of Environment and State Pollution Control Boards. Besides this, there also exist the other administrative mechanisms concerned with the implementation of policies on environment. The Panchayati Raj institutions have also become important instruments in rural India for environment protection and improvement.

There is no end to the debate on environment and development. However, instances of the preservationist approach is to be found in the local indigenous communities living in and around forests. In real life, such communities have been seriously affected as a result of both degradation of forest land and their reduced accessibility to forest resources on account of strict forest laws. Degradation of surrounding environment and rigid forestlaws have adversely affected food accessibility, livelihood options and quality of life of local indigenous communities. Such degradation has often caused periodic phases of hunger and malnutrition in the absence of supportive means of livelihood for acquiring basic essentials of life.

Forest plantations of eucalyptus and other species no longer provide the rich biodiversity available earlier in natural forests. Common property resources, in which groups of local people have co-equal use rights, such as community pastures, community forests, wastelands, village ponds, rivers, etc have declined at a rapid pace. Such phenomenon has led to a diminished role of local natural resources which have traditionally constituted invaluable asset-base for meeting basic needs and livelihood requirements of indigenous communities.

Such relatively undisturbed lands include forests, grasslands, wetlands, water bodies, etc which constitue habitat for indigenous communities, plants and animal species and thus contribute to maintenance of human and biological diversity. Such lands perform important environmental functions and also constitute essential means of livelihood. As far as fragility of such ecosystems is concerned, the indigenous communities have traditionally presented little threat to sensitive ecological zones, because their production systems have been sustainable, scattered over a large area, and they have traditionally kept encroachers, poachers and others out of the area.

The benefits provided by forests, trees and common property resources are basic to such communities and amongst direct benefits, the following are included:

— food such as nuts, wild fruits, vegetables, leaves, flowers, roots, stems honey, wild animals insects, etc;

— habitat and shelter;

— raw materials like bamboo, canes, fibres, oils, bhabbar grass, waxes, resins, gums, dyes and wood for furniture and capital equipment for agriculture, artisanship, etc;

— wood for building, fencing, tool making, etc;

— firewood;

— medicines and drugs;

— fodder such as grass, branches, twigs and leaves, grazing sites;

— means of livelihood, both seasonal and annual;

— shade;

— ornaments, religious items and cultural symbols; and

— drought relief.

Apart from direct benefits, forests, trees and common property resources also provide indirect benefits, such as preventing erosion, conserving moisture, conserving water, recycling nutrient, preventing drought or reducing its impact, providing leaf manure, fixing nitrogen by leguminous trees, regulating climate and rainfall, providing greenery and beauty and reducing pollution.

Forests as safety net: In short, forests, trees and common property resources provide safety nets to the local indigenous communities. In the presence of spiraling prices, reduced wages in real terms, unemployment, sickness, reduced productivity from land, and recurring shortages, forests, trees and common property resources act as a kind of safety net for local communities, protecting them from the harshness of market forces. They come to the rescue by providing a safety net against food and livelihood insecurity, drought attacks, pest attacks, illness, pollution, high prices, high rents, etc. They play a dominant role in providing alternative sources of livelihood and in offering coping strategies to local communities.

The strategy for development of the Scheduled Tribes is based on the TSP (tribal sub-plan) approach which came into operation since 1974-75 (V Plan) in 16 States (now 18 States) and two Union territories. The main objective of the tribal sub-plan is to (i) raise the socio-economic condition of the tribal population and strengthen infrastructure in the tribal areas, and (ii) to protect and promote tribal interests through legal and administrative support.

The programmes are now being implemented through (i) 194 Integrated Tribal Development Projects (ITDPs) comprising generally blocks/tehsils with 50 per cent or more Schedulied Tribe population; (ii) 277 pockets of tribal concentration (Modified Area Development Approach Projects) having a total population of 10,000 or more, and Scheduled Tribe population of 50 per cent or more; and (iii) 90 primitive tribe projects or micro-projects.

The tribal sub-plan has a two-fold thrust, viz (i) socio-economic development of the tribal areas, and (ii) socio-economic development of the tribal families.

It was expected that during the Seventh Plan period, there would be cent per cent coverage of Scheduled Tribe population under the tribal sub-plan. Benefits were also proposed to be extended to the scattered Scheduled Tribe population which was not covered by any specific project through family-oriented programmes. It may be mentioned that the tribal population coverage during the Sixth Plan period was only 75 per cent. During the Seventh Plan, the following were the objectives under tribal sub-plan approach: (i) taking up family beneficiary programme through raising productivity-level of the beneficiary families in the field of agriculture, horticulture, animal husbandry, small industry, etc. (ii) elimination of exploration of the tribals in the sphere of alienation of land, money-lending, debt bondage, forest, etc. (iii) human resource development through education and training programmes, (vi) infrastructure development, (v) development of vulnerable tribal areas and groups like, forest villagers, displaced tribes and tribal women; and (vi) upgradation of environment of tribal areas.

For the year 1985-86, the target of tribal families to be economically assisted was fixed at 8.35 lakh, and the achievement reported was 8.3 lakh families. For 1986-87, the target fixed was 8.35 lakh tribal families and for 1987-88, a tentative target of assisting 8.50 lakh tribal families had been kept.

Special Central Assistance: Under tribal development, Special Central Assistance (SCA) is an additive to the State Plan efforts for Scheduled Tribes. The Eighth Plan had a target to cover 46.50 lakh families. Against this, 28.69 lakh families were covered during the first three years of the Plan (8.88 lakh in 1992-93; 10.42 lakh in 1993-94; and 9.39 lakh in 1994-95). This constituted 61.7 per cent of the target. To improve the literacy rate among tribal women, a new scheme was introduced since 1992-93, and is being implemented through non-governmental organizations in 48 districts with tribal concentration where female population is less than two per cent.

Financing tribal sub-plan: There are four sources for financing tribal sub-plan programmes: (i) Special Central Assistance (SCA) administered by Ministry of Welfare, (ii) State Plan funds, (iii) centrally-sponsored schemes, and (vi) institutional finance.

Since the V Plan period, with the launching of the tribal sub-plan approach, special programmes for extremely backward tribe groups had been taken up. These were micro-projects or projects for primitive tribal groups. These primitive tribal groups had three criteria for their identification: (i) almost stagnant population, or extremely low growth rate facing the danger of extinction, (ii) having are pre-agricultural level of technology, and (iii) extremely low level of literacy.

Another important factor was the ecosystem in which they lived. There were also other factors which entered into the situation of each of these tribal groups calling for a sensitive and in-depth study of each, precedent to enforcement of any action plan.

The Planning Commission also mentioned that particular care need to be taken of the small primitive tribal groups, some of which were on the verge of extinction.

The Dhebar Commission (1961) alluded to them as the 'lowest layer}, and listed 50 tribes in various States which were in an extremely underdeveloped state During the V Plan period, the Ministry of Home Affairs identified 52 tribal communities as primitive, their estimated population being 10 lakhs. During the VI Plan period, an additional 20 tribal groups were identified raising their total number to 72 with an estimated population of 14 lakhs. Now the clusters of tribal concentration have gone up to 90.

There had been emphasis since the V Plan period on preparation of a project report for each of these groups relative to its situation. Nevertheless, there had been considerable neglect in this regard. Apart form the continued misery of conditions in which they lived, the risk of extinction of some of these tribes was also great.

One in every seven persons on this planet lives in India. With 16 per cent of the world's population and only 2.4 per cent of its land area, there is obviously a great demand on the natural resources including land. This is so in spite of the fact that an average Indian consumes a much lower quantum of resources than a person in the developed world. If an average person in the South were to consume as much as an average person in a developed country, the environmental crisis would be unimaginable. While, to a large extent, the lower per capita consumption is due to poverty, an important reason is also that a majority of the population in India follows a sustainable lifestyle which is based on environmentally sound practices evolved over thousands of years.

The environmental problem today is being precipitated partly because practices which were appropriate earlier, like shifting cultivation and unrestricted cattle grazing, are not so anymore. For instance, as a result of increasing population and decreasing availability of land, crop-fallow cycles in shifting cultivation have been reduced to a mere five years from a more sustainable 20-40 years in the past.

But just as there were learnings and difficulties with regard to traditional practices, so was the case with newly introduced technologies. Many measures, at one time seen as solutions, are today extracting an unanticipated price. The Green Revolution of the 1960s met India's growing demand for food. While it helped India to dramatically increase foodgrain production, what was not fully appreciated then was that the Green Revolution would on the one hand affect the country's natural resource capital, and on the other, create dependencies on inputs such as chemical fertilizers and pesticides. There are indications of soil health problems such as deficiency of micronutrients and organic matter, incidence of soil salinity and damage to the physical structure of the soil, apart from increasing dependence on chemical inputs, many of which are imported.

Today there is widespread realization that there can be no readymade solutions, that technology alone cannot solve problems, that we have to use all our ingenuity to find solutions which combine the best of the old practices with the benefits that modern science and technology can offer.

The challenges are staggering in number, scale and complexity. We need to develop and to modernize in less wasteful ways than is the current paradigm, but not lose our sound traditional values and practices. India will have to leap-frog over wasteful and polluting technologies and go for technologies which are the most environmentally sound, and are based on maximizing recycling and efficient use of resources practices which are inherent in India's traditions. It is when such development comes about that the population pressures will ease, as development brings down demographic growth rates.

The task is stupendous. For while the challenge of development might seem to be 'how to get there' the real challenges is 'how not to get there'. Urbanization, industrial growth, transportation systems, agriculture, housing... all have to stop imitating practices that are already being phased out in the developed world. With the North becoming more conscious about the condition of their own environment, 'dirty' factories are moving South. To cite only one example, the production of harmful and toxic dyestuff intermediates such as H-acid, K-acid, gamma acid and metanilic acid taken up in the 60s stands at over 41,000 tonnes in the country today, with an estimated Rs. 6 billion worth for export to the developed countries.

The forces which are taking India, and much of the developing world, on the conventional and largely imitative and unimaginative development path are many. But this path is not sustainable—for India or for the world. As Mahatma Gandhi remarked over 60 years ago. "God forbid that India should ever take to industrialism with an estimated Rs. 6 billion worth for export to the developed countries.

The forces which are taking India, and much of the developing world, on the conventional and largely imitative and unimaginative development path are many. But this path is not sustainable—for India or for the world. As Mahatma Gandhi remarked over 60 years ago. "God forbid that India should ever take to industrialism after the manner of the West. The economic imperialism of a single, tiny kingdom is today keeping the world in chains. If an entire nation of 300 million took to similar economic exploitation, it would strip the world bare like locusts.

When the West developed, it did so perhaps in ignorance of the environmental impact of its activities. Today we know that such a path is neither practicable nor desirable for countries which are raising their standards of living. We, along with other developing countries, have to find alternative paths to an alternative goal.

A goal which ultimately is the true goal of development—an environmentaly sound and sustainable quality of life, which is socially just and equitable. A goal that must be common to all citizens of the planet. A goal that is perhaps as distant from the developing world as it is from the over-consuming, wasteful societies of what is currently referred to as the 'developed' world.

It is this goal of development that we seek together as people, as organizations and as governments at the United Nations Conference on Environment and Development. It is this intermeshing of environmental and developmental concerns that must form the goal of humankind.

# 8

# Control of Pollution

Refining industry has been classified as one of the major industries in the country. The compliance with prescribed standards in respect of liquid effluents and gaseous emissions is, therefore, a statutory requirement. All the refineries in the country are fully equipped with adequate pollution control facilities to meet the prescribed environmental standards and pollution abatement measures are accorded top most priority by the Refinery management. The existing facilities are reviewed and upgraded as and when required and in the case of new projects / process units, actions are taken at the design stage itself to build necessary safeguards and facilities for improving the overall performance and compliance in the environmental standards.

The effluents generated in the refineries can be classified under 3 categories viz. (i) liquid effluents (ii) gaseous emissions and (iii) oily sludge. The compliance with respect to the statutory stipulations with regard to these as well as the actions taken by the refineries for environmental management are summarised as under :

*Liquid effluents*

The water used in the refining process gets contaminated with oil and other pollutants and has to be treated before discharging from the refineries. Government have prescribed Minimal National Standards (MINAS) for the discharge of effluents from refineries with respect to critical parameters, viz., oil and grease, phenols, sulphides Biochemical Oxygen Demand (BOD): Total Suspended Solids (TSS). The standard also specifies the quantum limits for discharge of these pollutants in terms of crude throughput.

All the refineries in the country are equipped with full fledged Effluent Treatment Plants, comprising physical, chemical and biological treatment facilities for removal/ control of pollutants from waste water. The treated waste water fully meets the prescribed stringent MINAS standards in all the refineries.

*Effluent reuse*

Keeping in view the growing shortage of fresh water, all refineries have accorded importance for maximising the reuse of treated effluent within their plants and thereby conserving the fresh water. With this objective, refineries have implemented various schemes to reuse part of their treated effluent within their plants in the cooling towers, fire water network, coke cutting operations, service water etc. Treated effluent from Mathura Refinery and treated domestic effluent from Gujarat Refinery township are being gainfully used by the local farmers.

*Gaseous emissions*

Controlling of gaseous emissions, particularly sulphur-dioxide (SO2), is one of the major tasks of the refineries. Government have prescribed standards for SO2 emissions from the three major processing units in the refineries in terms of SO2 emission per tonne of feed processed as well for the boilers in the Captive Power Plants. The stipulation for boilers is in terms of minimum stack height requirements to minimise the ground level concentration of SO2. Further, an overall limit for SO2 emission from the refineries is also stipulated by the State Pollution Control Boards/ MOE&F.

All the refineries in the country full. comply with the applicable process units' SO2 emissions standards a well as total SO2 emissions limits. The measures adopted by the refineries for controlling SO2 emissions include :

- Use of low sulphur fuel oil
- Desulphurisation of Refinery fuel gas in Sulpur Recovery Unit
- Advanced Process Control Systems
- Adoption of energy conservation measures for reducing fuel consumption which in turn reduces gaseous emissions
- Taller stacks for better dispersion of fuel gases etc.

***Management of oily sludge***

Treatment / disposal of oily sludge generated during the refining operations is of major concern to the refineries. Refineries have adopted various methods like installation of improved mixers for reducing formation of sludge. in the crude storage tanks and use of hot gas oil circulation / use of chemicals for the recovery of oil from the tank bottom sludge. Melting pits are used by the refineries to further extract the oil from the sludge. The treated sludge after gas oil treatment / melting pits is either stored in lined pits or disposed through land fill in low lying areas inside the Refinery. In some of the refineries like BPCL, HPCL-Mumbai and MRL, the oily sludge is sold to micro-crystalline wax manufacturers approved by the Technical Evaluation Committee of MOP&NG.

**Monitoring facilities**

All the refineries have full-fledged environmental cells to monitor the quality of effluents and emissions. Continuous ambient air monitoring stations / High Volume Samplers have been provided in and around the refineries to monitor the level of S02 and it has been observed that the emissions are well within the stipulated limits.

Mathura. Refinery located in the Taj-Trapezium area, has considerably reduced the S02 emissions over the years and is putting up a Once-through Hydrocracker Plant to increase the yield of middle distillates and also to reduce the S02 emissions from the Refinery.

**Accreditation with ISO-14001 environmental management system**

IOC-Mathura Refinery was the first Refinery in Asia and one of the few in the world to achieve the distinction of ISO-14001 accreditation in July, 1996. Since then, all the other IOC refineries, namely, Guwahati, Barauni, Gujarat, Haldia & Digboi and BPCL, Mumbai have also got accredited with this International Environmental Management System. As regards rest of the refineries in the country, actions have been initiated by these refineries for getting this accreditation.

**Introduction of unleaded petrol and low sulphur HSD**

In pursuance of the need for reduction of environmental pollution due to emission from vehicles, petrol with reduced lead content of 0.15 g/1 (maximum) has already been introduced throughout the country from December, 1996. As regards Unleaded petrol, Oil Companies have already made available unleaded petrol in the four metros of Delhi, Mumbai, Calcutta, Chennai and radial routes emanating from these metros and in the city of Agra from April, 1995. The availability of Unleaded petrol has been further extended to the Capital of State and Union Territories from June, 1998. By 1999-2000, unleaded petrol will be made available throughout the country. With effect from 1.9.1998, the entire petrol supplied in Delhi is unleaded.

Oil Companies have already started supplying High Speed Diesel (HSD) with reduced sulphur content of

0.5% maximum against the existing level of 1% from 1.4.1996 in the four metros and the Taj-trapezium zone. The sulphur content in HSD supplied in the Taj-trapezium zone was further brought down to 0.25% w.e.f. 1.9.1996. Government has made plans to supply very low sulphur HSD i.e. containing maximum of 0.25% sulphur throughout the country from 1.4.1999. However, keeping in view the growing pollution in the four metros Ministry of Petroleum & Natural Gas decided that the same should be introduced as early as possible in these cities. In pursuance of this, low-sulphur diesel of 0.25% was introduced in "Delhi Inner" with effect from 15.8.97 and with effect from 1.4.1998, the entire diesel supplied in the four metros, viz., Delhi, Mumbai, Calcutta & Chennai is of low-sulphur with maximum sulphur content of 0.25 %.